DESTINY HI
THE LOYALISM OF A

C000143380

DESTINY HIS CHOICE: THE LOYALISM OF ANDREW MARVELL

BY

JOHN M. WALLACE

Professor of English Literature,
University of Chicago

CAMBRIDGE UNIVERSITY PRESS

Cambridge

London   New York   New Rochelle
Melbourne   Sydney

Published by the Press Syndicate of the University of Cambridge
The Pitt Building, Trumpington Street, Cambridge CB2 1RP
32 East 57th Street, New York, NY 10022, USA
296 Beaconsfield Parade, Middle Park, Melbourne 3206, Australia

First published 1968
First paperback edition 1980

Printed in Great Britain at the
University Press, Cambridge

British Library Cataloguing in Publication Data
Wallace, John Malcolm
Destiny his choice.
1. Marvell, Andrew – Political and social views
2. Politics in literature
I. Title
821'.4   PR3546   68–10034

ISBN 0 521 06725 1 hard covers
ISBN 0 521 28042 7 paperback

To J. A. V. W. & M. W.

Contents

Foreword   *page* ix

Introduction   1

1 'The Spirits of all that were moderate': The civil war debates and the Engagement controversy   9

2 'How fit he is to sway': 'An Horatian Ode upon Cromwel's Return from Ireland'   69

3 'He seems a King by long Succession born': 'The First Anniversary of the Government under O.C.'   106

4 'The Country is the King': 'The last Instructions to a Painter'   145

5 'God send us moderation and agreement': The prose   184

6 'Destiny their Choice': 'Upon Appleton House, to my Lord Fairfax'   232

Index   259

The drawing under the dedication represents Marvell's stag seal, enlarged. It is based, by permission of Bodley's Librarian, on the seal on MS. Rawl. Letters 50, fol. 130v.

Foreword

History and literary criticism do not always make good mar-
riages, and I shall not know until later how happy they are
together in this book. No doubt I have committed faults
characteristic of both professions but will not make the mistake
that Marvell detested of offering any excuses. The method itself
of reading political poems in the context of their contemporary
background does not require a theoretical defence; but, if what
is usually called background in literary criticism sometimes
predominates, it is because the texts seem to me to call for a full
explanation, and because Marvell himself, when alive, played
a more significant part in the history of his period than he did
in its literature. I have been hoping to do justice to the man as
well as to his political poems, and believe that Marvell's
thought and changes of allegiance should have an archetypal
value to the historian, just as his best poems retain a perennial
freshness for the critic.

I should like to take this opportunity of thanking my parti-
cular teachers in the past for their instruction: the late Aubrey
de Selincourt, whom I remember with special affection as the
first; Graham Storey, Theodore Redpath, and F. R. Leavis at
Cambridge, whose supervisions were always better than I
deserved; and my friends and masters at Johns Hopkins. Don
Cameron Allen, Earl R. Wasserman, and Jackson I. Cope
remain still the teachers whose learning and acumen I try—
backwardly—to emulate. Mr Quentin Skinner of Christ's
College has most helpfully criticized the first chapter, and I am
also indebted to a correspondence with Professor Arthur
Barker for some shrewd questions which I fear I have in-
adequately answered. The Folger and Newberry libraries
assisted me with summer fellowships in 1961 and 1964, and I
am grateful to their staffs and their resources. The English
Department of Cornell University, through its grant-in-aid

fund, mercifully relieved me of some course-work in 1961–62. I should also like to thank the Clarendon Press, Oxford, for permission to quote from H. M. Margoliouth's edition of Marvell's poems and letters, the Bodleian Library for allowing me to reproduce as a curiosity a drawing of Marvell's stag seal, and The Johns Hopkins University for paying the expenses of typing the manuscript.

Chapters two and three appeared in earlier versions in *PMLA* and *ELH*. Other opinions and occasional sentences have appeared in articles and reviews in *The Bulletin of the New York Public Library*, *The Journal of the History of Ideas*, *Modern Language Notes*, *Modern Language Quarterly*, and *The Yale Review*. I gladly record their editors' permissions to reprint. Finally, this book is dedicated to my parents, because my filial obligations are of such long standing that I know of no other way to acknowledge them; I would also thank my wife, Justine, who has helped so much during the later stages of writing.

J. M. W.

Baltimore
August 1966

Introduction

Strange as it may seem to suggest a comparison between Andrew Marvell and Edward Hyde, the best model for a book on seventeenth-century loyalism that tries to alter some of the preconceptions about a particular man is Mr B. H. G. Wormald's classic study, *Clarendon*. At the heart of his thesis, which is developed and documented with extraordinary finesse, is the simple observation that when Hyde sat down to write the original *History of the Rebellion* in 1646 his attitude toward the past was already coloured by defeat. By that time he had acquired a deep insight into the King's difficulties and a willingness to excuse his mistakes; he was prepared to say that evil motives had guided the actions of the violent party from the start, and his loyalty to the crown led him to explain the King's actions so well that readers have been misled regarding Hyde's own activities during the period he described. In spite of the royalist cast thus given to the *History*, above all by his understanding of Charles and his unsympathetic treatment of the parliamentary leaders, the facts were otherwise, and Hyde's actions during those years were consistently directed at negotiation, bridge-building, and a settlement that would incorporate the results of the constitutional revolution of 1640–41. Defeat did not change these aims, although it altered the means whereby he thought they might be achieved, and the years to the Restoration saw him devising and managing a royal policy of patience that would not compromise the crown in the affections of the English people. He did his best to thwart the Scots alliance, he set his hand against all the schemes to invade England with a foreign army, and at the Restoration the wisdom with which he had waited on providence was rewarded. It is a moving and convincing story as Mr Wormald tells it, which destroys the old myth that Hyde changed from a parliamentarian into a royalist, or even into a constitutional royalist, in so far as the phrase implies a compromise with his parliamentary principles. Under such an analysis, Hyde draws nearer to the centre, further away from the true royalist extreme represented by the Queen and George Digby, and his ends and his methods are seen to be nearer to the desires of the majority of men concerned in the struggle. One of Wormald's conclu, sions is indeed that 'the true bridge between the non-resistance of the epoch of the Tudor rulers and the eighteenth-century constitution was the non-violent, the bridge-building parlia, mentarism of Hyde'.[1]

Loyalism, whether of Clarendon's or Marvell's variety, is intimately connected with this centre and may be said to arise from it. Politically both men were concerned with constitu, tional government, and both shared the conviction that a deep process was at work in history with which it was necessary for men to combine if providence were to bring good out of evil. The divergence of their paths after 1649 is to be explained not by supposing that Marvell apostatized from his royalism, any more than Hyde ceased to hold his parliamentary views during the long exile, but by recognizing that as each man sought to discern what God's part demanded of him, one decided that his only rôle was to be more patient, the other that he was called to an active participation in the reconstruction of public order. In January 1649 the country as a whole, Marvell and Hyde included, were appalled at the catastrophe which had occurred, and all moderate men were united in their grief and shame; at no other time in the century did the central position between political extremes hold so many men of a single mind. The crucial differences between the loyalism of Hyde and Marvell emerge later, and Marvell first defined his new stance in the Horatian ode. What Marvell argued for in that poem was the very thing that Hyde most feared—the legitimation of Crom, well's power—but Hyde feared it because he understood it to be the one alternative to the restoration of the Stuarts that the

[1] *Clarendon* (Cambridge, 1951), p. 153.

people might accept. His pondering over history had assured him early that the factions could be left to destroy themselves, and he thought he perceived that the people would never tolerate permanently an illegal rule by the generals. On this faith his waiting policy was based, but he watched anxiously the growing demand for a new dynasty of kings. If his original *History* reflects a difference between his new historical aware, ness, which dictated patience, and his earlier attitude, which was more actively political, so does Marvell's ode reflect a similar difference between his past and present attitudes. No ad, herent of the King could have regarded the execution with the poise Marvell achieves in the ode. His feelings would have been more shocked, probably more angry. But Marvell, like Clarendon, had been considering the historical process, and was persuaded that the Stuarts had gone for good. Defeat altered Clarendon's account of the revolution; Cromwell's victory altered Marvell's, as we can see by comparing the ode with the earlier poems. Wormald's simple observation that the past gets changed in the telling when men perceive its issue is as essential to a reading of the ode as it is to *The History of the Rebellion*.

By our contemporary standards, both Marvell and Hyde, with their whole generation, were whig historians, regarding and retelling the past with one eye on the present, and tending to see in the outcome of history a moral judgment passed by the Almighty. The whig historians of the nineteenth century, viewing seventeenth-century conflicts in the light of their own constitution, saw the revolutionaries of the 1640s and the whigs of the 1680s carrying the torch of progress, and con, sequently they dissolved many of the complexities of the period.[1] All books now concerned with seventeenth-century history are explicitly or implicitly devoted to recapturing the complexity

[1] The thesis is explored in the book which provided a programme for re, investigation, Herbert Butterfield's *The Whig Interpretation of History* (London, 1931).

of it all, and restoring to visibility the elements that vanished in the old versions of party politics. One of the most significant results of the new work has been to undermine the confidence with which historians once spoke of 'presbyterians', 'independents', 'royalists', 'whigs' and 'tories'; the terms are retained as indispensable for discourse but with the common understanding that they do not describe hard and fast categories of opinion, or parties with clearly defined limits. In other words, the fluidity of thought has been recognized, and the existence of a large area of common ground shared occasionally by people of every stripe has become more prominent at the same time that generalizations become more difficult to make. The Long Parliament will not divide along economic lines, as was once thought; Hobbes is being brought into relation with contemporary political thought instead of standing outside it; belief in the immemorial constitution or fundamental rights has been shown to cut across all party boundaries, and in a disputing age the occasions for conflict would appear to be outnumbered only by the common assumptions of the antagonists.

The movement against the whig interpretation of history, however, has not yet produced a book on the loyalists— thousands and thousands of them—who turned their coats with the times and followed with a clear conscience the changes of regime between 1649 and 1688. The dictionaries barely acknowledge their existence, the O.E.D. granting not so much as a paragraph, let alone examples, to the subsidiary definition of a loyalist as 'one who supports the existing form of government'. To Dr Johnson a loyalist was still 'one who professes uncommon adherence to the king', and the establishment to this day would appear not to sanction any definition of loyalty that implies a right to change one's allegiance if a usurper overturns the state. Common parlance, however, if I am not mistaken, grants a measure of loyalty to a man who defers the transference of his allegiance until after the death of his former sovereign; he may be loyal 'to the existing form of government' provided the old government is extinct. The word 'loyalist' is needed in this sense, because 'turn-coat', 'collaborator', and their synonyms are grotesque distortions for the kind of changing allegiance that Marvell typifies, and had they been thrown about by anybody except splenetic old cavaliers after the Restoration, orderly government would have been at an end. Buckingham, Shaftesbury, Carlisle, Hale, Downing, Hobbes, Locke, Waller, Dryden, Cowley: a long list could be compiled of men who had made a formal submission to the Common-wealth but who quickly obtained either office or recognition under Charles II. The Act of Oblivion does not explain the phenomenon, for it merely granted a formal status to the fact that most men neither judged nor felt that service under the Commonwealth was necessarily a stumbling-block to perfect loyalty to the restored monarchy. The Restoration as a whole admitted loyalism, in its second sense, as a genuine alternative to the more distinguished allegiance of the exiles. Why this was so, Marvell's example should demonstrate, but the nearest approach to a definition of loyalism during the Interregnum supplies one good reason why side-changing was so readily excused. Writing in 1656 to persuade England to elect Crom-well king, John Hall concluded: 'So then we may see the way to be a constant Royalist, is to be a constant Loyalist; not to respect the power or place for the persons sake, but the person for the place and power[s] sake.'[1] To Hall there was little difference between royalism and loyalism if properly under-stood, because both presupposed subjection to a single person as the head of state; but whereas the obedience of the royalist was to the king's person, the loyalist's was to his office and authority. Hall's remark is the logical outcome of the distinction between office and person which had served its purpose splendidly in justifying the rebellion, and which was to become the hall-mark of whig constitutionalism at the revolution of 1688. In

[1] *The True Cavalier Examined by his Principles* (London, 1656), p. 109.

between lies the effort of the Cromwellians to establish another mixed monarchy in which loyalism and royalism would have been as indistinguishable as they eventually became to Dr Johnson. Already by 1656 the difference was harder to main/ tain, or easier to break down, than it had been in 1649.

It is hard to understand why loyalism has not attracted the atten/ tion it deserves, although easy to guess why the earlier historians ignored it. The similarities in theory between revolutionaries and whigs were sufficiently plain to facilitate drawing a straight line from the democratic aspects of puritan politics to the more stable constitutionalism under William and Mary, and the timeservers in the middle appeared tangential. As Marchamont Nedham was their best/known representative, they doubtless seemed highly unpleasant also. Miss Robbins in her pioneering dissertation on Marvell's politics forty years ago called attention to the Cromwellian rather than republican background of whiggery, but her comments have never been followed up. Instead there has been what could be called a disproportionate emphasis on Milton's thought, had not the concentration produced some of the very best studies of seventeenth/century politics and religion. Milton, at any rate, has diverted literary critics from the loyalists because Milton's reaction to the execution was so different from theirs. Even the excellent new surveys by the editors of the Yale edition of Milton's prose pay only passing attention to Ascham, Dury, and Rous, whose opinions nevertheless were for a brief while more representative of popular sentiment than Milton's. The omission is more the fault of the Marvellians than the Miltonists, because the former have not produced an account of their poet that is clear enough to offer the basis for a comparison. Its general features would show the same striking similarities and important differences that mark the comparison with Hyde, but whereas Hyde and Marvell were most alike in January 1649, Marvell and Milton were most dissimilar. The evidence for their later friendship during the Interregnum is slight but indisputable, and the obvious grounds for it would be the depth of their religious feelings, their ecclesiastical prejudices and millenarian hopes, and the aristocratic bias of their minds. Marvell's unreserved support for Cromwell, however, suggests that in politics there must always have remained differences of opinion between them, and the course of their careers points to the basically different pattern followed by the loyalist and the revolutionary. Marvell's epic (as I attempt to show) was written in a retirement from which he emerged to join Milton in office, but while Milton retired to write his epic at the Restoration, Marvell continued in the House of Commons. The loyalism of one carried him over into an effective political career after 1660, while what may loosely be called Milton's republicanism forced him into political silence. In this pattern we find once again what we expect to find—that Marvell's political attitude overlaps with Milton's as it does with Hyde's, without ever becoming quite the same.

Hyde, Marvell, and Milton were all dead before the final settlement was made—final, that is, relative to the changes which had preceded it—but each stood for ideas that were embodied in the working solution that was eventually found to the constitutional difficulties. To pronounce which of them was more important is unnecessary and perhaps impossible, but as Milton's defences of liberty have been praised so often and his influence traced into later generations, and as Mr Wormald has not hesitated to say that Clarendon's parliamentarism is the bridge between two epochs, I hope I may be permitted to add that Marvell's loyalism embraces much that was best in each of them. He kept faith with the existing government until it disappeared, he worked like Hyde for peace and moderation, he defended toleration and even Milton himself. The central political experience and wisdom of the age that found expression after 1688 was also his wisdom, and the profound constitutionalism of Clarendon and the reforming spirit of Milton found a champion in his own life and works.

To substantiate fully the claims I should like to make for the importance of the loyalist spirit as an expression of the centre of moderation in seventeenth-century politics is beyond my capacities. The book that needs to be written would have to begin with the Wars of the Roses or with the upheavals that preceded the accession of Elizabeth to the throne. From that period the Vicar of Bray was resurrected at the Restoration as the prototype of the loyalist whose instinct for survival could be attributed by cavaliers to an easy cynicism. The history of a more scrupulous timeserving than the vicar's would also require the detailed biographies of many loyalists, and a study of the legal and other public office-holders who retained their posts from one cataclysm to the next. It would demand a considerable knowledge of English law and perhaps a talent for mind-reading, since loyalism is an ethical as well as a constitutional problem, and the motives of people who changed allegiances is a question one cannot escape. My own limited aim has been to clarify for other literary critics the political implications of some of Marvell's poems and prose tracts, but with the hope that they will thus become more available to historians as documents in a fascinating history that could be written. The first chapter is an attempt to sketch a background for the first change of allegiance that Marvell undoubtedly made within a year and a half of the King's execution.

'The Spirits of all that were moderate': The civil war debates and the Engagement controversy

The Civil War Debates

The narrative of the hostility between King and Parliament has frequently been retold as a struggle for sovereignty. Each side occupied an opposite corner, with Parliament defending common and statute law, and the King claiming that a more funda⁄ mental law of necessity enabled him to exercise his prerogatives in time of national danger. After a few rounds, these posi⁄ tions tended to be reversed until Charles was championing English law against Parliament's invocation of natural law and popular sovereignty. Concluding the most instructive of recent analyses of these changes, Professor Sirluck has employed a different metaphor: 'It would be easy enough to represent the whole complex debate⁄at⁄law...as a kind of comic ballet, a series of formalized movements, each purporting to be full of meaning, but when the sequence is completed seen to be only a dance.'[1] Sirluck is anxious, however, that the ballet be taken seriously, and we can so take it more easily if we insist that it is in the nature of casuistry, political and otherwise, to appear like a dance, and to end in the place where it began. As the science and the art of applying general principles to difficult cases, casuistry was committed to discussing the particular instance rather than the theory which both sides held in com⁄ mon. Ferne with his *Wounded Conscience*, and *Conscience Satisfied*, and *The Resolving of Conscience*, William Bridge with his *Conscience Cured*, Burroughes, Ball, Maxwell, Herle, and

---

[1] *Complete Prose Works of John Milton* (New Haven, 1953–   ), II, p. 51, from which the summary above also derives.

the other disputants for the two parties were perfectly aware of the rules of their method: the civil war presented itself to them as the most colossal case of conscience with which they had ever had to contend, and their assumption was that the solution could be found if men kept their tempers and honed their arguments to ever finer distinctions. Until the levellers came to dominate the Press and casuistical manners became impaired, casuistry provided the main support for the remonstrances, declarations, ordinances, and answers in which the parties' practical measures were put forward. Casuistry was peculiarly fitted for this task because the systematic treatment of cases had been developed in order to define, especially, the limits of Christian obedience in crucial instances, and to determine the guilt or excusability of particular actions. To all casuists, circumstances altered cases profoundly, so that two cases which looked alike might admit of very different solutions. Much of the confusion that one feels on first reading the constitutional debates may therefore be attributed to the air of relativity which casuistry casts over its subjects. Necessary as it is to ethical science, it may be said to have trained men in the seventeenth century to base their moral decisions on distinctions which are not always visible to the modern eye; it induced by its very nature an atmosphere in which the loyalists' choice in 1649 was easier to make, just as it had underpinned every possible allegiance during its vintage years with a wealth of argument and allusion. Arguments which had proved interchangeable during the war would be likely to effect similar substitutions later; casuistry was a system that could digest anything, and account for every circumstance. As one critic has said, 'means come to throw ends into the shade. In a word, the more self-conscious casuistry grows, the more its dangerous qualities tend to assert themselves.'[1]

[1] R. M. Wenley, 'Casuistry' in *Encyclopaedia of Religion and Ethics*, ed. James Hastings (Edinburgh, 1910), III, p. 242. My remarks on casuistry are indebted to this article and to Timothy Brosnahan's in *The Catholic Encyclopedia* (New York, 1908).

The course of the civil war may be said to confirm that statement, but the principal importance of recognizing the method for what it is is that it allows us to remove the emphasis from the difference of the principal parties and to appreciate more clearly what they had in common. In so doing one is following, as I have claimed, the trend of recent seventeenth-century historiography, which more and more has abandoned rigid party terminology, and has resorted to broader and more flexible terms such as violent and non-violent parliamentarism.[1] Casuistry was the natural mode of compromise, and the extent of it would suggest that the number of men who thought of themselves as moderate and peace-loving was yet larger than anyone has supposed. Moderation, however, was an extremely active virtue, unrelated to neutrality, and its casuistry was the most contentious of *genres* at the same time as it remained the least quarrelsome, simultaneously the organ of moderation and the servant of party subterfuge. Yet the arguments which the casuists proffered were meant to be, like Vane's, 'healing questions', and this aspect of casuistry's dual nature needs to be emphasized for the additional reason that the loyalist tracts of 1649 were begotten out of an overmastering desire for peace—the desire which is implicit in so many of the earlier works whose superficial appearance is wholly disputatious. The levellers nowhere proclaimed their revolutionary aims more conspicuously than in their rejection of the casuistical method and tone, for thereby they ignored the assumption, which the casuists took for granted, that civil war was the greatest tragedy that could befall the country, and peace the greatest good.

The common ground of the civil war debates was power, and Charles and Lilburne could have shaken hands on the fact

[1] See, notably, J. H. Hexter, *The Reign of King Pym* (Cambridge, Mass., 1941); B. H. G. Wormald, *Clarendon* (Cambridge, 1951); George Yule, *The Independents in the English Civil War* (Cambridge, 1958); and David Underdown, 'The Independents Reconsidered', *Journal of British Studies*, III (1964), pp. 57–84. Miss Margaret Judson's admirable study, *The Crisis of the Constitution* (New Brunswick, N. J., 1949), stops at 1645.

that all power was of God: the quarrel was about its distribu-
tion, not its origin. There was remarkable unanimity, moreover,
on the permissibility of all forms of government, the royalists
having no choice but to concede that no form was *jure
divino*, and all parties concurred that government itself was
necessary, and that every constitution needed somewhere an
arbitrary sovereign power from which no appeal could be
made. All that was left for many men at the end of the civil
war, it might be argued, were the certainties with which both
sides had started, and these alone were enough to induce a large
part of the population to accept passively the arbitrary power
that survived to govern in 1649. So broad a generalization,
however, would require too much qualification, and it will be
safer to look beneath the tendentious misrepresentation to
which casuistry is given, and to examine the major premise as
royalists came to interpret it.

Romans xiii. 1–2, as many have realized, was not only the
principal text for the royalists, but the heart of the matter, their
'main shelf-Anchor', as Parker called it. In St Paul's dictum
the theological and political halves of their argument found a
common base, and one of their important spokesmen, Henry
Ferne, made a major distinction which had long been more or
less explicit. There were, he said, three parts in the original of
power, which Parker and his allies had confused. First, there
was power itself, which in any form was enough to command,
coerce, and govern a people. The second part was the designa-
tion of the person to bear that power, which might on occasion
be accomplished by the people. Thirdly, the qualification of the
power was sometimes a contract between king and people, and
at others a limitation imposed by laws made by mutual consent.
But the power itself, he insisted—and by that he meant the
first part of his triad—was of God: 'That sufficiency of Autho-
ritie to govern, which is in Monarchy or Aristocracie, abstractly
considered from the qualifications of either form, is an efflux
or constitution subordinate to that providence, an ordinance of

that *Dixi*, that silent *Word* by which the world was at first made, and is still governed under God.'[1] The two sops which this definition threw to the parliamentarians had always been granted by royalists when they wished to take the edge off the absolutism inherent in their main claim, and they had become mandatory since the King's *Answer to the Nineteen Propositions*. As Miss Weston has shown, the *Answer* had been Charles's extremely influential statement that England was a mixed monarchy and the King, therefore, ruled in Parliament for all legislative purposes.[2] This qualification, which destroyed at one blow the absolute legislative (and hence sovereign) power which the King had once claimed by divine right, cleared the way for Parliament's natural law. In every possible way their apologists explored the designing and qualifying aspects of power and insisted on their applicability to Charles. One of their favourite tactics was to distinguish between power in the abstract, which parliament was not resisting, and power in the person of the King; this ancient stratagem had been employed by loyal Englishmen when they sought to dislodge Queen Mary, and it had been as vigorously denied by the same true subjects when later they asserted Queen Elizabeth's authority. The royalists now followed suit, as defenders of the new state in 1649 were to do again. To admit that power could be considered apart from the rulers who wielded it would have been to open a gap between lawful and unlawful power which the royalists could not afford. The parliamen⁄

[1] *The Resolving of Conscience* (Cambridge, 1642), p. 17. James I always claimed that he derived his power and authority as directly from God as the Pope did his. And cf. Roger Maynwaring's famous sermon, *Religion and Allegiance* (London, 1627), p. 8: 'All *Powers* created are of God; *no power, unlesse it bee given from above*: And *all powers*, that are of this sort, *are ordained of God*. Among all the *Powers* that be ordained of God, the *Regall* is most high, strong, and large.'

[2] Corinne Comstock Weston, 'The Theory of Mixed Monarchy under Charles I and After', *EHR*, LXXV (1960), pp. 426–43. Also Francis D. Wormuth, *The Royal Prerogative, 1603–1649* (Ithaca, N.Y. 1939), pp. 114–16.

tarians of course opened it anyhow, which drove the King's clerics to an even more fiercely literal interpretation of St Paul's text. The unity of person and power had to be maintained, or the disparity between king and tyrant, which royalists habitually denied when discussing obedience, would become impossible to control. Maxwell, for example, while he agreed as usual that kings were rarely appointed in modern times by God's fiat—an appointment which admittedly was special and immediate—would not relinquish the immediacy of the power enjoyed by ordinary kings:

The second way, we hold that all Kings really so, are immediately from God: for although some *Signum creatum*, some humane and created act, *as election, succession, conquest*, or what else in that kind is imaginable and possible interveneth, to *the designation of the person*, yet the *reall constitution, the collation of Soveraignty and Royalty* is immediately from God, for the act or condition presupposed or interposed containeth not in it that power to collate Royall and Soveraigne power: onely by Gods appointment it is inseperably joyned with it, or infallibly followeth after it, so that it referreth to God as the *proper donor and immediate author*.[1]

Maxwell's verbiage cannot disguise his mere repetition of Ferne, who in turn has but added his mite to the treasury of royalist assertion on the topic. Matthew Griffith summarized hundreds of pages of royalist casuistry when he wrote, 'Election doth not make him *King* although, unless he had been chosen he had not beene such';[2] and William Ball's *Caveat* to the parliamentarians was to the same effect. Professor Hughes is quite correct to draw attention to the increasing absolutism of these statements as the 1640s wore on, of which Filmer's *Anarchy* in 1648 and his recension of Bodin, *The Necessity of the Absolute Power of All Kings*, can be seen as the apotheosis.[3]

[1] [John Maxwell,] *Sacro-Sancta Regum Majestas* (Oxford, 1644), p. 22.
[2] *A Sermon Preached in the Citie of London by a Lover of Truth* (London, 1643), p. 19.
[3] *Complete Prose Works of John Milton*, III, pp. 60–1. Robert Weldon's *The Doctrine of the Scriptures, Concerning the Original of Dominion* (London, 1648) is another extreme statement which Hughes cites.

Despite the unusual naturalism of Filmer's theory, he accurately gauged the direction of royalist thought. Figgis described the civil war as the great period for the divine right of kings: 'As a popular force in politics', he remarked, 'the theory hardly exerted much influence until the time of the Long Parliament. Henceforward Divine Right becomes the watchword of all supporters of the rights of the Crown.'[1] One is puzzled at first to observe that expert and more recent historians regard the theory as having died out by 1640,[2] to be replaced by the less absolute doctrine of the mixed monarchy, but both views may be accepted if Figgis can be understood to have been expounding not the divine right of kings but the divine right of power.

Charles had settled for a mixed monarchy and could not go back on it, and by his *Answer* had tacitly accepted the revolution of 1640. His theorists had been left with the task of defending his sovereignty after he had admitted that in normal times he shared the legislative power, with which sovereign power was identified, with the other estates of the realm. Hunton in his now famous *Treatise* saw the problem precisely. Romans xiii was their godsend because, unlike the interpretations of natural law, revelation was incontrovertible, and the royalists had the advantage of a plain reading of the words which did not rely on subtleties of exposition. So long as they stuck to their text they could, in a sense, defy casuistry, and reiterate the necessity of obedience on the simple ground that any supreme power, however elected, derived directly from God. As England was a monarchy, it required only the minimum finesse to refute the argument that Parliament's power was similarly acquired. Thomas Swadlin managed very briefly to combine the royal truisms. The best government, he declared, is the mixture of monarchy, aristocracy, and democracy, 'but these three meeting in one, though severally, they

[1] J. Neville Figgis, *The Divine Right of Kings*, 2nd ed. (Cambridge, 1914), pp. 141–2.
[2] Judson, *The Crisis of the Constitution*, p. 386.

are equally and immediately from God, yet joyntly, the first onely, Monarchy, is immediately from God, and the rest from God, but mediately by the King'.[1] Yet Swadlin, on the previous page, had made an assertion which revealed the weakness of all royalist theory if the King should ever be deposed: 'His [St Paul's] perswasion is, *For there is no power but of God;* and my Proposition is, *Every power is of God.*' In the light of later events, the royalists' hapless but fatal flaw was the adoption of the language of St Paul, which committed them to dis-cussing not the uniqueness of kings or hereditary privilege but the doctrine of power, which was open to interpretations that neither they nor their enemies ever dreamed would become realities within a decade. Given the King's admission that the flowers of the crown were no longer as numerous as he had once supposed, the absolutism of royalist language during the 1640s may be regarded as partly a casuistical accident. The advising of the monarch, it is true, tended to fall increasingly into the hands of extremists, and Charles was unlikely to have objected to anyone who, like Michael Hudson, was eager to uphold his rights adamantly and at length, but royalists as a whole were not so absolute as they sounded, as their casuistry made them seem. The method of disputation, though contro-versial, remained an irenic mode, so that Quarles was quite consistent in prefacing one of the more uncompromising tracts with remarks to the honest-hearted reader which were all sweetness and peace.[2] The most genuinely absolute claims on behalf of the King derived not from St Paul but from Hobbes and his version of contractual theory, but with these we are not concerned, except to remark that both contract and the divine right of power were nearly related to the doctrine of election in which anglicans and puritans believed. An election, whether of king, priest, or presbyter, was not completed until the candi-

[1] Thomas Swadlin, *The Soveraignes Desire Peace: The Subjiects Dutie Obedience* (London, 1643), p. 20.
[2] *The Loyall Convert* (Oxford, 1643).

16

date's vocation had been tested, and the rites of institution into his office had been performed. At the moment of consecration, however, God conferred on him a spirit which was inde-pendent of the means of election. In ecclesiastical affairs, churchmen and presbyterians preserved the right to eject scandalous ministers, but in the political battle the royalists chose to emphasize the permanency of an election or contract once it could be presumed to have taken place. The analogies which they occasionally used were the soul's infusion into the seed after conception, or the grace received by an infant in baptism. Contract theory itself was the product of natural law, but its *modus operandi* was sufficiently similar to that of the divine law operating from day to day in the church for royalists to have had no difficulty in adapting it to their needs. The puritans, who had thought more deeply about Christian election than most anglicans, found the provisional nature of a king's election an easy subject to manipulate. It might have been wiser for the royalists if they had developed their contrac-tual ideas more fully, as their dogmas of power were open to very dangerous interpretations.

Unsurprisingly, it was Henry Parker who saw at once the weakness of the opposition's theory. He was later to complain that all men were slaves if the royalists' reading of Romans xiii was correct, and he opened his most original and important work with a characteristically bold sally:

In this contestation between Regall and Parliamentary power... *The King attributeth the originall of his royalty to God, and the Law, making no mention of the graunt, consent, or trust of man therein*, but the truth is, God is no more the author of Regall, then of Aristocraticall power, nor of supreme, then of subordinate command; nay, that dominion which is usurped, and not just, yet whilst it remaines dominion, and till it be legally again devested, referres to God, as to its Author and donor, as much as that which is hereditary.[1]

---

[1] *Observations on some of His Majesties Late Answers and Expresses*, in *Tracts on Liberty in the Puritan Revolution*, ed. William Haller (New York, 1933–34), II, p. 167.

Parker knew very well that this would cause trouble, because if the royalists were prepared to allow legality to other forms of government than monarchy, they certainly had no intention of granting it to usurpers. Parker, moreover, was not hinting that Parliament should usurp the throne, and he would have agreed that intruders could be resisted, but he had also perceived how embarrassing the problem of usurpation was to a party that upheld the privileges of a tyrant and denied any to his over-thrower. Few of the respondents to Parker's pamphlet failed to rise to the bait, and the best they could do was very little. Digges, with Herle from the other camp concurring, thought that usurpers could be resisted, but neither wished to discuss them.[1] Sir John Spelman dismissed the difficulty by asserting that 'with such absolute Dominion, *England* hath nought to doe',[2] but Bramhall was the most explicit:

We have been taught otherwise [than by Parker], before a few vaine upstart Empericks, in Policy troubled the world, that Dominion in a tyrannicall Hereditary Governour, is from God even in the concrete, (I mean the power not the abuse) that such an one may not be resisted with-out Sinne, that his Person is sacred: But contrarywise, that Dominion in a tyrannicall Usurper or Intruder is indeed from God permitting, wheras he could restrain it, if it pleased him; or from God concurring by a general influence, as the Earth giveth nourishment to Hemlocks, as well as Wheate, *in him we live, we move, and have our being*, or from God ordering and disposing it as he doth all other accidents and events to his own glory; but that it is not from God as Author, Donor, or Instituter of it. Neither dare we give to a Tyrannicall Usurper the essential Priviledges of Soveraignty; we deny not that any Subject may lawfully kill him as a publicke Enemy, without legall eviction. Much lesse dare we say with the Observer, that Power usurped and unlawfull, is as much from God, as Power Hereditary and lawfull. If it be so, cough out man, and tell us plainly, that God is the Author of Sinne.[3]

[1] [Dudley Digges,] *A Review of the Observations* (Oxford, 1643), pp. 2–4; also his *An Answer to a Printed Book* (Oxford, 1642), pp. 3–4; [Charles Herle,] *A Fuller Answer to a Treatise Written by Doctor Ferne* (London, 1642), p. 22.   [2] *A View of a Printed Book* (Oxford, 1642), p. 13.
[3] *The Serpent Salve, or, a Remedie for the Biting of an Aspe* (n.p. 1643), p. 10.

No distinction was more necessary or more standard than the one between God's permission and His ordinance, but none was more open to a purely subjective interpretation. Bramhall was unwilling to make consent the basis of a just title, but he did not elaborate why a tyrant was from God 'in the concrete', whereas a usurper might be assassinated. Having argued on the previous page that Charles's right rested ultimately on conquest, he was inconsistent in denying a right to the conquering intruder. Maxwell, having promised as his second topic a refutation of Parker's statement, wisely terminated his *Sacro-Sancta Regum Majestas* after an interminable discussion of the king's sovereign and God-given power. Bishop Williams, who was less cautious, found himself trapped into admitting that if a people deposed their king, the new ruler they instituted would obtain his power from God.[1] According to John Hall later, a popular royalist saying declared the crown was to be obeyed and fought for 'although it stood upon a May-Pole',[2] and the truth was that royalist thought leaned so heavily on the mystique of the crown and hereditary privilege that there had always existed, and remained, a fundamental ambiguity about the kind of title possessed by the institutor of a new dynasty. Bodin's conception of sovereignty led him to regard *puissance souveraine* rather than *droit gouvernement* as the essential mark of a state.[3] Monarchies, he said, cannot be distinguished from one another by the method of succession, but only by the way they are conducted—despotically, royally, or tyranically. A man who acquired power unjustly, but who ruled well, was a

[1] Griffith Williams, *Jura Majestatis* (Oxford, 1644), pp. 17–18. Noted in J. W. Allen, *English Political Thought, 1603–1660* (London, 1938), p. 489.

[2] *The True Cavalier Examined by his Principles* (London, 1656), pp. 101–2.

[3] J. W. Allen, 'Jean Bodin', in *Social and Political Ideas of Some Great Thinkers of the Sixteenth and Seventeenth Centuries*, ed. F. J. C. Hearnshaw (London, 1926), p. 48. M. J. Tooley discusses the matter in the introduction to Bodin's *Six Books of the Commonwealth* (Oxford, n.d.), pp. xxi–xxxix. Similarly K. D. McRae in the introduction to his ed. of *The Six Books* (Cambridge, Mass., 1962), p. A20, speaks of the 'moral neutrality' of Bodin's conception of sovereignty, with its allowances for the power of usurpers.

lawful king. Richard Hooker implied also that the usurpation
of a throne was less important than the government which
followed the intrusion, and the 'usurper of power' who might
be deposed was the ruler who abused the power he had lawfully
obtained.[1] Like Hooker, Lancelot Andrewes could preach
cheerfully before Queen Elizabeth on the subject of the Jews'
obedience to Tiberius, Caligula, and Nero, because he assumed
that the Emperors' authority had been justly gained by con-
quest.[2] Grotius, equally anxious to defend the royal prerogative,
admitted that if an invader gained possession of a kingdom by
force 'the right of war seemeth to remain'. Echoing his
predecessors, he concluded that no private man should take
upon himself to judge the title of a usurper, but should follow
the possession: 'Thus Christ bade that tribute be paid to
Caesar because the coin bore Caesar's image, that is because
Caesar was in possession of the governing power.'[3] Bishop
Overall's suppressed *Convocation Book* is perhaps the best, as it
is the most famous, evidence that royalists found it impossible
always to maintain the difference between *de facto* and *de jure*
government. Coke had ruled that treason could be committed
against usurpers, and even during the civil war Quarles can
be found referring to the 'De Facto Act' of Henry VII in
order to support his proof from Romans xiii.[4] Thomas Morton

[1] 'Supposed Fragment of a Sermon on Civil Obedience, hitherto printed as
part of the Eighth Book', in *Works*, ed. John Keble, 5th ed. (Oxford, 1865),
III, pp. 456-60.
[2] 'A sermon preached at Whitehall, 15 Nov. 1601', in *Ninety-Six Sermons*,
Library of Anglo-Catholic Theology (Oxford, 1841-43), V, p. 132.
[3] *De Jure Belli ac Pacis* I. iv. 20, trans. Francis W. Kelsey, *Classics of International
Law*, ed. James Brown Scott, no. 3 (Washington, D.C., 1913-25), II,
p. 163. All quotations from Grotius are from this ed. Christopher Hill in a
review (*Essays in Criticism*, x [1960], p. 208) has observed that Samuel
Daniel never made up his mind 'whether he was on the side of legitimacy or
de facto stability', although all his revisions of *The Civil Wars* tended towards
the latter.
[4] *The Loyall Convert*, p. 7. The ambiguities of the Tudor position have been
discussed by A. F. Pollard in *Factors in Modern History* (London, 1919),

was similarly oblivious to the implications when he remarked that Pontius Pilate had his power directly from God.[1]

Royalists, in fact, had habitually proved themselves unable to do more than assert a distinction between permission and right, and, as their treatment of the Roman Emperors shows, they could manage to prove it only by attributing a lawful title to every forced power which had ever succeeded in maintaining itself. Parker followed up his advantage in *Jus Populi*. He affirmed wholeheartedly that God's hand was to be seen in the crowning of princes—but He also dethroned them, and Scripture contained many proofs that 'God giveth and taketh away Scepters'. Therefore Jeroboam the usurper held his crown as truly from God as Rehoboam, Nebuchadnezzar as Josiah, Cyrus as Judas Maccabeus, and Richard III as his nephew Edward V. Wherefore, he concluded, we ought to be careful about what we ascribe to God's direction and what to man's.[2] The point of his argument, as it had been of Herle's discussing usurpation, was clearly to force the opposing casuists to grant that popular consent played a large part in determining the legality of any title; it was not, of course, intended as a personal threat to the King. The royalists were fortunate in that the topic could prove equally embarrassing to the parliamentarians were it pressed too far, and they were probably aided in the mid-1640s by the rise of the levellers, to whom usurpation became a word to be used indiscriminately to describe everything they disliked. Even they were at first reluctant to claim that their reforms necessitated the unthroning of the King, and they needed a conquest of their own to clarify their minds. The King's apologists were not unaware, I think, that their views on the King's right by

pp. 163–65, and in 'The "de facto" act of Henry VII', *Bull. Inst. Hist. Research*, VII (1929–30), pp. 1–12; and by Kenneth Pickthorn, *Early Tudor Government: Henry VII* (Cambridge, 1949), pp. 151–66.
[1] *The Necessity of Christian Subjection* (Oxford, 1643), p. 2.
[2] (London, 1644), p. 13. For Herle on usurpation, see *A Fuller Answer* (London, 1642), p. 22.

conquest were inconsistent with the little they were prepared to say about usurpation, and, until the King had lost the first civil war, it appeared that conquest was one of the most promising arguments with which to counter the parliamentary attack.

Older historians gave more credit to the importance of conquest theory in the civil war debates than their recent successors. It seems to be held now that royalists never gave it much credence, and that the frequency with which it was attacked by parliamentarians in the 1640s and by whigs in the 'eighties and 'nineties is one of the anomalies of seventeenthcentury history. Mr Laslett has been surprised at the seriousness with which Locke regards the theory, and Mr Pocock has purported to find a reason why it was never popular with the men who reputedly believed it. Filmer, he observes, deplored Hobbes, who in *Leviathan* made a fear of the sword the basis of consent after conquest, and thereby gave an equal right to the usurper and a peacefully instituted monarch. 'Hobbes's clarity of mind had exhibited to the perspicacious Filmer the two fundamental reasons why conquest could never be a theory long acceptable to royalists. Under close analysis it proved to be a mingling of force and covenant; and the royalists, especially under the Interregnum, could stomach neither.'[1] No great perspicacity was needed in 1652 to see that this was precisely what was wrong

[1] J. G. A. Pocock, *The Ancient Constitution and the Feudal Law* (Cambridge, 1957), p. 164; see also p. 149. Cf. Peter Laslett, ed., *Locke's Two Treatises of Government* (Cambridge, 1960), pp. 403–4 n. Recently, however, Quentin Skinner in an important article has put the conquest argument into a true perspective ('History and Ideology in the English Revolution', *The Historical Journal*, VIII [1965], pp. 151–78). He points out that seventeenthcentury historians consistently, though innocently, subverted the whole 'whig' view that no Norman conquest had ever occurred, and that Hobbes's views on the subject were anything but unique. Skinner's survey is now authoritative, and while our arguments touch at several places I would demur only at his contention that conquest was not important to the royalist casuistry of the civil war. Hughes, *Complete Prose Works of John Milton*, III, p. 201 n., notes that conquest argument was 'widespread'.

with conquest theory, but by that time there were many royalists who must have wanted to eat their words, or who wondered what history had done to their casuistry; Griffith Williams, for example, who in 1644 wrote a paragraph that had the seeming virtue of commencing with a point which Parker liked to make and of carrying it to a contrary conclusion. Williams wrote:

When *rightfull* Kings became with *Nimrod* to be *unjust* Tyrants, then God that is not tyed to his *Vicegerent* any longer then he pleaseth, but hath right and power *Paramount* to translate the *rule*, and transferre the dominion of his people to whom he will; hath oftentimes *throwne downe the mighty from their seat*, and given away their crownes and kingdomes unto others, that were more *humble and meeke*, or some other way fitter to effect his divine purpose, as he did the kingdome of *Saul* unto *David*, and *Belshazzar's* unto *Cyrus*; and he doth most *commonly* by the power of the sword, when the Conqueror shall make his *strength* to become the *Law* of justice, and his *ability* to hold it, to become his *right* of enjoying it.[1]

The King's casuists badly needed the conquest theory, although they would not have required it at all if their belief that a king's power was directly from God had been generally acceptable; and they might have been more cautious while playing with swords. They were beset, however, by the argument that power devolved on the king through the people, and conquest enabled them to reply that, on the contrary, the people once they had submitted to a conqueror had surrendered their rights and could not regain them except by the voluntary gift of the new king and his successors. The beauty of the notion was that it appeared to utilize the consent of the people—because even a forced consent was a legal submission—while depriving them of every particle of sovereignty. In Bramhall's view, His Majesty's title rested on 'a Multitude of Conquests, the very last whereof is confirmed by a long Succession of foure and twenty royall Progenitors and Predecessors';[2] and the Observator could not deduce from this that England was a

[1] *Jura Majestatis*, pp. 16–17. [2] *The Serpent Salve*, p. 8.

land of vassals because there had been an equally long line of charters, good laws, and free acts of grace. Maxwell believed that a king might be a lawful ruler by conquest without any consent at all, and William Ball argued that William I could have made far greater changes in the constitution than he did: he might have acted as the King of Spain had done in the West Indies.[1] Thomas Dymock also awarded the King absolute rights by ancient conquest, while Sir John Spelman held the more moderate opinion that modern kingdoms originated from a mixture of paternal and martial power—the quarrels among the first families having led to the election of a strong man. When kingdoms were founded naturally, as by Shem and Abraham, or violently, as by Nimrod, the people had no choice in the institution of their governor. In the mixed form they did, but by no means did they have the exclusive choice.[2] For Henry Ferne conquest theory was one of the corner-stones of his several 'cases'. God, he affirmed, has a perfect power to dispose of sovereignty by ordinary providence, without waiting for a people's consent. 'If this Answerer should looke through all Christendome, he would scarce find a Kingdom that descends by inheritance, but it had a beginning in Armes, and yet I thinke he will not say the Titles of these Kings are no better then of Plunderers; for though it may be unjust at first in him that invades and Conquers, yet in the succession, which is from him, that providence which translates Kingdomes, manifests it selfe and the will of God; and there are *momenta temporum*, for the justnesse of such Titles, though we cannot fixe them.'[3] Even the impartial Hunton was willing to concede

---

[1] *A Caveat for Subjects, Moderating the Observator* (London, 1642), p. 6; see also p. 12; and Maxwell, *Sacro-Sancta Regum Majestas*, p. 158. William Ball later changed sides.

[2] *Certain Considerations upon the Duties both of Prince and People* (Oxford, 1642), pp. 2–3; Dymock, *Englands Dust and Ashes Raked up* (n.p. 1648), p. 72.

[3] *Conscience Satisfied* (Oxford, 1643), p. 32. Also p. 7: 'The Governing power was from God, not only as an ordinance of the precept that commands

that conquest 'may give a man title over, and power to possesse and dispose of the Countrey and Goods of the Conquered; yea, the Bodies and lives of the Conquered are at the Will and Pleasure of the Conquerour'.[1] But for Hunton subjection was a 'morall condition' involving consent, though he allowed that the consent paid to a victor, in exchange for life and servitude, was morally binding. Such a concession was grist for Digges's Hobbesian mill, and in a long analogy about the marriage of king and people, he exclaimed: 'So the consent of the people is now necessary to the making [of] Kings (for Conquest is but a kinde of ravishing, which many times prepares the way to a wedding, as the Sabine women chose rather to be wives, then concubines, and most people preferre the condition of Subjects though under hard lawes to that of slaves).'[2]

Pocock, looking at the royalists from the Interregnum period of their misery, has concluded that 'conquest struck few roots in royalist thought',[3] but a longer root would be hard to find. James I was tactfully brief but quite explicit on the origin of new empires in the power of the sword,[4] and Arthur Hall had been thrown into prison by Parliament in 1581 for dismissing the antiquity of the House of Commons on the same grounds. John Speed, the historian, described Caesar's conquest of the Britons, after which every man had 'departed, thinking it better to secure every private by his owne meanes, then by a generall power to hazard all, as hopelesse any more to uphold

Government, but also as an Efflux or issue of that providence, which sets up & pulls down, which translates Kingdomes, and governs the whole world, Creatures Reasonable and unreasonable.' See also his *A Reply unto Severall Treatises* (Oxford, 1643), pp. 18–21, 55, and *The Resolving of Conscience*, p. 19.   [1] *A Treatise of Monarchie* (London, 1643), p. 22.

[2] *The Unlawfulnesse of Subjects Taking up Armes Against their Soveraigne* (n.p. 1647), p. 113.

[3] *The Ancient Constitution*, p. 149. This is a small mistake in an excellent book.

[4] *The Trew Law of Free Monarchies*, in *Political Works*, ed. C. H. McIlwain (Cambridge, Mass., 1918), pp. 62–3.

that which the heavens (they saw) would have down'.[1] Bodin was uncompromising about the origin of all societies in force and violence, and the Jesuits admitted a right to form a lawful government by conquest, although (like others, including the later parliamentarians) they thought that the justness of the preceding war determined the lawfulness of the new authority. Most writers on the *jus gentium* inclined to discuss conquest as one of the means by which empire is transferred, and the progress of the world's four empires presupposed the effectiveness of the sword. Conquest was merely one of the facts of life, which in times of constitutional stability could plainly be seen to have changed titles in the course of history. The ardent discussion of the rights of William the Conqueror, protracted throughout the seventeenth century, is meaningless without a recognition that it was a matter of great urgency to the parliamentarians, and later the whigs, to prove that William was not a conqueror but a lawful claimant to the English throne. The researches of the feudalists were barely available during the 1640s but one finds Digges quoting Camden to the effect that only the King has *directum dominium*, 'this being reserved by the conquerour, who changed many of our lawes'. So far as they could, they developed the argument from feudal tenure, stating that tenure was 'manifestly a derived right, and founded in him who hath supreame right'.[2] One of Sir Robert Cotton's tracts was published posthumously at the same time and, in spite of the great scholar's parliamentary sympathies, his research curtailed the immemorial antiquity of parliaments: 'To search so high as the *Norman* Conquest, it is necessary to lay downe the forme of Government of those times, wherein the State of affaires led in another forme of publique Councels: For the people (wrought under the Sword of the first *William*, and his followers, to a subjected Vassalladge) could not possesse in such Assemblies the Right of their

[1] *The Historie of Great Britaine*, 2nd ed. (London, 1626), VI. ii. 8, p. 49.
[2] *The Unlawfulnesse*, p. 81.

26

former Liberties, Divisions and Power having mastered them, and none of their old Nobility and Heads, being left either of credit or fortunes.'[1]

Royalists had no desire to alienate the people's affections still further by rubbing in *ad nauseam* the prerogatives that Charles inherited by conquest, but so long as the war was going well they were happy to leave the issue to God's decision in a trial by battle. Edward Bowles declared plainly in *Plaine English* (1643) that only conquest could settle the matter now,[2] and the same year a medal was struck with Charles's head on one side and a crossed sword and olive branch on the other; it bore the motto 'in utrumque paratus'. William Bridge was quick to reflect that this kind of argument opened the door to more resistance than the royalists complained of,[3] and of course after Naseby the parliamentarians turned increasingly to the providential justification of their actions by the sword. By 1647 the royalists were backtracking rapidly, until the unfortunate Michael Hudson, one of the extreme exponents of the divine right of power, was holding that while conquest was an instrumental cause and means of supremacy, it was also one of the Lord's severest curses and judgments on a nation. 'For as it is an affliction and punishment to the passive party, so it is a sinne and injustice in the active party.'[4] If the conqueror was not legitimated by immediate revelation or by the extinguishing of the lawful issue, Hudson continued, he is a usurper, and the people are duty bound to resist him. Allegiance must remain with the King until God had shown His will in one of the two ways.

The royalists were hoist with their own petard, as they well knew, and the glee of the army writers in 1648 was ill concealed. They returned again and again in their declarations,

[1] *The Forme of Government of the Kingdome of England* (London, 1642), p. 3.
[2] Noted by Sirluck in *Complete Prose Works of John Milton*, II, p. 46.
[3] *The Wounded Conscience Cured* (London, 1642), p. 26, misnumbered 42.
[4] *The Divine Right of Government* (n.p. 1647), p. 123.

27

remonstrances, intelligencers, and other tracts to their right by conquest, and Henry Hammond was unable to persuade them that a trial by battle had not occurred.[1] Cromwell was incensed, as Professor Haller has remarked, that Charles would not accept his defeat as a judgment on his cause, but it was still possible as late as November 1648 for the army to appeal to conquest for its right while denying that it aimed at over-throwing the monarchy or intended to rule by the sword. The more typical line was taken by *The Moderate*, which announced 'that all Tyrannous Laws, and Arbitrary Govern-ments being imposed upon the people of this Land by the sword, are now forfeited by two severall conquests which God hath given his people, on purpose to make them free'. To a later royalist, Parliament intended to enjoy its conquest, and those who would not submit could 'goe seeke their living where they can get it'.[2] *The Armies Modest Intelligencer* in January 1649 reminded its readers that English kings had claimed their right by conquest for five hundred years. The air was full of such statements, and they cannot be explained away as a temporary lapse on the part of men who knew better, nor as the euphoria of victory. There had in truth been an appeal to arms, and the manœuvres of the casuistical battle had revealed that both sides had accepted conquest theory as a reality.

The practical application of conquest theory was the gravest

[1] *To the Right Honourable, The Lord Fairfax... The Humble Addresse of Henry Hammond* (London, 1649), pp. 4–5. *A Declaration of the Commons of England* on 18 January 1649 is explicit: 'We hereupon despairing of any good return of Justice from the King, did appeal unto the great God of Heaven and Earth for the same; who after four years of Wars, did give a clear and apparent sentence on our side...' (p. 6). With great foresight, Thomas Povey had written in *The Moderator Expecting Sudden Peace or Certaine Ruine* (London, 1642), p. 11, that 'the question hereafter will be, not so much, where is the Right? But where is the Power? For the Right of Power must carry the businesse.'

[2] *The Moderate: Impartially Communicating Martial Affairs to the Kingdome of England* (31 Oct.–7 Nov. 1648), no. 17, sig. R1, and *Mercurius Melancholicus* (25 Dec.–1 Jan. 1649), no. 1, p. 6.

threat to Parliament and to peace in 1648, 'the Climacterical year of this Kingdome'. In April the House voted by a large majority not to alter the fundamental constitution of King, Lords, and Commons. The strained relations between the army and the two Houses, however, divided all counsel, and people were in two minds whether to regard the impending invasion of the Scots as a hostile or a helpful act. The more revolutionary members of the army did not intend to let their opportunity slip, but the overwhelming feeling of the country was expressed in the determined efforts during the spring and summer to arrange negotiations for a Personal Treaty with the King. Charles was imprisoned, and still civilly dead by virtue of the Vote of No Addresses, but neither he nor his present friends in Parliament were thereby hindered from continuing a semi‑public diplomacy, and the Thomason tracts show how active was the wish to come to terms. Sir Francis Nethersole in parti‑cular awoke after many years of political dormancy and pro‑pounded scores of perplexing questions of conscience which tended to distribute the blame for the past on both parties; he seemed to believe that a general pardon, an oath of allegiance, a day of national humiliation, an assurance of annual parlia‑ments, and a remarriage of the sword and the sceptre would heal the breaches. If these were insufficient, he concluded, would any other remedies be successful 'but their confessing their faults one to another, forgiving one another, praying for one another, burying all harsh passages in oblivion without repitition, and beginning the world anew with the good old Scottish Proverbe; *Let bygans be bygans*'?[1] A sympathizer with the presbyterians in religion and the King in politics, Nether‑sole spoke with a typical voice. His charity extended to everyone except the levellers, and he reprinted a declaration of June 1647

[1] P. D. [Nethersole], *Parables Reflecting upon the Times* (n.p. 1648), p. 5. See also his *A Project for an Equitable and Lasting Peace*, his *Problemes Necessary to be Determined*, and *Another Parcell of Problemes Concerning Religion*, all at this time.

to illustrate how closely his propositions matched earlier resolutions of the army. He hoped, as many did, that a compromise could be found to modify the three conditions which the House of Commons insisted the King must accept before treaty negotiations could be initiated. By the end of July the propositions had been abandoned in exchange for an agreement not to treat in the vicinity of London, and the final effort for peace was thus initiated. Marvell, I like to think, was an anxious spectator of these events, and his *Elegy upon the Death of My Lord Francis Villiers*, who was killed on 7 July, shows plainly that his animus was directed against the army and its leaders, 'heavy *Cromwell*' and 'long-deceived *Fairfax*'. To be against the army at this juncture of affairs was to proclaim one's allegiance to Parliament and the hopes of a treaty. Villiers himself had been an important participant in the Earl of Holland's abortive royalist uprising, and the aims of that suicidal group may be gathered from a paper they left in exchange for some stolen horses 'repudiating absolute monarchy, and declaring for peace and a Parliamentary constitution'.[1]

If this was the profoundest hope that animated all negotiations during the summer, July 1648 was also the single most important month for the subsequent development of loyalist thought, for it was on the 28th that Thomason recorded Anthony Ascham's *A Discourse: Wherein is Examined, What is Particularly Lawfull during the Confusions and Revolutions of Government*. Ascham had supported the presbyterians and taken the Covenant, but had then followed the trend towards the independents, who had appointed him tutor to the future James II. Anthony à Wood declared he became a 'great Creature of the Long Parliament'. The mysterious medal which was found around his neck at his death may signify that he considered the King to have forfeited his rights of

---

[1] S. R. Gardiner, *History of the Great Civil War, 1642–1649* (London, 1886–91), III, p. 408. I accept Marvell's authorship of the elegy on Villiers, but my main argument does not depend on it.

allegiance when he surrendered to the Scots at Newark in 1646. The crown pierced with a dagger certainly did not imply, as his enemies later claimed, that he proposed to murder Charles, and Milton wrote in *The Second Defence* that Ascham was 'not even suspected' of having had any connection with the King's death.[1] Ascham also desired peace, and eloquently described 'the cholericknesse of war (whereby the lustfull heate of so many hearts is redoubled)'. It stirs up the lees of a commonwealth, he said, 'as a tempest doth weeds and slimy sedement from the bottome to the top of the Sea, which afterwards driven to the shore, together with its foame, there covers pearles and precious stones'.[2] Or, as Marvell had written a little earlier, 'Our times are much degenerate...Our Civill Wars have lost the Civicke crowne.' The sense of lost order, of 'an unhappy War, as unhappily ended', and of the inscrutable providence which had directed the issue was the shared feeling of many, even most, of the commentators on these times, but Ascham was unique in the way he chose to meditate on the army's conquest. To my knowledge, he alone of those who spoke for the independents was prepared to acknowledge that their army was a usurping power. No revolutionary theory could pretend that the change had not been unconstitutional, and the only recourse now open to the people was to accept the fact as accomplished. The laws concerning just titles had always been ambiguous, but the laws of evidence were not, and England must witness what had happened with her own eyes. As Ascham declared in another context, 'the evidence of the Christian Religion depends on the evidence of the History of fact',[3] and so, he argued, does the evidence of empire. Ascham's astonishing candour is not, however, the direct result of hard thinking about

---

[1] *Complete Prose Works of John Milton*, IV, p. 647. A reproduction of the medal is to be found as the frontispiece to Irene Coltman, *Private Men and Public Causes* (London, 1962). It would be a pity if Miss Coltman's denigration of Ascham in her chapter on him were to pass for an unbiased appraisal.

[2] *A Discourse*, Preface, sig. *4r.

[3] *Ibid.* p. 139.

the implications of conquest theory and the divine right of power, but the first serious attempt to apply the principles of the *jus gentium* to the outcome of the civil war. The *Discourse* is no less than a selection, paraphrase, and embellishment of the *De Jure Belli ac Pacis* by Hugo Grotius, but with the emphases so drastically redistributed that Ascham's book has no relation, except a Grotian forebear, to the more famous work of Richard Zouche, published two years later, that has become one of the classics of international law. The *Discourse* is a piece of special pleading, but is also an original in its own right, and deserves to become a classic of another kind. Moreover, it marks the beginning of the real influence of Grotius in England.

The two opening chapters define the 'cases' he wishes to solve according to the principles of natural law. The questions are 'how farre a man may lawfully submit to, and obey opposite parties, during the confusions of Warre actually formed and introduced' and 'what may be lawfull for a man to submit to upon the issue of a Warre, which may end to the advantage of him who by unjust force hath possest himselfe of anothers right'. A brief history of the Wars of the Roses (the fictional subject-matter for his inquiry), and remarks about the power of the sword then precede the ordinary distinction between the certainties of natural and mathematical causes and the uncertainties of civil law. The latter is a fallible system of rules assembled to give guidance in the vast area of human activity which lies between the absolute dictates of right and wrong that have been eternally revealed. They are concerned more with 'public quiet and repose' than with 'inward piety and vertue', and they punish petty theft, for example, more severely than great prodigality. It was necessary, therefore, to inquire 'what right or liberty we have naturally in our owne actions, as also how wee were originally invested with lawfull possession of the gifts of Nature'. Chapters III and IV then carefully outline, from Grotius, the right enjoyed by primitive people of acquiring property merely by occupying land or

possessing the fruits of the earth; on the other hand, in periods
of famine or other desperate necessity, the original right by
which all things were held in common was restored, and people
were permitted to infringe the rights of ownership. At this
point, in the concluding two chapters of Part I, Ascham
launches his main thesis. Englishmen are now in a state of
extreme misery, totally possessed by the invading party, and may
therefore look out for themselves and do what they can to
preserve their lives. Their transcendent right of self-preservation
overrules 'all those rights, priviledges and obligations which
others may pretend upon us'. In such extremities, men are not
bound to question the lawfulness of their obedience, although
they may have no doubt that the power which afflicts them is
unjust. Part II of the *Discourse* is a reworking of various sections
in *De Jure Belli* in order to prove that obedience may lawfully
include the paying of taxes, personal service, or the swearing of
oaths of allegiance to a usurper.

Now it is transparent that by taking Grotius' arguments out
of context, Ascham has found a use for them which Grotius
never intended. In an earlier work, which Ascham quotes,
Grotius had declared that the two sides in a civil war could be
reckoned as two nations, but in *De Jure Belli* Grotius was not
even concerned with civil war, and in treating the dual rights
of possession and common ownership he was explaining
that one of the principal causes of war—a subject that Ascham
declined to discuss—was an injury received to that which
belongs to us: 'some things belong to us by a right common to
mankind, others by our individual right'.[1] He admits elsewhere
that nations may be possessed by conquest, but that is far from
his mind in the chapters which Ascham found most useful.
Similarly, his application of the rule from the *Digest* that 'in
pari jure melior est conditio possidentis' was not to usurpers, but

[1] II. ii. 1; trans. Kelsey, II, p. 186. Nedham later picks up Grotius' and
Ascham's point about two sides in a civil war being equivalent to two nations
in *Mercurius Politicus* (24–31 October 1650), no. 21, pp. 342–3.

to the doubtful causes of war, in which a king in possession should be judged to hold the better cause.[1] Nevertheless, Grotius was examining the principles of natural law, and these were open to the interpretation Ascham gave them. The essence of Ascham's argument, which determined the nature of his selections from *De Jure Belli*, is to be found in one of Grotius' paragraphs on the alienation of sovereignty:

Likewise in turn it is not right for a part to withdraw from the body unless it is evident that it cannot save itself in any other way. For, as I have said above [II. ii. 6], in the case of all rules of human devising, absolute necessity seems to make an exception, and this reduces the matter to the strict law of nature. In the eighteenth book of the *City of God*, Augustine says: 'Among almost all nations this utterance of nature has in some way been heard, that they should prefer to yield themselves to the conquerors rather than to be exterminated with every kind of war's destruction'. And so in the oath of the Greeks, in which those who have yielded to the Persians were devoted to death, there was added the exception, 'unless they should be actually forced'.[2]

Ascham found Grotius' chapter on usurpers less amenable, because of course they had no rights, and resistance to them was often permissible. But once again, Grotius' humanitarian instincts were in sympathy with the belief of Cicero and others (whom he quoted) that 'peace on any terms between citizens seems more advantageous than civil war'. With very few exceptions, private persons should not kill a usurper, because 'it may happen that he who holds the sovereign power by right would prefer that the usurper should be left in possession rather than that the way should be opened for dangerous and bloody conflicts'.[3] That is to say, a subject should presume his true governor's concurrence in the usurpation, and Ascham seized on this point for the capstone of his argument, even adding a long

---

[1] *Ibid.* II. xxiii. 11; trans. Kelsey, II, p. 564.

[2] *Ibid.* II. vi. 5; trans. Kelsey, II, pp. 261–2.

[3] *Ibid.* I. iv. 19; trans. Kelsey, II, p. 161. See also II. iv. 15 (II, p. 159). By 1659 Baxter had accepted this point of view, although he would not have done so ten years earlier. See *A Holy Commonwealth* (London, 1659), p. 161.

illustration from Guicciardini's *History*. Ascham's intention
was to conclude his thesis not only with the suggestion that
Charles could be presumed to have abdicated, but that it
would save considerable trouble if he did so. Charles's deposi-
tion had been one of several remedies proposed to overcome
the impasse between the parties, but whether Ascham favoured
a republic or the crowning of one of the King's younger sons it
is impossible to say.

Ascham's *Discourse* is the more remarkable in that English
loyalism found its first clear voice not in a disaffected royalist
but in a supporter of the revolution. He perceived that the
natural-law doctrine of necessity, which had done such excellent
service in the cause of constitutional change, could now be
employed to resist further changes and to uphold the virtues
of passive obedience and acceptance. Looking back, he could
observe, as royalists had done before, that in the search for
authority 'the familiar canvasing of these supreme Rights
appeares...to be the dangerousest. For it unloosens the very
pinns of Government, and so lets all the Frame fall into confusion,
and by that into the extremity of dangers.'[1] England, as Hobbes
was to remark later, had returned to the primitive state of nature,
where the only lawgiver was God. 'Princes cannot by their
commands change the nature of humane condition...[or]
pretend to a power of obliging us to morall impossibilities',[2]
so Englishmen were now absolved from obedience to an autho-
rity which war had destroyed. Necessity had first made all
laws, and by necessity the law should continue to be interpreted.
The revolution had been made theoretically possible by an
appeal to the original rights of mankind, 'not those rights of this
or that Country', and, with the help of Grotius and his own
training as a lawyer, Ascham discovered the other statute-books
of natural right which had lain neglected while the revolution
was in progress. This procedure afforded him a vocabulary by
which 'conquest' became known as 'possession', and was

[1] *A Discourse*, p. 75.   [2] *Ibid.* p. 38.

therefore deprived of the aura of Nimrodic violence which surrounded it in the *jus gentium*: one word invoked the glorious providences which had trodden the ungodly underfoot, the other asked the victims what they were going to do next. Casuistry has its own rhetoric which may disguise personal ends, and Ascham was conceivably another Ireton, adamant about the justice of the army's cause; but the position he chose to adopt proclaimed his sympathy with the sufferers, not the victors. His words could be expected to find echoes in the hearts of all those who despaired of any immediate solution to the constitutional crisis, and who, in Christian fashion, brought their problems to God for His answer. The future belonged to Him, as it had always done, and England now required an act of faith. 'The time present is governed by the wils of men, which are mysterious one to another, & are so covert and serpentine, that *they who sit in Councill together, rarely penetrate themselves*: As for the future...that depends solely on his Providence, who never tooke humane reasons into his Counsell, and for the most part produces events contrary to, or beyond our hopes and machinations.'[1] If the King were deposed, no damage would be irreparable, and Ascham is extraordinarily circumspect about the future. Monarchy, he said, is best, but northern climates seem best suited to senates and diets. No other statement would have consorted with his call to faith. As he justly remarked, 'all governments carry with them the causes of their Corruption, and a complication of their Infirmities', and no government which men can imagine 'hath not in the very constitution of it a power to wrong us'.[2] These old political truths had come home to roost on the wings of Ascham's turkey-cock's quill (as an enemy called it), and with them they brought a reminder that government was still indispensable, and the great danger was a chaotic levelling multitude which already threatened to flood the country.

The two historians who have paid more than passing notice

---

[1] *Ibid.* p. 85.   [2] *Ibid.* pp. 72–3.

to Ascham have studied the *Discourse* in its more elaborate version published the following year, and they have concluded that he suffered either from a 'low opinion of wounds' (an unflattering adaptation of Hobbes's definition of courage as 'the contempt of wounds') or the 'malaise of the sceptic';[1] neither phrase takes sufficient account of the orthodoxy of his Christian sentiments, the rationality of his treatment of natural law, the casuistry which dictated his form of address, or the peculiar and historical context of his argument in 1648. He captured in some of his graphic sentences the sadness with which many people watched the King's sun decline, and he caught the elegiac mood which was to sweep the country on the publication of the *Eikon Basilike*. It is no accident, I believe, that Marvell's poems in 1648–49 are either elegies or lamenta/tions. The civil war and the King's execution enhanced as noth/ing else was ever to do again in English history a general sense of the world's mutability. Like all catastrophes, men slowly forgot it, but not before loyalism had been reborn. Feeling, not intellect, was its efficient cause, although reasons, as I am suggest/ing, were not lacking. When Cato and Scipio declined to yield to Caesar after Pharsalia, Plutarch commented that they were 'to be blamed for the needless destruction of many good men in Libya'.

Life, to be sure, which affords the basis for all temporal and the occasion for eternal blessings, is of greater value than liberty. This holds true whether you consider each aspect in the case of an individual or of a whole people. And so God Himself reckons it as a benefit that He does not destroy men but casts them into slavery. And again, through the prophet He advises the Jews to yield themselves as slaves to the Babylonians that they may not perish of hunger and disease.[2]

[1] Coltman, 'Anthony Ascham and the Low Opinion of Wounds', in *Private Men and Public Causes*; Perez Zagorin, *A History of Political Thought in the English Revolution* (London, 1954), p. 66. For a corrective view with which I am in substantial agreement, see Skinner's article cited in the note on p. 22.

[2] *De Jure Belli*, II. xxiv. 6; trans. Kelsey, II, pp. 573–4. A sample of other comparisons with Grotius which may be made are as follows (Grotius refs.

Thus Grotius, writing about war in the calm of his regained liberty; and the same conviction animates Ascham's *Discourse*: 'A mans life is that which can be lost but once, and after that, nothing can make it good to us againe'; 'no man is of such a captivated Allegiance, as by reason of it to engage himselfe to a party, believing upon the engagement that he shall be certainly destroyed in it'; 'besides all this wee doe but abuse our selves in presuming of a pleasant condition to be recovered in this life, bee it either in Sense, Riches, or Honour'.[1] In the midst of confusions and revolutions Ascham pretends to do no more than offer a little helpful advice so that the people may 'weather out such stormes, and in the midst of so many swords find an *inculpata tutela*'. To sleep in the tempest, like Christ before them, they should keep 'quiet all within'.[2]

Had Ascham not himself been of the conquering party, his theme would appear to have been begotten by despair upon the impossibility of resistance. Judging from the royalist anguish at this time, the *Discourse* could not have failed to strike a few responsive chords. 'We are all in an Egyptian darkness,' moaned Richard Farrar, and the King's subjects 'are ready every minute to precipitate themselves into the Gulf of Despair'.[3]

first): II. xxiii. 1 / p. 6 (Aristotelian distinction between mathematical and natural causes); II. ii. 2 / p. 11 (reasons for loss of common ownership; one of the few places where Ascham acknowledges a Grotian source); II. ii. 6 / pp. 14–20 (the right of common ownership in times of necessity); III. viii. 4 / p. 39 ('Surrender in fact voluntarily permits what force would otherwise take'–Grotius); II. xiii. 10, 13 / pp. 46–7 (definitions of oaths, quotation from Chrysippus); II. xiii. 8 / p. 53 (we cannot swear to perform impossibilities); II. xiii. 15 / p. 55 (swearing to pirates); II. xiii. 5, and xvi. 2 / p. 58 (the correct interpretation of an oath by common usage); II. xiv. 1–2 / pp. 63–4 (the oaths of Kings); I. iv. 13 / p. 78 (an acknowledged borrowing); III. vi. 4 / p. 88 (the price of fields near Rome; see also vi. 3 and p. 88).

[1] *A Discourse*, pp. 43, 4, 73.

[2] *Ibid*. Preface sig. *4ʳ and p. 73. Incidentally, the lay-out of Ascham's chapter-headings, with numbered summaries of contents, appears to be based on a similar custom in some of the earlier editions of Grotius, e.g. the Amsterdam 1631 ed. and the Paris 1625 ed.

[3] *An Expedient for the King* (n.p. 1648), p. 3.

With their crosses standing at all four points of the compass, the royalists might have listened to Sir Robert Filmer's advice that in the case of usurpation 'the subjects' obedience to the fatherly power must go along and wait upon God's providence, who only hath right to give and take away kingdoms'.[1] Filmer was not an altogether typical royalist, and he seems to have been the only one in 1648 who might literally have agreed with Ascham's argument; but in the autumn, during the negotiations at Newport, the King assembled as many of his favourite clergymen round him as Parliament would permit, and some of their surviving sermons reveal how accurately Ascham had judged the prevailing mood. On 8 October Dr Thomas Turner preached on the text 'Sin no more, lest a worse thing come unto thee'.[2] The following week William Haywood preached his *Sermon tending to Peace*; on the 25th Brian Duppa expatiated on the need for a tranquil conscience; on the 29th Turner took as his text 'Come unto me all ye that are heavy laden'. Other sermons on less promising subjects were also delivered, but one of Sanderson's is the most interesting. His burden was the fainting weariness of the soul, and the loosening of the spiritual joints. This appalling malady was one possible consequence of heavy afflictions, when the people, like David, felt themselves to be hunted like a partridge upon the mountains. Greater troubles might still be in store and his congregation were to remember that, Januslike, every affliction has two faces. 'It looketh backward, as it cometh from God, who layeth it upon us as a correction for some past sin. And it looketh forward, as it cometh from Satan and the world, who lay it before us as a temptation to some new sin.' However, Sanderson had the aim of a treaty in mind, and it was no part of his intention to suggest that these afflictions could only be

---

[1] *The Anarchy of a Limited or Mixed Monarchy*, in *Patriacha and other Political Works*, ed. Peter Laslett (Oxford, 1949), p. 289.

[2] The names of most of the preachers and their texts may be found in Nicholas Oudart, *A Diary of Passages at the Treaty of Newport*, in *Desiderata Curiosa*, ed. Francis Peck (London, 1779), Book x, pp. 387–413.

suffered and not amended. The greatest anglican casuist suddenly reminds us of Ascham. Christ 'doth not bid us undo ourselves when His service requireth it not, nor make ourselves Crosses when we need not'; 'a man may without disparage/ment to his fortitude, decline dangers, according to the dictates of prudence, provided withal that nothing be done but what is according to the rules of justice'. In a plain case of either sinning or suffering, there could be no choice, 'but where there is a *medium*, or third thing, as an outlet or expedient between both, as many times there is, nothing hindereth but we may, and reason would we should, make choice of that, and so neither sin nor suffer'.[1] Ascham had company in seeking the *inculpata tutela*, and his reasoning differed from Sanderson's only in the interpretation of the middle way. Sanderson was preparing the King's mind to make concessions to unreasonable demands, Ascham the minds of his followers to abate their afflictions according to a similar principle. Both recognized that God's penalties could be met only by an act of faith—an act which would suspend judgment about God's purposes but make prudent concessions to necessity.

Neither was alone in his opinion of the most profitable sub/jects for the royal meditation, and in the last sermon which it was the King's fate to hear, Henry Ferne preached what could well be called a manifesto of loyalist thought. 'Though it tarry, wait for it', he said, quoting a verse from Habakkuk, but although deliverance was assured, the present prospect was hopeless. 'Flesh and bloud weary of restraint, looks out for reliefe, as *Sisera's* Mother from the windows... *crying, why doe the wheels of his Chariot tarry?*' And supposing, he asks, deliverance tarries so long that a man is cut off by death before he sees it? Then 'we must know, that Temporall promises are not alwayes made good in the same kind, and he that has not faith to look beyond the very thing assured by them, may misse

[1] 'Sermon XVI' in *Works*, ed. William Jacobson (Oxford, 1854), I, pp. 417, 419, 420, 418.

of his desire and expectation'. The righteous man can only wait, solacing himself with the thought that if he never lives to see the 'wish'd-for Nationall deliverance' he cannot fail to enjoy the crown of glory that fadeth not away.[1] When Ferne preached, the effort for peace had breathed its last gasp, so he had no alternative but to envisage a future strong in faith but devoid of foreseeable blessing. The man of faith was he who *against hope can believe in hope*', contemplating in silence the inscrutable administration of providence. God had gathered up the reins of empire into His own hands, and Ferne knew the futility of proposing any further course of action. At the moment of truth, he recognized that the events which had occurred were not merely by God's permission, but derived 'out of great wisdome, and upon good reason', and Charles on the scaffold was to make a more grudging admission of the same fact. By tacit consent, and only for a brief period of total fear, the conquerors were the undisputed agents of divine judgment, whose title could not be challenged without challenging God's decree. Like the proud champions of the revolution, loyalists were to take providence as their watchword, but while the former proclaimed the joyful evidences of their election to power, the latter waited faithfully under the scourge. Loyalism was created from chaos, in those moments of desperation when the only conceivable action is the performance of the daily routine; or, as Ascham put it, the doing of those just deeds which would be permissible at any time. On the day of crisis itself a few of the armed bands may have clapped their bloody hands, but we do know that a great groan went up from the crowd, and I do not think I exaggerate much in suggesting that, except for a few men like Hugh Peters, the nation as a whole was in a loyalist frame of mind. With the constitution in ruins, every deed of self-perpetuation was in effect a loyalist act. Certainly, to judge from the sermons to which it listened the

[1] *A Sermon Preached before His Majesty at Newport...November the 29. 1648* (London, 1649), pp. 4-5, 19-20.

next day, the House of Commons was extremely chastened. 'You see [preached Owen] what variety of plagues are in his hand. Changing of condition will do no more to the avoiding of them, than a sick man's turning himself from one side of the bed to another; during his turning, he forgets his pain by striving to move—being laid down again, he finds his condition the same as before.' Owen spoke of ruin, and 'nation-destroying sins', and warned that if 'the present administration with sincere humiliation do not run across to unravel this close-woven web of destruction, all thoughts of recovery will quickly be too late'.[1] In the real emergency, royalists and moderate parliamentarians thought, felt, and expressed themselves in very similar terms, which Fairfax echoed in his poem on the execution:

> Oh lett that Day from time be blotted quitt
> And lett beleefe of 't in next Age be waued
> In deepest silence th'Act Concealed might
> Soe that the King-doms Credit might be saue'd
> But if the Power deuine permited this
> His Will's the Law & ours must acquiesse.[2]

It remains to trace the history of this acquiescence in the first years of the Interregnum, because of course by the time of the Protectorate acquiescence had changed into widespread confi-dence that only Cromwellian government could check the excesses of the sectarians. If Charles II had not at his Restora-tion maintained a gentleman's memory he would have had very few people to serve him. The origin, however, of all the active obedience to the Commonwealth which Charles had to forget was the passive obedience of 1648–49. The acquiescence of many godly ministers who had sworn to protect not only the King but his heirs should not be regarded as a lamentable exhibi-

[1] 'Righteous Zeal Encouraged by Divine Protection', in *Works*, ed. William H. Goold (London and Edinburgh, 1851), VIII, pp. 135, 138.

[2] *The Poems of Thomas Third Lord Fairfax*, ed. Edward Bliss Reed, *Trans. of the Conn. Academy of Arts and Science* (New Haven, 1909), pp. 281–2.

tion of human weakness, but as a deeply religious response to the sadness of the times and the responsibility of government. The casuistry of the civil war, and especially the royalist dogmas of power and conquest, reveal that the foundations of the constitution were more shakable by argument than anyone had imagined, and the dying cadences of the reign already pro-phesied a future of inescapable trial, and a necessary compliance with an act of God.

The Engagement Controversy

The opening chapters of Gardiner's *History of the Commonwealth and Protectorate* expose very clearly the government's dilemma during the early months of the Interregnum, in which first the members of the new Council of State and then the judges had to decide whether they would serve or not. Naturally, the House felt an oath of allegiance was necessary for anyone entrusted with public office, but it proved to be difficult to get anyone except the regicides to swear approval of what had been done. *The Moderate Intelligencer* for 22 February 1649 discussed the Engagement oath for the Council of State in terms which were reminiscent of Ascham's, and which looked forward to the dispute that was to follow later. Passivity said the writer, was the best posture in times of change and war, and relieved the most miseries, 'but to be passive is to approve, No, not the passive', because

there is in Common-Wealths or States, two capacities, and in that regard care should be had to distinguish of Impositions [;] for the generality of the people, who act in their callings, there needs no more but this, that you shall not do any thing to the prejudice of the present Govern-ment, and this is the common practice of the Conqueror in parts abroad, who takes Towns or Countries, when so taken, and it may be re-taken, and again taken; all that the generality are sworn unto is, that they shall doe nothing to the prejudice of the present possessor or Government.[1]

[1] 22 Feb.–1 March 1649, no. 206, pp. 1909–10 (cf. Ascham, *A Discourse*, pp. 92–3).

No man was compelled to work for the new government, but he who chose to be active for it could reasonably be expected to 'subscribe his approbation of the way he is to act in...though it seems not requisite that any man acknowledge all the wayes and steps to bring about such or such an alteration'.[1] Two weeks later, John Dury published his *Case of Conscience Resolved: Concerning Ministers Medling with State-Matters in their Sermons* which besought private persons, as Calvin had directed, to refrain from generating heat on political questions. Dury, or his double, was also the author of another tract, recorded by Thomason on 20 March, which attempted by invoking the power of providence to allay the fears of those who had sworn the Covenant. While he confessed that he had been unable to pray for the King's restoration to his throne, he had sworn to preserve his person with all his heart: 'And I can take God to record, I did performe here, as I was bound to my utmost, for my bowels yerned towards him, so as I could have been contented to put my body (could I by so doing have advanced the name of my God, the peace of his people, and the soule of the King) betwixt the instrument of Death and his body.'[2] These painful and self-conscious admissions of the government's crime by its supporters are not, however, very common during February and March, when the Press was at the mercy of the true believers in the revolution. Their protestations of righteousness are too fervid to be quite believable, and they found their official voice on 22 March when the Rump published *A Declaration of the Parliament of England, Expressing the Grounds of their Late Proceedings, and of Setling the Present Government in the Way of a Free State*. It had been ordered to be printed five days earlier, and appeared in Latin as *Parliamenti Anglia Declaratio,*

[1] *Ibid.* p. 1910. There follows the text of an Engagement oath for the Council of State.
[2] *The Sense of the Covenant...Especially Intended for the Vindication of our Heads, Judges, and Officers, Heavily Charged at that Point* [of Covenant-breaking] (London, 1649), p. 16.

and in other languages also. Twenty-seven pages long, it was a full-scale rehearsal of propaganda in the old style. An agreement of the people was the foundation of government; Charles's tyrannical record was reiterated and his anointment denied special significance; the son was disinherited with the father, and various objections—such as the unrepresentative nature of the House and the danger to the pre-Norman laws—were dealt with in a conventional way. The *Declaration* closed with a catalogue of Parliament's noble intentions, the pious expectation of fair dealing from abroad, and the hope of a 'cheerful concurrence' at home.

The *Declaration* was much touted and occasionally cursed in the newspapers, but otherwise seems to have fallen on ears so inured to its brand of platitude that nobody deigned to answer it for over a year. Francis Rous read it, however, and felt that it did not meet the case of men, like himself, who had very recently decided to offer no resistance to the Parliament, although his sympathies had for many years been in harmony with those of the now secluded members. Rous has been called one of the two deepest-dyed presbyterians in the Commons, and he had played an important part in curtailing the King's prerogatives. Nevertheless, there is no evidence that he was concerned in any way with the execution, and his conversion to the independents probably occurred after that event; he was a loyalist in a sense that Ascham was not. He also saw his role as a peacemaker's, and his tract, *The Lawfulnes of Obeying the Present Government*, was specifically addressed to the presbyterians, who could not have been expected to approve of the *Declaration*, and it closed with an exhortation for the same 'calme, cleare, and peaceable spirit, without prejudice or partisanship' which had led its author to the truth. Romans xiii was his text and he made the old royalist assertion that the 'power' could not be abstracted from the persons who held it. Hence the usurpers Claudius and Nero had been obeyed, and 'in this Nation many persons have been settled in supreame power and authority by meere force without title of inheritance or just conquest'; five English kings in succession had retained the allegiance of their subjects, although none of them had a title by lineal descent. Rous then enlisted the aid of a battery of divines to prove the obligation of obeying present magistrates, and he believed that nothing existed in any former oath or covenant, properly read, which prohibited obedience to the government, 'much lesse when no other can be had, and so the Common-wealth must goe to ruine'. The structure of Rous's argument, consisting of histor-rical examples, biblical exposition, and a section on oaths, was to form the basic pattern of the controversy he initiated, supple-mented though it soon was with Ascham's version of natural law and the *jus gentium*. The impassionate presbyterians lost no time in exploiting Rous's tacit admission that the government was an unlawful power, and within two months five pamphlets had attempted his rebuttal.[1] Rous soon enlarged his *Lawfulnes* in order to add some further authorities, and included a marginal reference to 'Master *Aschams* Discourse (that hath in it both judgement and learning) concerning possession'. In his seventieth year, however, Rous had no desire to involve himself in further controversy, and in the postscript to his second edition he firmly declared that he was returning to his accustomed employment. Hence his cause now belonged to others, and it was Ascham, I am sure, who decided to come to the old man's support. In *A Combate betweene Two Seconds* he elaborated Rous's positions and referred to his own *Discourse*, and he also confirmed that Rous had been a spectator of events 'untill he saw a Government set on foot, and that justice might be had this way, and no other. And then having a right to act, he beleeved that he might exercise it in just things; yea he beleeved that it was a duty, though the Government

[1] The titles of these tracts, and others, with brief summaries of their contents, are recorded in 'The Engagement Controversy, 1649–1652: An Annotated List of Pamphlets', *Bull. New York Public Library*, LXVIII (1964), pp. 384–405.

had been taken by designe, and force, that those who had taken it and excluded all other, should give Justice.'[1] Six weeks later Ascham was ready with a longer reply to the presby-terians in which he summarized at length his earlier argument from plenary possession and extended his consideration of the limitations of promissory oaths. Nothing had fundamentally changed since Ascham first advanced his thesis a year earlier, but his sense of the mutability of all 'morall & civill things' had been enhanced ('those various accidents which perplex our actions, and make them like that famous flower the Marvell of *Peru*, which changes the colour of it's Leaves every day')[2] and he wrote one of the most emotional descriptions of the alternative to a willing compliance:

But I pray you what doe people get when warres for recoveries of dubious rights are long and calamitous? What are the people of *France* or the people of *Spaine* better for the long and hereditary anger of their two Kings? Or what was the world better for *Alexanders* Conquering it? The Houses which are burnt, and the millions of bodies left dead in the field, are the peoples; and Princes scorning to derive from them, still trample them to dung. We talke of some Titles wronged, as if their rights were so certaine, and so necessary to live under, as God almighties is, who yet disposes of the changes which are made here among his chiefe Officers, and not we; Who is it then that can right wronged Titles, but he alone who makes all Titles right?[3]

Like Rous, Ascham defended only the right to obey an un-lawful government in lawful things, but he concluded that such permission 'virtually extend[s] to our acting under such a Government'. The distinction between active and passive obedience was a nicety: 'They are in a manner the same thing,

[1] (London 1649: recorded by Thomason 2 July), pp. 2-3.
[2] *The Bounds & Bonds of Publique Obedience* (London, 1649), p. 15. The evidence for Ascham's authorship of this pamphlet, invariably attributed to Rous, is given in the annotated list cited in the note on p. 46. In addition, three lines on p. 66 of this tract are repeated verbatim in Ascham's *Of the Confusions*, p. 28, later in the year.
[3] *Ibid.* p. 34; see also pp. 36-7.

derive from the same Principle, and differ but gradually, just as the morning and the noone light do, which derive both from the same planet.'[1] This is the language of common sense, as was Ascham's remark that the demurrers in fact rendered the obedience which, to cause public desolation, they would not allow to others. As one of his opponents was later to observe, Ascham might have the sun in his eyes, but the ground and the wind were with him.[2]

There the matter stood in August, and there it might have remained had not the Parliament run into increasing difficulties with the levellers as the summer wore on. At the end of September the House issued a *Declaration* aimed at rebuking their pretensions, and two weeks later, on 11 October, it passed a resolution which was to carry the themes of Rous and Ascham to the country. The *Resolves of Parliament Touching the subscribing to an Engagement, by or before the First of January next* proclaimed that an oath similar to the one proffered to the Council of State in February, and calling for a vow to be 'true and faithful to the Commonwealth of England, as it is now Established, without a King or House of Lords', was to be taken not only by the generals and the army, but by all ministers, aldermen, masters of colleges, fellows, schoolmasters, clerks, and others. Almost the entire literate population, and certainly all the classes of men who would be able and vocal enough to denounce it as a hindrance to tender consciences, were thereby asked to become loyalists. The House had learned from earlier mistakes, and sought no approval for its past actions, but the presbyterians, whose ministers were to offer the sole vocal resistance, had much justification for regarding the oath as an attempt to make an illegal government lawful. Lilburne regarded it as a trick, and the levellers as a whole could have seen it as a ghastly parody of their own determination to seek a universal Agreement of the People. Theoretically, with

[1] *Bounds & Bonds,* p. 66.
[2] [Nathaniel Ward], *Discolliminium* (London, 1650), p. 1.

48

the oath to support it, Parliament need have feared no dis-
obedience, and might have misguidedly imagined that it now
had the people's assent to its constitutional inadequacies. If
this was the purpose which the presbyterians attributed to the
Engagement, it was not realized in practice, and the House
appears to have been happy to settle for a much less positive and
affirmative reading of its oath of allegiance. From 11 October,
however, the battle was joined in earnest, and before the end of
the year the most learned attacks on the oath and the most
influential defences of it had appeared. The extension of the
Engagement on 1 January 1650 to all male persons aged eighteen
or over, on the pretext that another war seemed imminent, did
little more than perpetuate the quarrel and lend an excuse for
preaching on the subject everywhere.[1]

The importance of the dispute is, as I have suggested, that it
involved the whole nation in the question of loyalism, because
anyone who wished or needed to hold a public position of any
kind, or who had any cause to seek for redress of grievances at
law, was obliged to take the oath. Whatever the private reserva-
tions and casuistical deceptions with which, say, many fellows
at the universities swore to be true and faithful in order to
keep their posts, they were technically loyalists if their swearing
reversed an earlier allegiance. The Cambridge Platonists to a

[1] The October *Resolves* has not been reprinted. Gardiner, *The History of the
Commonwealth and Protectorate* (London, 1903), I, pp. 193–4, outlines the
circumstances of the general Engagement Act, the text of which is given in
Acts and Ordinances of the Interregnum, 1642–1660, ed. C. H. Firth and R. S.
Rait (London, 1911), II, pp. 325–9. 'An Act for Giving Further Time for
Subscribing the Engagement' was passed two days before the deadline of
25 February 1650, and in February 1651 an 'Act Constituting a Council of
State' contained a clause banishing city ministers who had refused to swear
the oath (II, pp. 348, 500–3). In spite of a possible confusion with an earlier
group of the same name, 'Engagers' would seem a better title for the defenders
of the oath than the more historically accurate 'Subscribers'. The oath was
the centre of their loose alliance and the major spokesmen were quickly
rewarded by Parliament. The Rump thus accepted their interpretation of the
meaning of the oath.

man took the Engagement, although only Henry More is
known to have been a warm supporter of the King's cause.
However, the taking of the oath cannot be applied too
literally as a test of loyalism, because, if William Prynne
reported correctly, many royalists made no bones about
swearing lies to such old enemies. There was, he said, 'a
most wicked and base Maxime of theirs, lately taken up among
them, that, *He is a fool that will not take it, and he is a knave that
will not break it*'.[1] Eventually, the exiled King was widely
reported to have given way to the Engagement,[2] so former
royalists obtained a respectable reason for obedience. As every
Engager knew, an old oath could be rendered invalid by the
consent of the person to whom it was sworn. The presbyterians
were in a more anomalous position, because, having brought
the King to the block, as was said, they had as a body re-
affirmed their loyalty to the crown and the King's person in the
year before his death; they were also conscientious by nature,
and the Engagement at least tested their brand of loyalism, if
not that of the old malignants. The Rump had several notable
conversions to its credit besides Rous, and the example of these
leaders was probably the most effective argument for loyalism
that arose. The names of thirteen of them, all of whom had
taken the Covenant, and most of whom had been members of
the Westminster Assembly, were nailed to church doors in
London in November 1649. John Lightfoot was one of them,
and he had written 'murder'd' when recording Charles's
execution; Joseph Caryl was another and he became one of the
Engagement's 'busie Champions' and licensed many of the
tracts. Of the four divines who had accompanied the parlia-
mentary commissioners to Newport—Richard Vines, Caryl,
Lazarus Seaman, and Stephen Marshall—only Vines refused
the Engagement and lost his appointment at Cambridge. The

[1] *A Briefe Apologie for all Non-Subscribers* (London, 1650), p. 14.
[2] Robert Sanderson, 'The Case of the Engagement', in *Works*, v, pp. 19, 23-4.

notorious Marshall, who confirmed his presbyterianism on his deathbed, was already working for the Rump by April 1649, and Seaman's support for the oath in pulpits in London and Cambridge must have been the more impressive to his congregations in that he had preached the *de jure* nature of presbyterianism and had been one of the signers of *A Vindication of the Ministers of the Gospel* who at the last moment had disclaimed wanting either to condemn or to execute the King. Cornelius Burges, the first signature on the *Vindication*, must also have taken the Engagement as he received a lectureship at Wells in 1650, and William Jenkin, another and important member of the group, refused the oath at first but later made a public submission which was printed in at least three versions. John Dury, however, was to become the busiest champion of all for the new oath, and at the Restoration he wrote an account of the reasons for his decision, having first recorded how desperately he had tried to prevent His Majesty's trial and sentence:

But when the *Engagement* was proposed to be taken, a greater difficulty did arise, in the Spirits of all that were moderate; and a more eminent danger was like to fall more fully, upon the Body of the Nation, and chiefly upon that party in it, which did acknowledge the Kings just Right and Prerogative; and might in due time be a means to restore the same. For certainly it was the design of some, by the Engagement, to oblige al by Pole, to exclude at least indirectly the King and Lords for ever from having a hand in the Government, by removing al that would not take the Engagement *in terminis* from having any safety & protection in the Nation. Yet the words of the Engagement being so laid; that they could not inforce the sense which was aimed at, but could bear a clear sense, of a duty; which not being directly opposite to the Royal Interest, was advantagious to the welfare of the Nation; which two things should never be separated (though their aim was to separate them) I was moved to own the Engagement so far as I found it contained a clear duty.[1]

Considering all the Interregnum service that Dury by 1660 had to excuse, his statement is surprisingly truthful and undistorted;

[1] *A Declaration of John Durie* (London, 1660), p. 18; on p. 17 he refers to 'the moderate party'.

but then Dury's painful sincerity habitually verged on the maudlin, and to it may be attributed the obfuscation of his great abilities by a tangle of verbosity. He is the seventeenth-century's great exponent of the woolly style. However, his *Considerations Concerning the Present Engagement* went into four editions in four months, and, together with the eight other pamphlets he wrote on the subject, exerted an influence on both the government and the country. The one he assisted by reducing the implications of the oath to a few acceptable commonplaces, the other he did much to persuade that its scruples might be eased.

Dury approached the Engagement with a series of casuistical arguments which shielded his central notion that the oath was basically a 'harmless pledge'[1] to be faithful to 'the Peace and publick welfare of the People of this Land', which at the present time was secured only 'under the power & Government of the Parliament & Counsell of State that now is'. Hence the oath asserted nothing against kingly rule *per se*, or against the heirs of Charles I; it would have been quite conceivable to institute a new king tomorrow,[2] and Dury uttered a solemn warning that resistance would jeopardize a happy settlement in the future. Subjects who scrupled about the future were resisting what providence had already ordained, and they forgot that God invariably directed acts of usurpation or tyranny to a good end. The political changes of the late times were events in themselves neither good nor evil, 'and everie power in his own time was to bee submitted unto, by those that were under it, because it was of God for the time over them'.[3] Holding this

---

[1] The phrase is Minton Batten's in *John Dury, Advocate of Christian Union* (Chicago, 1944), p. 122.

[2] *Two Treatises Concerning the Matter of the Engagement* (London, 1650), p. 58. Quotation from *Considerations concerning the Present Engagement*, 3rd ed. (London, 1650), p. 26. The latter was the most printed and quoted of all Dury's Engagement pamphlets.

[3] *A Second Parcel of Objections against the Taking of the Engagement Answered* (London, 1650), pp. 23–4.

conviction, it was a matter of indifference whether Dury argued that former oaths had been voided by new circumstances, or that the intention of the Covenant to preserve the nation was now fulfilled by, and consistent with, the new oath. On the one hand, a more immediate good or necessity nullified former oaths, and, on the other, essential equity remained the same. If Herod had denied Salome the Baptist's head, 'he had been true to his duty, without being false to his Oath'.[1] More thoroughly than any other Engager, with the possible exception of Samuel Eaton, Dury was conversant with the casuistry of oath-taking, and to the really embarrassing question, whether the oath meant that a more rightful party offering resistance must be opposed, Dury fell back on his old contention that private persons were not called upon to judge questions of right. Subsequent emergencies were no part of the existing crisis, and could safely be left to the decision of the superior powers. Dury also indicated that he had read Ascham by employing the argument from plenary possession, but his most valid and personal contribution to the cause was his insistence on the simplicity of the oath. None of his fellow Engagers failed to explain the relationship of the Covenant and the Engagement, and most of them were endowed with a better prose style, but Dury did more than anyone to interpret the oath in such a way that it commanded no more 'beyond that which is clear and known duty'.[2] Dury *felt* peaceably towards his opponents, and pained surprise was his typical reaction to Prynne's calling him a 'time-serving Proteus, and ambidexter divine'.[3]

Dury takes one kind of precedence in the controversy not only by virtue of his voluminousness but because the brief first edition of his *A Case of Conscience* received Caryl's imprimatur

[1] *A Disingag'd Survey of the Engagement* (London, 1650), p. 16.
[2] *Just Re-Proposals to Humble Proposals* (London, 1650), p. 11.
[3] Prynne's anonymous attack was *The Time-Serving Proteus, and Ambidexter Divine*, and Dury's self-defence *The Unchanged, Constant and Single-hearted Peacemaker* (London, 1650).

only six weeks after the execution. Rous could have claimed the actual leadership of the Engagers on the grounds of age, experience, and the importance of his *Lawfulnes* pamphlet, but he clearly did not seek the preferment. Ascham, however, believed correctly that his *Discourse* was the true forerunner of the loyalists' case, and in 1649 he worked hard to ensure that he was heard. His *Combate* and *Bounds & Bonds* referred his readers to the earlier work and by November he was ready with a second edition of the *Discourse* which contained nine additional chapters. Two of them, inserted into Part I, contained a further disquisition on property and a defence of the use of money;[1] they were intended to protect Ascham's theory from the levellers and other more communistic groups who might have found his argument that possession returned to a common ownership in critical times useful to their still rebellious aims. Natural law, and the law of necessity in particular, had been the source of revolutionary principles for so long that they were not easily adaptable to the maintenance of the status quo. Two further chapters made deeper excursions into the difference between assertory and promissory oaths, and were especially emphatic about the ways in which the latter were rendered void, but it was in the remaining five that Ascham contributed a view of political justice that was as original an emphasis in 1649 as his theory of possession had been in the previous year.

Ascham grounded his argument as before in the mutability of human affairs, and no Engager turned this lament to better advantage. To speak of well-founded rights and original compacts was to overlook the fact that 'no infallible records of the actions of the world from the beginning, [were] kept any where safely and certainly but in heaven'.[2] Glancing, I think, at Filmer, and explicitly at Hobbes, Ascham declared that

---

[1] *Of the Confusions and Revolutions of Goverments* [sic] (London, 1649), pp. 17–31. Ascham's additions to *A Discourse* are clearly signalled in the text, and comprise these two chapters and pp. 85–95, 103 (bottom)–159. There are also minor verbal changes.

[2] *Ibid.* p. 111.

government was doubtless of patriarchal origin, although contracts had since proved a better means of cementing societies, but in the course of empire many accidents had intervened, and all titles were obscure. Prescription gave the opinion, not the actuality, of a just title, and canon law clearly ruled that a wrong never became a right through the passage of time. Other Engagers, notably Rous, had observed how unstable in law were the claims of many English kings to a perfectly legal crown, but Ascham transformed this palpable truth into a principle. The Jews had been fortunate, because in their confusions and revolutions 'they presently had a voyce from heaven to assure their actions, and secure their consciences', but nations now looked in vain for divine guidance in their public affairs; and the sources of their most cherished institu- tions, together with the terms and conditions under which they had been established, were lost in the past: 'The Evidence of ancient facts have—*Vestigia nulla retrorsum*, no infallible marks of their pre-existence (one step doth so confound and obliterate another) and that time it selfe is but an imagination of our owne, and an Intentionall, not a reall measure for Actions, which passe away concomitantly with that measure of time in which they were done; for which reasons we talke of ancient things, but as blinde men doe of Colours.'[1] Ascham may have exaggerated the irrelevance of prescription to the making of a lawful authority, but the absolute claims about their origins made by both parties during the civil war sounded in his ears as they do in ours; they were largely a matter of opinion, and the attempt to anchor royalty and resistance to either irrefutable principles or indisputable historical evidence left both open to doubt. No temporal power could claim a right unquestionable in origin, any more than it could pretend to be impervious to time. Hence usurpation differed from hereditary kingship only in lacking the prescription which would give the appearance of justice, and Ascham implied that time, in its undestructive

[1] *Ibid.* p. 127.

aspect, would remedy that defect as it had so often done before. In changes of government 'there is nothing that really affects us so much, as the Novelty and the Opinion of it, to which if the circumstance of a Little time be added, all our wonder is gone'.[1] Plenary possession, therefore, did not confer a just title on a usurper, nor would a long occupation of the throne remove the injustice, but it did afford the people a right to obey him if they chose. No other right *existed* for them in a confusion, and critics who have held that Ascham thereby confused might with right have not seen that Ascham, like Rous, rigorously confined himself to a right of obeying, and that the right to rule (supposedly confused with might) was no part of his argument. Granted his premises, it was the genuine, original right in natural law that everyone had been looking for, not a mere doctrine of expedience supported by historical precedents—a criticism which might fairly be made of the *Lawfulnes*. Ascham believed also that expedience called for compliance, because the natural liberties of the people, which could only be preserved within the context of a state, would be gravely endangered by disobedience, but he propounded his thesis as a real and serious alternative to the contending systems of political theorists. So far *Of the Confusions* serves to confirm the theory of the *Discourse*, but the two final chapters of Part II of the later work reveal the interesting connection between loyalist acquiescence and the familiar ideal of political and religious independency.

The abandonment of prescription put, as a second conse-quence, a new emphasis on the natural-law doctrine that equity was above the law. Developing this commonplace to a logical conclusion, Ascham affirmed that 'where all Justice is distributed by the same internall equity, the same fixt Lawes, and the same Tribunalls' it could be of only minimal importance whether the law was legislated by a monarchy, an aristocracy, or a democracy, or whether the subordinate magistrates who administered justice were changed. Justice was the 'form' of a

[1] *Ibid.* p. 133.

state, that 'which gives it life and being', and while it was necessary for a people to live always under 'a superior will and Government', it should be irrelevant to them what outward shape their government took, so long as equity was preserved. Ascham's was the most extreme statement ever written by an English political casuist on the indifferency of forms of govern⁄ ment: 'The difference which is betwixt Monarchy, Aristocracy, and Democracy, is no more then is betwixt one Jacobus piece of Gold, twenty two shillings, and forty foure six⁄pences, which put together are equivalent one to another, and of the same intrinsick valew.' 'A Christian may be perfect in any State of Government', and he would give account at the Last Day 'concerning the things themselves, just or unjust, which [he] did here in the flesh; not under what Person, Titles or Politicall formes [he] did them'.[1] Ascham manifests in his last chapters a Hobbesian grasp of the need for civil government, and a passionate independent's sense of the indifference of all outward forms, whether legal or religious. In the most Hobbesian passage of his book he asserted that public authority must depend on the peremptory will of the governor, who was not obliged to reason or persuade in the execution of his office;[2] but Ascham's preference was clearly for what he called the 'private' evidencing of religion and justice, that is, the motions of the spirit which 'hath the greatest proofe for it selfe within, but hath the least Evidence for it selfe without'.[3] Justice needed both reason and arbitrary will, but the end of man's creation was to glorify the supreme magistrate and to do good to his neighbour and fellow citizens. The earthly magistrate had chiefly various negative functions, enabling the people to live peaceable and godly lives, and it followed that the least govern⁄ ment was best. Equity, like the doctrinal succession of truth claimed by the protestant churches, survived all the vicissitudes of temporal authority, which were no worse than changes of

[1] *Ibid.* This paragraph so far is a summary of pp. 130–35.
[2] *Ibid.* p. 151. [3] *Ibid.* p. 150.

diet; a deficiency in a prince's title need not affect the justice he dispenses, and casuists had long recognized that not every defect vitiated a true title, any more than every sin made a man cease to be a true believer. Those who would insist that justice was injustice unless administered by a particular third person unwittingly inferred that equity and justice must be resolved into human authority as a direct principle. A Christian's immediate allegiance might be to his plenary possessor, 'but in and above all to God, the Universall Eternall Magistrate, under whose Jurisdiction we are to live eternally in another world'.[1] If it is possible to discern in Ascham's eloquence, described by the Exercitator as his 'pythagoricall magisteriousnesse',[2] a sympathy with the opinions of true revolutionaries like Milton, who consistently exalted equity at the expense of particular persons, one must add that nowhere does Ascham remotely attempt to describe bloody occasions as equitable. On the contrary, the very danger of losing all equity in a continuing confusion is the catastrophe of which he was most apprehensive. The over⁄turning of constitutional forms had threatened the moral con⁄tinuity of English law, so that only a return to obedience and the practice of justice in individual courts and by private men could save the country from final chaos. The revengeful casuists who would persuade the people to continue the quarrel 'think they do God good service in acting that which will at last oblige men neither to give nor take quarter all the world over'.[3]

Ascham, Rous, and Dury had selected the weapons for the debate, and their initial advantage was sustained by the general willingness of the country to take the oath, with or without mental reservations. It was to be expected that the principal

[1] *Ibid.* p. 131.
[2] [Edward Gee,] *An Exercitation Concerning Usurped Powers* (n.p. 1650), p. 54. Gee's authorship of this pamphlet is doubtful. It has also been attributed to Herle and Hollingsworth, and my copy has 'Geree' written on it in a con⁄temporary hand. Geree, who would also be a good candidate, died apparently in 1649, but there seems to be some doubt about the date of his death.
[3] *Of the Confusions*, p. 144.

attack of the presbyterians would be directed at the unlawful ness of both the government and obedience. A usurper, they said, was a self created power, and as such 'like an Idoll, that is, *nothing in the World*, a meere nullity',[1] and was in capable of tendering oaths or of commanding obedience except by force. Authority and obedience, magistrate and subject, were terms of relation, and inseparable from one another: 'if there be no Magistracy in him, there can be no obedience properly, and formally in me to him'.[2] Lawful power is founded on the wills of the governed, usurpation on the arbitrary will and power of the governor, which, as they were the only title of the present rulers, could be the only measure of their government. All force should presuppose a right, without which violence could not deprive a lawful magistrate of his title. Rebellion were no treason if its successful completion overthrew the legal right; and if private property was not lost by the dispossession of its owner, public property could not be. To obey a usurper was to participate in his sin, and to deny the right of the lawful prince to attempt to regain his throne. Power and right were always separable, and Romans xiii could refer only to lawful magistrates. In short, the presby terians held tenaciously to some of the main parliamentary positions of the civil war, emphasizing the elective and repre sentational nature of all government and insisting that the English constitution remained intrinsically intact. In this latter claim, absurd on the face of it, they were enormously helped by the oaths of allegiance to the King and his heirs which they claimed were still in effect. In fact the Covenant, which was their chief text, had only incidentally contained clauses to protect the King's person and his successors, but they afforded the opportunity now to indict the Rump for com pounding its impiety. To a God fearing nation the presby terians offered the alternatives of non compliance or damnation.

[1] [Edward Gee,] *A Plea for Non Scribers* (n.p. 1650), p. 28.
[2] *An Exercitation*, p. 9.

The opposition had answers, also, to the Engagers' specific arguments. They distinguished between different kinds of providential right and concluded, conventionally enough, that the providence enjoyed by the Rump was merely permissive, and no affirmation of God's favour. His providential acts could be followed only when they concurred with His revealed precepts. As for conquest, they held that victory proved nothing unless preceded by a right and confirmed by popular consent. They denied the innocent interpretations put on the words of the oath, and argued that 'commonwealth' meant more than 'the country as a whole', and 'true and faithful' more than 'to sit still and quiet'. They ignored, however, the government's apparent willingness to settle for these explica-tions. They refused to agree that the failure of one party in a mutual relationship freed the other side from his duties, and they periodically affirmed that Charles II neither had released nor could release his subjects from their allegiance. In the historical field they held their own, managing to show that every usurp-ing Roman emperor or English king never lacked a precedent right or a subsequent mandate. It is doubtful if these matters were susceptible of final proof, and the presbyterians could have made more of the inexpediency of the oath, where their case was probably incontestable. One of the most telling attacks on the oath was consequently *Some Considerations in relation to the Act of 2 January* (23 October 1650), which listed succinctly a number of reasons why the oath was untimely, including its offensiveness to scrupulous men, its inevitable inconsistency with one or another of the previous engagements, the unlikeli-hood of its effectiveness, and the bad consequences generally of laying obligations on the people. The author concluded that the magistrates should trust God with their government, because the oath would not hinder incendiaries, and people who had seen God's hand at work were aware that these trivial measures were unnecessary.

On these matters, as on the intention of the oath and its

wording, the presbyterians spoke the clear truth, and Dury in particular can be accused of canting insufferably about the consistency of the Engagement with the Covenant. He and his allies were on much firmer ground when they argued that former oaths had been abolished by an act of God. The presbyterians canted, on their side, in pretending that circum/stances had not radically altered since the first civil war, and while they had a reasonable contention in the mere permissive/ness of present providence, they were weak in answering the argument from conquest. They had themselves, as the Engagers informed them, taken up the sword in a just cause, and were now objecting to the consequences. Their fundamental limita/tion, however, was that they were not prepared to argue for immediate resistance or further rebellion, and they conceded nearly all the points which the Engagers maintained. Even Sanderson, besides Reynolds and the Exercitator, concurred in finding it lawful to pay taxes, to bear arms for the sake of self/preservation, and to complain and petition before the law, and generally to obey the power in all lawful things—with the single proviso that its authority must not be recognized.[1] All they really denied was the right to serve in any official capacity under the Commonwealth and the right to take an oath which could be interpreted as regularizing the status quo. Their principal assault was on a fact which the Engagers were not prepared to defend, and they relieved their feelings in ribald sarcasms. *The Man in the Moon* expostulated that 'now are the Rebells ty'd together by their late wicked combination (called the Engage/ment) as fast as Dog and Bitch, which the Saints thinke will beget a new Litter of Independent Puppies to barke for their Masters at *Westminster*, and give them warning that King *Charles*

[1] *Ibid.* pp. 22–4; also [Edward Reynolds,] *The Humble Proposals of Sundry Learned and Pious Divines within this Kingdom* (London, 1649), pp. 1–2, and Sanderson, *Works*, v, pp. 28–31, 34–35, and his anonymous *A Resolution of Conscience (by a Learned Divine) in Answer to a Letter Sent with Mr. Ascham's Book* (n.p. 1649), p. 1.

is comming to claime his Right'.[1] Three months later the same source reported that rats were being pilloried for gnawing the Engagement, and one victim had lost both his ears; a taker of the oath was known to have hanged himself, and Henry Hall wrote ominously of the increase of crime in recent days, and of an explosion which had killed seventy people on the night the Engagement was announced.[2] He contended that, by the Engagers' lights, Joseph could have slept with Potiphar's wife if he had claimed that providence put her in his way. The indignation of the opposition may be summarized in the outraged utterance of Clement Walker:

So that it fareth with the People of England as with a traviler fallen into the hands of thievs....they Robbe him by Providence, And then Murder him by Necessity, and (to bring in their Third Insisting Principle) they may alleadge; They did all this upon Honest Intentions; to enriche the Saints and rob the Egiptians. With these 3. Principles they Justify all their Villanies. Which is an invention so meerely their owne, That the Devill must acknowledge: They have propagated his Kingdome of Sinne and Death more by their Impudent Justifications, then by their Turbulent Actions.[3]

Presbyterian wrath was of little avail against the tide which was to flow for ten years. For every minister who refused the oath there was another to take it, and in argument the non-compliers were outnumbered. Ascham's influence was widely apparent in the number of references to 'possession', and one clergyman even published a sermon entitled *Plenary Possession Makes a Lawful Power*, which was not what Ascham had argued at all, although it was a legitimate misunderstanding of it.[4] Hobbes

[1] *The Man in the Moon*, 2–9 January 1650, no. 37, pp. 293–4.
[2] [Henry Hall,] *Digitus Testium* (London, 1650), p. 30. Baxter claimed to be the author of the queries about the Engagement in this book. See list cited in the note on p. 46.
[3] *The High Court of Justice; or Cromwell's New Slaughter House in England* [*Hist. of Independency, Part III*] (n.p. 1651), pp. 58–9.
[4] Richard Saunders, *Plenary Possession Makes a Lawful Power* (London, 1651), a sermon preached, he says, in March 1650.

contributed indirectly to the debate with the publication of *De Corpore Politico* in May 1650, which contained sections on conquest and the alienation of sovereignty which Nedham recommended 'together with the whole Treatise' to the nation at large.[1] Hobbes's influence is more directly discernible in what became a popular exposition of the reciprocal relation of protection and obedience. Ascham demonstrated that he had read *De Cive* before enlarging his *Discourse*, but his promised chapters on protection and obedience came to little, and other Engagers, including Dury, were to make more use of this proposition than he. They were also less cautious than their leaders, and more ready to look to providence for the determina- tion of a right to rule, rather than a permission to obey. Nedham, Francis Osborne, R. Fletcher, and others unabashedly de- clared that all governments originated in foul beginnings, and that crowns were but gallant robberies at first. They flaunted the conquest which had always been at least implicit in the idea of providence in political tracts, and in so doing they tended increasingly to return to the mode and manner of the die-hard revolutionaries. The success of the Irish, and later the Scottish, campaign bolstered the confidence of the govern- ment's apologists in God's immediate approval of the new regime, and even the sober *Memorandums* of a conference held in the North in February and March 1650 record that the old republican justifications were aired at the last meeting. As time went on, republican and loyalist argument became inextricably mixed—as they are, for example, in Peter English's *Survey of Policy* (1653)—but until the government was firmly established the most typical attitude of the Engager was what the Reverend A. Palmer called 'the waiting posture'. 'If we would serve providence intentionally and regularly, it must be in Gods way, sutable to his revealed will; but when God walks in the waters, there we cannot follow him: we can only stand still, and

---

[1] 'An Appendix, added out of Salmasius, and M. Hobbs', *The Case of the Common-Wealth of England, Stated*, 2nd ed. (London, 1650), pp. 103–11.

admire him, and wait upon him.'[1] Or, as the Northern Subscribers first agreed,

we judg it our duty, to stand up with those few heads and stayes of our Tribes, kept together by Gods providence in this strait of time for our support, and to engage with them for the strengthening of their hands, till the Lord hath accomplished his great work, planting the Heavens, and laying the foundations of the Earth amongst us; till he give us rest from the days of adversity, and still the enemy, and the avenger; till judgment return unto righteousness, and all the upright in heart follow it; till he throughly plead our cause, and roll away our reproach; till he ordain peace in our borders, making our walls salvation, and our gates praise.[2]

These sentiments Sir Robert Filmer publicly endorsed in his *Directions for Obedience to Governours in Dangerous and Doubtful Times* (1652), in which he resurrected the old royalist doctrine that it was better to sit still and suffer some injustice than to disturb the state with a multitude of pretences. He borrowed ideas without acknowledgment from Grotius, Ascham, and Hobbes, and his main proviso, that nothing must be acted against the person of the rightful governor, may have placated his friends and his conscience without hindering his submission to the present power.

To enhance the sense of the world's mutability, as the civil war and its aftermath did, is to deepen the sense of history. Clarendon became an historian in defeat, and Ascham, Rous, and Marvell turned to their history books as they meditated on the inevitable changes they experienced. 'All change argues imperfection', as Ascham commented, and the testing of this truth upon their pulses led to their perception of the significance of the present moment, and the need of that moment for law

[1] *The Saints Posture in Dark Times* (London, 1650), p. 10. John Wilkins's submissive *Discourse Concerning the Beauty of Providence* (London, 1649) was entered with the Stationers' Company five days after the execution.

[2] N. W., *A Discourse Concerning the Engagement: or the Northern Subscribers Plea* (London, 1650), p. 4. Known by the second half of its title, this was one of the tracts to which other writers most often referred.

and order and discipline and private virtues. The past became less important at the same time that thoughtful men became more aware of it, and the greater the nostalgia for the realm that had passed away, the greater the urgency became to preserve what was possible. Shakespeare had felt in similar terms when he wrote the history of Richard II, the last of the divine kings, and of Henry IV, the first of modern usurpers. Shakespeare too, in his first tetralogy, had brought the English history play to life with a profound inquiry into the meaning of a title, and the Engagement controversy confirmed the suspicion that all titles were ambiguous. Possibly the oath had been intended to obtain that consent of the people which all parliamentarians had declared to be necessary after a conquest, but it effectually alerted the government to the inadequacies of a virtually forced compliance, and to the necessity of a strong government that would render such measures otiose. Throughout the early years of the Interregnum, and culminating in the offer of the crown to Cromwell in 1657, the conservative and traditionally minded elements in Parliament moved towards the stabiliza-tion of the status quo. As the movement came to a head, there was hardly a poet who did not belong to it. They looked not to republican theory, which had come into its own again by 1653, but to Cromwell as the likely founder of a new dynasty who would restore the old constitution with a minimum of alterations. In 1660, when God by a miracle had restored the Stuarts, shame was lost in the contemplation of God's surprises. Moreover, there was no need for shame, as once again winners and losers were folded in a single party. History exonerated and justified not only the providential patience of Clarendon in exile, but the political quietism of the Engagers, whose patience also had contributed to the happy settlement they had desired. In 1688 their views were revived intact, and the future Dean of St Paul's was of the company.[1] One may enjoy the

---

[1] These writers have been studied by Gerald Straka, *Anglican Reaction to the Revolution of 1688* (Madison, Wis., 1962).

irony of observing the non-jurors occupying the seat of the presbyterians, and the conforming anglicans that of the Engaging independents, but beyond irony one may conclude that the loyalist opinions were not an irrelevant side-shoot of Interregnum thought but the foundation of passive obedience and respect for order on which the contractual theories of democratic government came to be built.

Marvell assumed political office after the Engagement oath had been abolished, and was probably never faced with a crisis of conscience about taking it. Apart from Milton's suggestion to Bradshaw in 1653, however, that Marvell would make a useful replacement for Ascham,[1] it is impossible to believe that Marvell could have changed his allegiance from the royal to the puritan cause for reasons that were unrelated to the Engagement arguments. Admittedly, a number of very prob-lematical questions are involved even in the statement that Marvell 'changed his allegiance', because, if his remarks nearly twenty-five years later are to be credited, the cause was always 'too good to have been fought for', and his hatred of ecclesiasti-cal tyranny appears then to have been a life-long obsession. In one sense, we might infer, Marvell had always been a supporter of the revolution, and he may have viewed the downfall of the anglican establishment, for which Charles had given his life, with some complacency. It would seem better not to speculate about what Marvell may or may not have thought, and to discuss his opinions as they arise in given texts, but the evidence of the ode and the royalist elegies is at least clear about his allegiance to the King's person, and his dislike of the specifi-cally 'democratick' aspects of the successful rebellion. Equally certain is his devotion throughout his life to providential ex-planations of political events, which alone makes his sympathy with the Engagers highly probable. Mr Skinner has concluded of the Engagers that 'it is they, first of all, who present us with a fully articulated and rationalist theory of sovereignty for the

[1] *Complete Prose Works of John Milton*, IV, p. 860.

first time in the history of English political thought',[1] and his own proper emphasis falls on the rationalism which is the special attribute of Anthony Ascham's theory; but it would be equally true to emphasize the religious basis for the acceptance of a usurped government, and to see the conflict with the presbyterians as arising from different interpretations of providence. The opposition between might and right, which the Engagers have been accused of confusing, is better seen as a struggle between the belief that God had merely permitted the new regime, as He had always permitted (without justifying) evil, and a conviction that it might prove later to have been His express design. The Horatian ode points back along the intervening years since Cromwell left his private gardens and accepts the apparent verdict of history on the royalist cause. By June 1650 Marvell could have taken the oath, although by that time he was already one step ahead of the Engagers' main concern.

The problem is to define, as well as one can, a context which will not only make Marvell's early political judgments and decisions intelligible, but which will help to make his subsequent development appear more normal and less random. The recrudescence of pure Engagement theory was not to reoccur until after Marvell's death, when loyalty to a *de facto* king was again interpreted as fidelity to a God-given dispensation, but Marvell's identification of England's destiny with Cromwell's in 1650, and then again in 1655, in which he was later followed by a majority of Parliament, is a natural growth of the Engagers' support for the principal power in the country, wherever it might reside. The necessity of regularizing the power, and the expectation of doing so in the near future, was as much the belief of the Engagers as it was of the men who urged Cromwell's kingship in 1657. With extraordinary prescience, Clarendon had foreseen such a movement as early as 1646, and dreaded it as the time approached for its

[1] *The Historical Journal*, VIII, p. 169.

consummation.[1] He himself clung to the hope that England would never be satisfied with anything less than a restoration of the royal family, but he also recognized that a substitute might prove just as acceptable to a majority. A love of the constitution proved not incompatible with an acceptance of the principal power, and his attribution of the success of his own ideals wholly to providence is in part his acknowledgment of how lucky Charles II had been, and how narrowly men of Marvell's mind had missed seeing their own interpretation of the times come true.

The matrix of Marvell's political thought, about which we are likely to remain, strictly speaking, ignorant, lies in the months between the King's death and the writing of the ode. Everything else, I believe, follows naturally from the commitment which was the upshot of his cogitations during that period. Changes of loyalty after the Restoration have never presented difficulties to an historian, and Marvell's was as unexceptionable as Sprat's, or Baxter's, or Fuller's, or Wilkins's, or Jeremy Taylor's. The task for a critic of his opinions after 1660 is to persuade readers that he meant what he said, and that his constitutionalism then was no less real than during the Interregnum.

[1] Wormald, *Clarendon*, p. 176; see also pp. 199–203.

2

'How fit he is to sway':
'An Horatian Ode upon Cromwel's
Return from Ireland'

The Horatian ode, by centering its attention on Cromwell and his part in English politics, represents a departure from the principal concern of the Engagers. Yet the preceding chapter will have served much of its purpose if it has manifested how acute the constitutional dilemma was which faced many moderate men, and how arduously they struggled to reconcile their desire for peace and a firm settlement with their clear perception of the illegality of the present power. The fracture of the old order divided their minds in a fashion which Milton, with confidence in his cause, either never felt or was never forced to admit; it took a prayerful suspense of condemnation and constant self-reminders that God's ways are not our ways to convince them that opposition to the regime was not a bounden duty on moral and legal grounds. Whether one accepts their arguments as an honest alternative to Milton's gloating and the equally righteous indignation of the royalists, or rejects them as the subtleties of ambidextrous and time-serving divines is not the question; what matters is the cruel choice of loyalties which the separation of justice and power had brought about. Neither alternative could be called happy, and each required resolution to follow. A decision was inescapable, however, and its consequences had to be accepted, because, even more sharply than the civil war itself, the situation did not permit an attitude of strict neutrality. To withhold consent while still paying taxes to preserve one's liberty and property, or to engage with mental reservations, was a reluctant form of involvement, not an opting out of the political mess.

The ode, written in the summer of 1650 when the highest winds of the controversy had begun to subside, reveals as firm a commitment to the established fact of the revolution as is to be found in the most positive of the Engagement pamphlets, and it also makes a proposal for the amendment of the constitution, which the pamphlets never did. Historically the ode, or anything like it, would have been impossible to write in 1649, and Cromwell's return from Ireland, I am convinced, marked a decisive moment in Marvell's political thought, and brought him to the point of formulating an opinion about England's best course which had been inevitably delayed until the first threats to the government's stability had been repulsed. As a response to a particular event which had confirmed Cromwell's power and prompted speculations about its future employment, the ode is not ambiguous at all, any more than the Engagement tracts were ambiguous about their proposals for submission. Yet the dichotomies of resolution and regret, apology and affirmation, power and justice are clearly as much a part of Marvell's reflections on Cromwell as they are of the thoughts of the Engagers about the unlawful government they supported. There are two Cromwells in the poem, the scourge of God and the leader of His troubled people; and, in proposing that the second of these figures is the predominant and controlling theme, it is no purpose of this chapter to explain the other away or to pretend he doesn't exist. On the contrary, the history of the eighteen months between the execution and the poem show that a divided awareness was intrinsic to much political writing, especially of the loyalist kind that Marvell would have read most sympathetically.[1] Hence, as Mr Wormald has argued about Edward Hyde's 'royalism' in 1646, we need not so much a revision of accepted commonplaces as an addition which will serve to place them in an historical perspective. One may welcome Miss Syfret's

[1] Marvell discusses Samuel Parker's father's contribution to the dispute in *The Rehearsal Transpros'd*, in *Works*, ed. Grosart, III, p. 332.

observations about Cromwell's likeness to Lucan's hated Caesar without accepting her tentative conclusion that 'in so far as there is a moral or emotional judgement made in the poem, it goes against Cromwell'.[1] The emotional force of the ode nobody disputes, or the tension engendered by the comparison between Charles and Cromwell, and the most satisfactory readings have been, and should remain, those in which the antithetical aspects of Cromwell's career are left intact. The only error is to suppose that the 'conflict' between the flattering and unflattering lights under which he is observed originates in a unique Marvellian quality of impartiality, and not in the nature of circumstances which were popularly understood to be contradictory; or, on the other hand, to imagine that the poet's cool appraisal of Cromwell's past and present actions is inconsistent with a decided political stand. No critic for many years has believed in Marvell's complete neutrality, but the debate cannot be profitably continued unless we relinquish introspection into our personal responses to the poem, and concentrate once again on the meaning of a Christian providence which could bring good out of evil. Anthony Ascham's eloquence may serve to reintroduce the subject:

This we know by Prophecie in generall, that God as universall governour of the world, will still make change of his substituted Vice-Roys, yea, and of governments: men not moving in that station by chance this way or that way, as Pis-mires doe upon a mole-hill. *Nec tanquam tali ex fritillo temere huc illuc volventes*; not like dice which come at haphazard out of the box, and runne some higher then another by the same chance. But because there is an O *Altitudo* in Gods wayes; and that he may use the obliquities of our actions to a good, though secret end (just as we our selves may strike a right stroke, with a stick that is crooked).[2]

[1] R. H. Syfret, 'Marvell's "Horatian Ode"', *RES*, new series, XII (1961), p. 172. Miss Syfret herself has pointed out that Cromwell in the second half of the ode bears some resemblance to Lucan's more favoured Pompey. Her analysis of the emotion in the ode, apart from the line quoted, is exceptionally fair.

[2] *Of the Confusions and Revolutions of Governments* (London, 1649), pp. 109–10.

The Horatian ode, both implicitly and explicitly, conveys Marvell's belief that God 'may use the obliquities of our actions to a good, though secret end', and that Cromwell had been sent by God to be first the punisher and then the deliverer of his country. The theme of the ode is the deliverance, and Marvell envisaged, in accordance with the concept of the *dux bellorum* which permitted dictators at the commencement of new empires, Cromwell's election to the constitutional dictatorship of England. With the passage of time, and after more laurels for the victorious general, the meaning of the previous tragedy had begun to reveal itself, and the end to which God's judgments pointed had, to Marvell at least, been made clear. The signs could not have been read before, when the destruction of ancient rights would have appalled all just men and enlisted their resistance, but a purpose had now emerged of which Cromwell was the embodiment. The duality of his rôle in the poem reflects the bitter impressions of the past, not fears for the future, and there was no confusion in Marvell's mind about the way in which he should be greeted on his return from Ireland. The opening stanzas, however, with what the rhetoricians might have called an insinuation, tacitly concede that his homecoming raises grave questions about the dangers of his supreme power which Englishmen ought to consider.

If Cromwell had not behaved with exemplary modesty, his triumphant return from the Irish campaign could well have been the prelude to his assumption of supreme power, and many of his enemies were convinced that his ambition was boundless. His return posed distinct choices, for himself, for Parliament, and for all interested spectators who were wondering how this new Caesar would act. Marvell dramatized the possible conflict of attitudes by an allusion to a passage in *Pharsalia* (1. 239 ff.), a book long recognized as a source for phrases in the first part of the ode. Lucan described the desperate plight of the inhabitants of Ariminum, on the day Caesar crossed the Rubicon, when they awoke to the blare of

Caesar's trumpets in the market-place. In Thomas May's translation,

> With this sad noise the peoples rest was broke,
> The young men rose, and from the temples took
> Their arms, now such as a long peace had mar'd.
> And their old bucklers now of leather's bar'd:
> Their blunted Pi[k]es not of a long time us'd,
> And swords with th' eatings of black rust abus'd.[1]

Caesar had presented the people of Ariminum with a *fait accompli*. Their weapons, defective with 'th' unused Armours rust', were rendered yet more futile by the surprise with which Caesar had struck. The morning was dark (the 'Shadows' of line 3 of the ode) and Caesar declared that he had left peace behind him (the 'inglorious Arts of Peace' of line 10), and henceforth would follow fortune and 'adventrous War'.[2] Instead of attacking Caesar, the armed but terror-stricken youths had been too frightened to complain, and, in languishing numbers, they had silently bewailed the fate of their city, which bore the brunt of every new invasion.

It is not at once clear whether Marvell's youth who is exhorted to reach for his armour should do so to join Cromwell's army, or, like the youths in Rimini, to oppose the Caesar invading across the Bristol Channel. Marvell might be, like Lucan, the laureate of a madman he detested as the disturber of the peace, but on the other hand he is also writing an ode, the normal vehicle of praise for victorious generals. The title of the poem suggests that Marvell is to be another Horace to Cromwell's Augustus, while the exordium could imply the poet's hostility towards his subject. Subsequently, the parallel with Lucan is seen to function as a means of establishing the

[1] *Lucans Pharsalia: or the Civil-Wars of Rome*, trans. Thomas May, 4th ed. (London, 1650), p. 8. Marvell's 'Removing from the Wall' is closer to Lucan's 'Deripuit sacris adfixa penatibus arma' than May's 'temples'.

[2] Lucan, *De Bello Civili* I. 225-7: '"Hic", ait, "hic pacem temerataque iura relinquo;/Te, Fortuna, sequor. Procul hinc iam foedera sunto;/Credidimus satis his, utendum est iudice bello."'

poet as a just and thoughtful man: he knows that Cromwell appears to some men to be a tyrant, and it is at once plain that the ode is not to be a piece of panegyric flattery.

'So restless *Cromwel* could not cease/In the inglorious Arts of Peace.' The analogy between Cromwell and the forward youth of the opening stanzas is the measure of Cromwell's greatness, because he too had once taken his corslet from the wall, and had succeeded, unlike the youths in Rimini, in opposing a Caesar's tyranny and blasting his imperishable laurels. Inevitably, having defeated a tyrant single-handed, he was now himself able to tyrannize, but the providential nature of his power is confirmed by the comparison. History repeats itself at the start of every civil war, but with essential differences, and Cromwell's achievement of the seemingly impossible task of overthrowing an absolute power distinguishes the events in England from a comparable occasion in ancient Rome. Cromwell has made actual the resistance which the boys in Rimini only imagined, so a greater than Caesar is here, wielding more force and offer-ing a more terrifying prospect than that which confronted the Romans. Hence the forward youth who *would* appear—that is, who has not yet appeared, but who now has his chance—is also each and every one of Marvell's readers, who is invited, after the contemplation of the past and the present, to rewrite history in the way that Cromwell has already done. The moment has arrived for a brave man to oppose Cromwell, and in 1650 the unthinkableness of the idea provided its own answer. Rational readers are forced to concede that Cromwell's eminence is secure, and must therefore be accepted. Marvell shows his own inclination to accept it by implying that the choice for him is not between muse and armour but between 'languishing' and more public or masculine numbers.

The multiple ironies of the opening twenty-four lines con-tain no overt praise of Cromwell, although they tend to re-inforce a view of his special and ordained mission from the 'angry heavens' as a scourge. Not even Cromwell's enemies

could have disagreed with this opinion, for just as to the
victors all victories were marks of God's approval, so to the
defeated were all defeats a punishment for past wickedness.
The semblance of Marvell's impartiality is thus retained until,
with a marked redirection of his attention, the poet turns to an
analysis of Cromwell's personal qualities: 'And, if we would
speak true,/Much to the Man is due.' The following section
(lines 27–56) divides Cromwell's virtue into the four cardinal
varieties, thereby matching his character against a classical
ideal. His temperance is exhibited in the 'reserved and austere'
life he once lived in his 'private Gardens'; his fortitude has
been revealed in his 'industrious Valour' on the field of battle,
and his wisdom or 'wiser Art' displayed itself in his capacity
for crafty hunting. Only in one category of virtue does Crom⁄
well appear initially to be seriously deficient, in justice:

> Though Justice against Fate complain,
> And plead the antient Rights in vain:
>> But those do hold or break
>> As Men are strong or weak.
> Nature that hateth emptiness,
> Allows of penetration less:
>> And therefore must make room
>> Where greater Spirits come.   (37–44)

Neither Marvell nor the Engagers wished to pretend that the
'antient Rights' embodied in English common and statute
law were on Cromwell's side, and recent interpreters of the ode
have responded variously to the challenge of the lines. Professor
Mazzeo finds 'the pinnacle' of Marvell's Machiavellianism in
them; Professor Hyman comments, 'The question of what is just
is kept on an ideal plane of what ought to be, and this poem
deals with the world of action, with what—at least to Marvell—
must be'; and Professor Williamson, with a Senecan brevity,
has explained thus: 'If Justice without strength is powerless
against Fate, then rights depend upon power. But the poet can
at least call things by their right names: events may become

necessary without being right. The order of nature depends upon such necessity.'[1] Certainly, a doctrine of necessity is being employed to counter the cause of justice, but in the context of the cardinal virtues, and the legal imagery of complaining and pleading, it may be more accurate to emphasize Marvell's own appeal to a higher justice, embodied not in a constitution but in natural and revealed law. Cromwell's detractors may listen to necessity if it is presented to them under the proper rubric. The Engagers, and especially Ascham, with their support for the power of usurpers, also defended the status quo by natural law, and Henry Parker had even, like Marvell, found analogies between the laws of physical matter and the laws of political change. 'When Nature', he wrote, 'permits heavie bodies contrary to the Law of heavie bodies to ascend, for the prevention of some greater breach of some law that concerns all the Elements, and peace of the universe: it teaches us, what we are to do in politicks.'[2] The law of impenetrability was Marvell's happy selection, because though in science it was an incontrovertible rule that no two bodies could occupy the same place at the same time, in theology the materiality or immateriality of spirit could in Hobbes or Henry More excite a lively debate about its properties. To Marvell, Cromwell's usurpation could be defended by a justice that was no less scriptural than natural, for had not Christ declared more than once that lesser spirits must give way to greater? On one occasion He had added with peculiar aptness: 'When a strong man armed keepeth his palace, his goods are in peace:

[1] George Williamson, *Milton & Others* (Chicago, 1965), p. 125; J. A. Mazzeo, *Renaissance and Seventeenth-Century Studies* (New York, 1964), p. 174; Lawrence W. Hyman, *Andrew Marvell* (New York, 1964), p. 79.

[2] *Scotlands Holy War* (London, 1651), pp. 77–8. A similar analogy of Parker's is quoted in F. D. Wormuth, *The Royal Prerogative, 1603–1649* (Ithaca, N.Y., 1939), p. 113, which also occurs in Robert Sanderson's 'Judgment Concerning Submission to Usurpers' in Izaak Walton's *The Life of Dr. Sanderson* (London, 1678), pp. 16–17. Natural law could always find the exception to itself.

But when a stronger than he shall come upon him, and over come him, he taketh from him all his armour wherein he trusted, and divideth his spoils.'[1] The text was familiar to the loyalists, because Francis Osborne glanced at it in *A Perswasive to a Mutuall Compliance under the Present Government*, and Nathaniel Ward, in the wittiest of the anti-Engagement pamphlets, had tried to laugh Marvell's kind of argument out of countenance: 'I never read in all my Law-books, that sole possession begat a true right. Certainly if it doth, *Christ* did the devils great wrong to cast them out of the *Dæmoniacks*: Possession may be II. points of the Law, but not half a point of the Gospel.'[2]

Apart from his justice, which required a peculiar and, from an unsympathetic point of view, a controversial defence, Crom well's other virtues were beyond dispute. But Marvell has still not raised openly the question of Cromwell's dictatorship, contenting himself, in the justice lines, with the re-formula tion of a providential justification for Cromwell's power. It may have been recalled by some of his readers, however, that the four virtues, common alike to the pagan and Christian traditions, had invariably figured in the mirrors for princes as attributes of the Christian prince—often with a concatenation of other qualities which Cromwell may or may not have possessed. Cromwell, moreover, combined the virtues of wisdom and valour, of knowledge and experience, to an exceptional degree, and those combinations had long been felt to constitute the indispensable equipment of a good governor. Malvezzi summarized the belief when he stated: 'To the third [kind of prince], namely to him that hath both [strength and understanding], the Scepter, in my opinion is due, and to him indeed, for the most part, People have granted it, when it

---

[1] Luke xi. 21–2; also Matthew xii. 26–9.
[2] *Discolliminium* (London, 1650), p. 13. The tract is signed 'B' but is generally attributed to Ward. For Osborne, see *Somers Tracts*, ed. Walter Scott (London, 1809–15), VI, p. 157.

hath bin in their power to give it: as to *Saturne, Iupiter, Hercules, Romulus,* and so many others; The Gentiles so highly esteeming him that hath those two characters of valour and wisdome (which both goe to the framing of true Fortitude) that where they have found them both united, they have even adored them.'[1]

By turning deliberately from a scrutiny of Cromwell to an account of Charles's dignity at his execution, Marvell initiated a comparison which has dominated interpretations of the ode. The movement of the poem, however, is not determined by an opposition between Charles and Cromwell; Charles is merely an incident in a narrative which begins with Cromwell's extraordinary past and concludes with the expectation of his glorious future. Nor does the comparison, which also isolates Charles 'upon that memorable Scene', serve to belittle Crom-well. Charles, through Cromwell's subtlety, had trapped him-self, and he steps onto the scaffold as one who accepts with superb humility the consequences of his own mistakes. The image of the tragic theatre was one of the commonest meta-phors employed to describe the events of the late times, and to the royalists Charles was indeed the '*Royal Actor*', the medieval *Christomimetes*, who went to his death like a second Jesus. 'I have now done with my text,' wrote Leslie, 'but not with the Princes of this world; for I am now to present unto you another sad tragedy, so like unto the former that it may seem but *vetus fabula per novos historiones*, the stage onely changed, and new actors entered upon it, other Princes of this world, yea, of *the darknesse of this world,* Farre worse than then [sic] Pilat.'[2] But Ascham could use the metaphor also, and castigate an oppos-ing casuist for wishing to see the play continue: 'For, lest we of the People should bogle at comming on the Stage to Act our

---

[1] Virgilio Malvezzi, *Considerations upon the Lives of Alcibiades and Coriolanus,* trans. Robert Gentilis (London, 1650), p. 193.

[2] Henry Leslie, *The Martyrdome of King Charles, or his Conformity with Christ in His Sufferings* (The Hague, 1649), pp. 11–12.

late Tragedy over againe, hee would impose it on our beliefes, that we are still in the middle act of it and that we ought to finish it.'[1] Dury lamented the execution also, and Marvell's particular blend of reverence and pity for Charles was in fact captured most nearly by John Sadler, a friend of Cromwell's, writing in 1649 to defend the new government:

Yet in That juncture of Time, and every Circumstance, I am not ashamed, to confesse my selfe, to have been So Tender of Blood, that I would gladly have spoken, All that I justly might to have saved him from Death...Must we confesse the way to be a Narrow Strait, between the Mighty Rocks of Fear, and Love of Justice, with the Kingdoms Safety? Or can Any Cleere it, that it may appear, and be, a fair and plain High Way, that was the Kings by Right, although not used much of late.[2]

A sense of the national tragedy was not the prerogative of royalist elegists, as we have seen, and there is no reason to suppose that a poet could not write an ode to Cromwell and retain a profound regret for Charles's murder. The list of independents who were willing to try Charles, or to govern after his demise, but who would not sign his death warrant, is a long one,[3] and Lord Fairfax is the classic example of a man who never condoned the King's execution but who remained on friendly terms with Cromwell. Marvell's feelings meet the historical probabilities, yet the lines are not a simple concession to sentiment but a continuation of an argument which began by confronting the reader, as dramatically as possible, with a picture of Cromwell's power.

Mr Lerner has observed that when Charles 'bow'd his comely Head,/Down as upon a Bed' he was making a gesture

[1] *The Bounds & Bonds of Publique Obedience* (London, 1649), pp. 36–7.
[2] *Rights of the Kingdom* (London, 1649), sig. ¶¶ 4ʳ. Dury in his *Declaration* (London, 1660), pp. 10–11, comments on Charles's trial: 'I made it a serious part of my work, first to prevent the Sentence, & Secondly the execution of it; in the first to save his reputation, in the second his life. For I did conscionably judge myself bound to do for him, all which I could or should have done for mine own Father if he had been in his case'.
[3] George Yule, *The Independents in the English Civil War* (Cambridge, 1958), p. 129.

of 'perfect acquiescence'.[1] The phrase has a happy accuracy and its implications are profound, because Charles's consent to his fate, his willingness to make his destiny his choice, leaves the way open for the conqueror to assume command, and for loyal subjects to accept the new dispensation. 'This was that memorable Hour / Which first assur'd the forced Pow'r'. Marvell suppressed the very mixed emotions with which the King faced his death, but he cannot be said to have invented Charles's acquiescence. Apart from his bearing on the scaffold, Charles's inaudible address to the crowd had contained the statement, 'Yet for all this, God forbid that I should be so ill a Christian, as not to say that Gods Judgements are just upon me';[2] he later qualified this remark with reflections on the 'unjust sentence' and the injustice of a title acquired by conquest, but then also, in his self-conscious martyrdom, he forgave his enemies for what they did. The verses he was reputed to have written in prison also show a man desperately hoping and resigning himself at the same time:

> In all things here Gods providence,
>   and will alone commands,
> The life of my poore spirit sad,
>   is only in his hands.
> Oh, that the Lord would me restore,
>   my strength then I would give,
> To serve my God in humbleness
>   whilst he would let me live.[3]

[1] L. D. Lerner, 'Andrew Marvell: An Horatian Ode...', in *Interpretations*, ed. John Wain (London, 1955), p. 68.

[2] *King Charls his Speech made upon the Scaffold at Whitehall Gate* (London, 1649), p. 6. Charles's statement is taken up by the writer of *A Crowne, A Crime: or, the Monarch Martyr* (a single sheet dated by Thomason 13 Feb. 1649) to gloss the phrase 'Heav'ns judgment's just!' in one of the verses attributed to the King. Christopher Hill, *Puritanism and Revolution* (London, 1958), p. 360 n., notes other contemporary accounts of Charles's submissiveness.

[3] *The Kings Last Farewell to the World, or the Dead Kings Living Meditations, at the Approach of Death Denounced against Him* (a single sheet dated 1648 [old style]). The punctuation has been amended.

Marvell chose to isolate the aspect of the execution that most became its victim, and the significance of Charles's resignation is made the more pointed by his refusal to call upon the gods 'with vulgar spight/To vindicate his helpless Right'. In the seventeenth century, 'vindication' generally carried legal overtones, since in Roman and civil law it meant an assertion of one's legal right or the recovery of a right by legal process. It was with the law in mind that Edward Hyde wrote a declaration for Charles II in the first months of 1649 in which the young King promised to bring his father's murderers to justice, to 'recover our owne rights and just power', and 'vindicate the knowne and confessed Lawes of the Kingdome'.[1] In a fine providential sermon on the King's death, Thomas Fuller prefigured the use of the word in the ode. He is reprimand/ ing the fretters, the droopers, and the arguers at the sad occasion and instructing them that they should not count their ignorance God's injustice:

If one conceive himself wronged in the *Hundred*, or any inferiour Court, he may by a *certiorari*, or an *accedas ad curiam*, remove it to the *Kings/Bench* or *Common/Pleas*, as he is advised best for his own advantage. If he appre/ hendeth himself injured in these Courts, he may with a *Writ of Error* remove it to have it argued by all the Judges in the *Exchequer/chamber*. If here also he conceiveth himself to find no justice, he may with an *Injunction* out of the *Chancery* stop their proceedings. But if in the *Chancery* he reputeth himself agreeved, he may thence appeal to the *God of heaven and earth*, who in another world will vindicate his right, and severely punish such as have wilfully offered wrong unto him. And so much to assert Gods justice in suffering the *righteous man to perish in his righteousness*.[2]

In the ode, by not appealing his case to the gods, Charles has surrendered his right both to fate and to Cromwell, and 'the forced Pow'r' now rules with his permission.

[1] S. R. Gardiner, ed., 'Draft by Sir Edward Hyde of a Declaration to be Issued by Charles II in 1649', *EHR*, VIII (1893), p. 304.
[2] *The Just Mans Funeral* (1649) in *The Collected Sermons* (London, 1891), I, p. 523. Fuller also has an image of just men being hasted to bed betimes 'even before their ordinarie hour' (I, p. 531).

Of all the ways of changing a government, the resignation of power by the holder to the new ruler was considered the least painful. 'Voluntary change', as Bodin remarked, is 'the smoothest and easiest of all',[1] and in 1650 the question of oaths had revived an awareness of the easiest means by which old obligations could be dissolved. One Engager suggested that 'the Kings yielding is an absolution of the Subjects from the allegiance formerly due to Him by them, and so makes it law‿full for them to yield the same to another'.[2] John Rocket added: 'If he that made the *covenant* or *promise* dissolve it, it is dissolved, I mean him to whom it was made, and by whose power it was made: the reason is good; he sees no necessity of such an *obligation* to him, and it being for his sake, his safety, honor, &c. and a burthen to the *obliged*; the one party may part with *his own right*, to ease another.'[3] And Hobbes summarized with his usual succinctness: 'In transferring of Right, two things therefore are required, One on the part of him that transferreth, which is a sufficient signification of his Will therein; The other, on the part of him to whom it is transferred, which is a sufficient signification of his Acceptation thereof. Either of these failing, the Right remaineth where it was.'[4] The surrender of right is also the transferral of right, and the acceptance of defeat an acknowledgment of the conqueror. What the En‿gagers were implying when they wrote in these terms was that Charles could be presumed to have abdicated, thereby dis‿solving the bonds of the old covenant. A similar argument, of course, was to prove of the utmost value in 1688, but in 1649–50 it was no more than a suggestion thrown out to ease the pressure on overworked consciences. If we are to call things by their proper names, abdication is also the informing idea of the description of Charles in the ode, although historically it would be more accurate to use another word. We might remember, however,

[1] *Six Books of the Commonwealth*, trans. M. J. Tooley (Oxford, n.d.), p. 110.
[2] *A Briefe Resolution of that Grand Case of Conscience* (London, 1650), p. 4.
[3] *The Christian Subject* (London, 1651), p. 121.
[4] *De Corpore Politico* (London, 1650), p. 11.

that in 1648 'dethroning' had been a practical possibility, one writer declaring, 'We cannot but be sensible of his Majesties grace and goodnesse to us, who was pleased to condescend *even to the dethroning of himselfe*, for our Peace and quiet',[1] and that Ascham had related the story of Ferdinand of Naples with obvious persuasive intent. Nor did he fail to revive the anecdote after the execution, and his extract from Guicciardini's *History* may be quoted, because it conveys exactly the tone which informs Marvell's verses:

But because things can not be put to triall, without committing the common patrimony to desperate perill, I am determined rather to give place to fortune, and keep hid my vertue, then in striving [not] to lose the kingdom, to be the causer of effectes contrary to those ends for the which I have alwaies desired to be King. Therefore with teares I give you this councell, that standing no more against the fury of the time, you send with speede to make your accord with the french King. And to the end you may be in better power, to do it without staine to your honours, I absolve you willingly of the homage and oath which you made to me a few daies past: wherein I exhort you according to the necessity of your fortune, not to defer your obedience, humility, and readinesse to receive him, as by that meanes to stay the course of your proper adversities, and helpe to moderate the naturall pride of that nation.[2]

Ascham commented on this passage that 'here was the true duty both of a man, and of a King; yea the Action was more then Kingly: For to lay down a Crowne is more Majesticall then to weare it...Though other places in the like or worse condition have not so cleare a Declaration of their Princes and Governours wils, yet *the same is to be presumed from them*, rather then that they should occasion a fruitlesse and a calamitous confusion in their behalfs: For he who spits against the wind, spits but in his owne face.'[3] The final maxim distinguishes

[1] *The Returne of the People of England: Tendred to the Speaker of the House of Commons* (n.p. 1648), p. 6.
[2] *The Historie of Guicciardin*, trans. Geffray Fenton (London, 1599), end of Book 1, p. 54.
[3] *Of the Confusions*, p. 102. Also his *A Reply to a Paper of Dr. Sandersons, containing a Censure of Mr. A. A. his Book* (London, 1650), pp. 7–8, and

Ascham from Marvell and from Grotius, but the presumption of the monarch's concurrence has been actualized in the ode and is at the heart of its unforgettable cadence. As the ode moves nearer to the explicit announcement of its theme, the King's prior consent to a change of loyalty is important, as it was likely to be one of the first concerns of a royalist who wished to support a new leader, just as the report that Charles II had given way to the signing of the Engagement was a belated tribute to an accomplished fact.

The smaller space allotted to a second and third argument—the evidence of the bleeding head and the loyalty of the con-quered Irish—may suggest their somewhat lower status as proof of Cromwell's inheritance of the kingdom. The original head was found in the reign of Tarquin the Proud, the last of the Roman kings, at the time when he was building a temple from the spoils of captured cities. The temple was not dedicated until the first year of the Republic, and, as a prognostication, the head was taken to mark the end of Rome's infancy, the begin-ning of the Republic and of Roman liberty, and, universally, as a sign that Rome would be the head of a new world empire.[1] In these respects the death of Charles could be proclaimed a 'happy Fate' for England, although the head would be a callous and grisly detail were it not that the ode is pervaded by a sense of recurring history. But who, then, are the frightened architects, for they are Marvell's embellishment of the familiar story? The architects of the Capitoline Temple, if we follow the

A Combate betweene Two Seconds (London, 1649), p. 12. Richard Baxter was an opponent of the Engagement, but by 1659 he gave it as his opinion in A Holy Commonwealth, p. 161, that it was the duty of an injured prince to resign his government, 'and if he will not, the people ought to judge him as made uncapable by providence, and not to seek his restitution, to the apparent ruine of the Commonwealth'.

[1] Livy, Annals I. lv. 6; Servius, Comm. in Verg. Aen. VIII. 345; Arnobius of Sicca, The Case against the Pagans, VI. 7; Cassius Dio, Roman History, trans. Earnest Cary (London, 1914), I, p. 77 (Zonaras's epitome, vii. 11); Isidorus of Seville, Etymologiarum sive Originum, XV. ii. 31. Margoliouth annotates the passage from Pliny and Varro.

logic of the poem, were the founders of the Republic, and in England these men were the regicides, the members of the governing Parliament, and the Council of State. Marvell implies that their 'fright' has created a hiatus in the construction of the new building, and the founding of the republic is endangered by the confusion wrought by Charles's death. A fearless architect is now required to bring the work to completion and achieve the happiness augured by the execution. Marvell's nomination for such an architect cannot be in doubt.

The rhetorical intention of the Irish testimony is not obscure. As Lord Lieutenant of Ireland—a position to which he had been appointed a year before, and from which Parliament would not now release him—Cromwell had already exercised an authority of 'highest Trust'. If a conquered people were willing to grant that his administration had been good and just, no more convincing recommendation for supreme office could be obtained. The supposition that Marvell invented the Irish praise is based, in the first place, upon the assumption that the Irish are congratulating him on his exploits as a general, rather than on his behaviour as Lord Lieutenant; secondly, the massacres at Drogheda and Clonmel have always made it easy to forget that the campaign as a whole was waged according to a more gentlemanly code than has operated in many wars since. Terms were regularly granted to cities willing to capitulate, looting was forbidden, and the discipline Cromwell maintained among his troops was as much his concern in Ireland as it had always been. Thirdly, the reports that filtered back to London and were reported in the weekly newspapers exonerate Marvell from being guilty of more than a mild exaggeration, the purpose of which the poem explains. From the start, the government had been anxious to publish accounts of submission from all over the British Isles, and Ireland was no exception.

In September 1649, the *Perfect Occurrences* recorded that 'other letters from *Ireland* say, that divers come in daily to the

Lord Lieutenant, so that his Lordship is likely to be more in want of Armes then of men, to make his Army great. The Lord Lieu. hath so gallant a Discipline of his forces, that where his Lordship comes, he doth much get into the affections of the people.'[1] At the fall of Cork in January 1650, one writer commented that 'the generality of the Townsmen [were] wel affected to the English, and enemies to the Irish',[2] while a more sceptical reporter wrote that 'the well-affected of this City of Cork entertained us with very much cheerfullnesse and free-nesse', but, he admitted, 'the honester part is allwayes the fewest... we cannot say we over abound with fast friends'. The same issue of *A Perfect Diurnall*, however, carried a letter from Holyhead in which it was noted that 'the Gentlemen and Commonalty of *Ireland* do generally comply and submit to the Lord Lieutenants orders'.[3] Proof of widespread compliance was provided by an extremely hostile witness, 'the Ecclesiasticall Congregation of the Archbishops, Bishops, and other Prelates'. In the last of three declarations which were reprinted in London the prelates confessed 'that many of our flock are mislead by a vain opinion of hopes, that the Commander in chiefe of the Rebels Forces, commonly called the Parliamentaries, would afford them good conditions, and that relying thereon they suffer utter distruction of Religion, lives, and fortunes, if not prevented'. They continued with a fair warning that contains, nevertheless, the reason why they considered it necessary to urge the people to continue the war effort: 'And for the common sort of people, towards whom if they shew any more moderate usage at present, it is to no other end but for their private advantage, and for the better support of

[1] *Perfect Occurrences of Every Daie Journall in Parliament*, 7–14 Sept. 1649, no. 141, p. 1285.

[2] *Severall Proceedings in Parliament*, 31 Jan.–7 Feb. 1649 [1650], no. 19, p. 248. The surrender of Cork 'did also give an incouragement to *Youghall* to declare for the Parliament' (p. 250).

[3] *A Perfect Diurnall of Some Passages and Proceedings of...the Armies in England and Ireland*, 28 Jan.–4 Feb. 1649 [1650], no. 8, p. 67–8.

their Army, intending at the close of their conquest (if they can effect the same as God forbid) to root out the Commons also, and plant this land with Colonies to be brought hither out of England...'[1] A letter in June 1650 acknowledged that the Irish were still ready to do mischief, 'although through the wisdome of the Lord Lieutenant, and the Commanders under him, they have been dealt with in such a way, as that if it were possible they might be won to peace and subjection, and do injoy al liberties as freely as others, save only in point of tolleration of the exercise of their popish Idolatry'.[2] It would be a great mercy, the writer continued, if God would open their eyes, which, at about the same time, He appears to have done for the people of Londonderry: 'Our Army and Garrison have alreade subscribed the Engagement with a most unani/mous consent, and likewise our Co[r]poration, to wit our Mayor, Alderman, Common/Councell and the rest of the Inhabitants (though not required there unto by any Orders of Parliament or my Lord Lieutenant that I know of) have very willingly and chearfully subscribed it; so that (thanks be to God) we are here in a very conformable temper, expecting good Rules of Civill Government from the State of *England*, which I hope will in due time be conveighed to us.'[3] By August Ireton was writing to the House of Commons to explain the miracle which God had performed at Waterford and Carlow —the people had not been forced to surrender, but God had worked in their hearts.[4] The news from Ireland was mixed, as we should expect, but the evil Cromwell did there has lived after him far longer than the prudence he exercised, for which

[1] *Severall Proceedings in Parliament*, 25–31 Jan. 1649 [1650], no. 18, pp. 236–7.
[2] *Ibid.* 13–20 June 1650, no. 38, p. 553.
[3] *A Perfect Diurnall of...the Armies in England and Ireland*, 10–15 June 1650, no. 27, p. 302.
[4] *Severall Proceedings in Parliament*, 22–29 August 1650, no. 48, p. 707. Someone else may be able to find from Ireland a 'Humble Acknowledgement' such as was presented to Parliament in June 1650 by the people of South Wales, signed by 19,000 names, and thanking the authority for its clemency.

he received some credit at the time. The ode, however, is not about Ireland, and the satisfaction of her people is plainly recalled to witness to Cromwell's fitness for another task. The only trust which can reasonably be construed as the 'highest' must be that of Governor of England and Supreme Head of the Commonwealth. Lest there be any mistake, Marvell immediately recalls one of the most famous and un-ambiguous of all political maxims: 'How fit he is to sway/ That can so well obey.'

The *sententia* was attributed to Solon, repeated by Plato, and confirmed in the canon of political thought by Aristotle, who observed, 'It has been well said that "he who has never learned to obey cannot be a good commander"'; he con-tinued to make a clear distinction between governing and obeying: 'The two are not the same.' Cicero, in a statement which was later to be frequently quoted in the lexicons, wrote that 'the man who rules efficiently must have obeyed others in the past, and the man who obeys dutifully appears fit at some later time to be a ruler'. A paraphrase attributed to Seneca, 'Nemo bene imperat, nisi qui ante paruerit imperio', became the first proverb in Richard Taverner's translation of Erasmus' *Adagia*, and was later quoted by Charron and incorporated into Barbeyrac's great edition of Pufendorf. It figured in Florio's *Firste Fruites* and Thomas à Kempis's *De Imitatione Christi*. The Christ of *Paradise Regain'd* refuted Satan with the same argument, and the dying Charles II in Dryden's *Threnodia* could pass on his authority to his brother with the words 'Well for so great a trust, he chose/A Prince who never disobey'd'.[1] No one could have read Marvell's lines without

---

[1] The references for this paragraph are as follows: Diogenes Laertius, 'Solon', in *Lives of the Eminent Philosophers*, I. 60; Plato, *Laws*, VI. 762E; Aristotle, *Politica*, trans. Jowett, in *Works*, ed. W. D. Ross (Oxford, 1952), III. iv. 1277b; Cicero, *De legibus*, trans. C. W. Keyes, Loeb Library (London, 1951), III. ii. 5; Richard Taverner, *Proverbs or Adages by Desiderius Erasmus* (Gainesville, Fla., 1956), p. 3; Charron, *De la Sagesse* III. ii. 1; Pufendorf, *Of the Law of Nature and Nations*, trans. Basil Kennett, 4th ed. (London,

at once recognizing the gist of the poem, and perceiving that Cromwell's obedience was but an apprenticeship to rule. His submissive and affable behaviour on returning from Ireland, at the hour when England was at his feet, was the final proof that he would not violate a higher trust.

On this section of the poem Margoliouth must have based his contention that Marvell saw in Cromwell 'the civic ideal of a leader'. Since then, however, the theoretic background to Marvell's proposition has been explored by Professors Fink and Kliger. Parts of their work may need revision, but they have documented the concept of the *dux bellorum* in England, and it is on this idea that Marvell's plea for a dictatorship depends. Fink, working chiefly from Machiavelli's ninth *Discourse*, which declares that a dictator may be necessary for the institution of a new republic, went on to argue that both Milton and Harrington believed Cromwell to be the natural legislator and institutor of the Commonwealth. This opinion, he claims, informs the eulogy of Cromwell in the *Second Defence*, the purpose of which was to prepare the way for the general to found the ideal mixed state of Milton's dreams.[1] Marvell was never a republican, but his later association with Harrington and the Rota would suggest that he was sympathetic with some of their ideas. Kliger subsequently demonstrated that the figure of the *dux bellorum* was not confined to the classical tradition,

1729), p. 734, n. 7; John Florio, *His Firste Fruites* (London, 1578), p. 28ᵛ; Thomas à Kempis, *De Imitatione Christi*, part 1, ch. 20; Milton, *Paradise Regained*, III. 195–6; Dryden, *Threnodia Augustalis*, ll. 233–4 (ed. Kinsley, 1, p. 448). See also Baldwin's dedication to *The Mirrour for Magistrates*, ed. L. B. Campbell (Cambridge, 1938), p. 63; *Gorboduc* I. ii. 226–30. Thomas Starkey, *England in the Reign of King Henry the Eighth*, ed. J. M. Cowper, E.E.T.S. (London, 1878), p. 3; S. Guazzo, *The Civile Conversation*, Tudor Translations (London, 1925), II, p. 97; Andrew Ramsay, *The Travels of Cyrus*, 3rd ed. (London, 1728), I, pp. 5–6; I cannot find the paraphrase attributed to Seneca, although in 'De Ira', II. xv. 4, he writes, 'nemo autem regere potest nisi qui et regi'.

[1] Zera S. Fink, *The Classical Republicans* (Evanston, Ill., 1945); see index under 'dictator' and 'law-giver'.

but had a life of its own in the Gothic or Germanic back-ground of English parliaments. According to the puritans, who were searching diligently for means to curtail the King's prerogatives, the Saxon sovereign had been elected only in time of war and only for a limited period. Kliger has shown, from numerous and varied sources, that the gothicists believed that all kings, because originally elected, could be deposed if they violated their trust.[1] However, the theory, which was called upon by the prosecutor in the speech he prepared for Charles's trial,[2] could work both ways, and Marvell could count on it to support him in designating Cromwell as dictator elect. In 1650 after the Irish, and still more after the Scottish, campaign, feeling ran high that Cromwell was 'elect and precious in the sight of God', and that God had made him 'the man of his right hand'.[3] One of Cromwell's correspondents, who lamented that England was still the old state with the head of monarchy cut off and the name of Commonwealth stuck on the headless trunk, went so far as to inform the general that he had prepared a detailed plan for the recovery of national stability, which lacked only an institutor: 'Of humaine ways [of getting the free commonwealth started] my observations have left me only this doore of hope, a returne of your honour, accompanied with some choyce number of those officers, that adventure there [sic] lives to mayntayne this government, they have helped to brings us to; the more the better.'[4] Hickman's letter reveals especially clearly that the *dux bellorum*, the institutor, and the servant of the Lord met easily in the providential figure of Oliver Cromwell.

The letters to Cromwell which have survived are generally eulogistic, but they are not typical of most of the contemporary

[1] Samuel Kliger, *The Goths in England* (Cambridge, Mass., 1952); see index under 'dux bellorum'.

[2] John Cook, *King Charls his Case* (London, 1649), pp. 8–9.

[3] John Nickolls, ed., *Original Letters and Papers of State, Addressed to Oliver Cromwell* (London, 1743), pp. 6, 22–4.

[4] *Ibid.* p. 33.

evidence for the vitality of the dictatorship issue. Gardiner records two serious calls for a stronger executive which would be less dependent on the deliberations of Parliament,[1] but Cromwell's enemies seem to have agreed unanimously that he desired supreme power and could hardly be stopped from obtaining it. Their hatred began early, for by 1647 Lilburne was already turning against Cromwell, and by 1649 the levellers were in uniform opposition to him. Their 'principal object of attack for the moment', writes Abbott of the summer of 1649, 'was the growing ascendancy of Cromwell'.[2] In 1649 appeared the famous *The Hunting of the Foxes from Newmarket and Triploe Heath to Whitehall, by Five Small Beagles*, which contained an open attack on Cromwell's ambitions. In the broadside *A Coffin for King Charles: A Crowne for Cromwell: A Pit for the People* (Thomason's date, 23 April 1649), Cromwell was made to declare from the throne, 'We (the *Elected* ones) must guide / a thousand years this land; / You [the people] must be props unto our pride, / and slaves to our command.'[3] On 30 January 1649 had appeared a Dutch caricature with a descriptive verse entitled *The Coronation of Oliver Cromwell*, and in August was published another attack by Lilburne on Cromwell's aspirations, *An Impeachment of High Treason against Oliver Cromwell and his Son-in-Law, Henry Ireton.* Before Cromwell sailed for Ireland, presbyterians and royalists were agreed that he would never consent to the lessening of his power by leaving England, the royalists adding that he would become instead 'Lord of the new Republic'.[4] The royalist *Man in the Moon* (28 May–5 June 1649) 'printed a detailed account of how Cromwell was making a deal with the Jesuits and the

---

[1] *History of the Commonwealth and Protectorate, 1649–1656* (London, 1903), I, pp. 244–6.

[2] W. C. Abbott, *The Writings and Speeches of Oliver Cromwell* (Cambridge, Mass., 1937–47), II, p. 45. Hereafter cited as Abbott.

[3] *Political Ballads of the Seventeenth and Eighteenth Centuries*, ed. W. Walter Wilkins (London, 1860), I, p. 83.

[4] Abbott, II, p. 46.

Pope in order to get himself crowned king of England',[1] and Clement Walker decided that Cromwell would be created King of Ireland. He would then return and subdue England likewise. 'Then let all true Saints and subjects crie out with me, *God save K. Oliver and his brewing Vessels.*'[2] By May 1650, when Cromwell was daily expected back from Ireland, the French agent, Croullé, and the royalist newspapers were talking of schemes to make Cromwell Constable or Protector, and on 11 June *Mercurius Politicus* hailed Cromwell as the 'only *Novus Princeps* in History'.[3] Cromwell's absolute refusal to supplant Fairfax scotched any motion to make him *novus princeps* in actuality, but clearly the movement which was to culminate in the Protectorship and the offer of the crown had begun.

In the light of the opposition to him, Marvell's account of Cromwell's humility should be read not only as part of the proof that a man rules well who least seeks to govern but also as a refutation of the attack on his alleged ambition: 'Nor yet grown stiffer with Command, / But still in the *Republick's* hand'. There can be no objection to reading in the ambiguous 'yet' a hint that unless Cromwell's power is kept within the republic's hand it may well grow more arbitrary, but the adverb may more confidently be asserted to introduce the reasons why the denigration of Cromwell has been ill founded. Marvell has seized on the very fact that Cromwell has refused to become a dictator to argue that this is his true destiny. Opponents might think of him as a hypocritical Richard III standing with a Bible in his hand and declining the proffered crown he meant to grab—but Richard knew the form he had to follow,

---

[1] Joseph Frank, 'Some Clippings from the Pre-Restoration Newspaper', *HLQ*, XXII (1959), p. 353.

[2] *Anarchia Anglicana: or the History of Independency. The Second Part* (n.p. 1649), p. 203.

[3] Abbott, II, pp. 250, 264; also p. 43 for a comment by the Frenchman Graymond: 'They designate Cromwell as the author of the great design and the reformer of the universe.'

and Cromwell's refusal in the ode is unquestionably sincere. The poem begins with the evocation of a new Caesar and proceeds with great tact to the point where the implications of Marvell's descriptions can be fully revealed. Caesar *de facto* should become Caesar *de jure*. The persuasiveness of the sug-gestion was illustrated with peculiar aptness in 1654 by the ex-Engager Anthony Norwood, who wrote in defence of Cromwell *A Clear Optick Discovering to the Eye of Reason; that Regality is not Inconsistent with the Ends of Government:*

Sir, I have heard that one of the bravest Generals that ever commanded the *Roman* Legions, after he had victoriously asserted the peoples liberty, and put an end to a Civil War, offered up his power and Commission to the then assembled Senate, by whom he was re-invested and gratified with more triumphant dignities. Here was a fair and honorable correspondence. And this procured a present and lasting peace to that Empire, and ren-dered it flourishing and formidable.[1]

Cromwell's forbearance should, precisely, be followed 'with more triumphant dignities', and Marvell *may* have intended a more elaborate parallel to be drawn between Cromwell and the victorious Caesar. Certainly he allowed to Cromwell in this section three of Caesar's main attributes—his speed in action, his generosity, and his restraint after victory—but a chronological analogy is also possibly implied. As the ode begins with the crossing of the Rubicon, and there are simi-larities (pointed out in Margoliouth's notes to the poem and in Miss Syfret's article) between Marvell's description of the death of Charles and Lucan's account of Pompey's beheading

[1] (London, 1654), p. 19. John C. Coolidge, 'Marvell and Horace', *MP*, LXIII (1965), pp. 111-20, points out that this passage refers to Octavius before he became Caesar and suggests that Augustus is the model for the Caesar whom Marvell celebrates in the second half of the poem. Certainly the regularizing of Cromwell's power makes him in effect a kind of Augustus but, if the image is explicit, Coolidge then ought to explain why the future which Marvell envisages for England is warlike and not a Golden Age. I am happy to agree with Professor Coolidge that the 'ambiguities of power and right' are classical as well as contemporary.

shortly after Pharsalia, it is tempting to view Cromwell's conquest of Ireland in one year as analogous to Caesar's conquest of North Africa, prior to his receiving a series of triumphs in Rome, greater dictatorial powers conferred by the senate, and a commission to subdue Spain forthwith. The invasion of Scotland would then become equivalent to Caesar's march on Spain.

The main argument of the ode is now complete. The peroration looks forward first to the more distant consequences of Cromwell's reign, and then to the immediate prospect of war with Scotland. The new wave of millenarianism, with which all parties were touched, had revived the hopes of a protestant alliance and a united onslaught against the forces of papal Rome. England had now achieved her liberty from royal and clerical tyranny, and 'to all States not free' Cromwell would prove that God had sent him to bind Satan and foreclose his kingdom. Cromwell was never to lead an army into France or Italy, but he was later to become in the hopes of many men the natural successor to Gustavus Adolphus. In this vision of the future, Cromwell is no longer the hubristic Caesar who crossed the Rubicon, but the champion who leads a united nation to foreign wars, obedient to the wishes of the state while holding the reins of government.

It was one matter, however, to conquer Europe 'ere long', another to invade Scotland the next week. Fairfax had resigned, or was about to resign, thus frustrating parliamentary hopes for a reconciliation with the moderate presbyterians, and opinion was as divided over the invasion as it was over the Engagement. In fact, the two issues were closely related, as the Covenanters objected to both Act and action on the ground that they violated existing oaths. A separate and fairly extensive literature exists on both sides of the Scottish question, which began to gather momentum in May 1650 and continued uninterrupted throughout the summer. The principal document for the English party, which, as Parliament's war manifesto, summed up the official attitude and determined the course of the subsequent argument, was *A Declaration of the Parliament of England, Upon the Marching of the Armie to Scotland. Die Mercurii Junii 26 1650.* Only justice and necessity, it began, could justify the misery of war, and it went on to aver that England had made all possible offers for a composition, whereas the Scots had shown a total aversion to amity. The justice of the cause was proved on five counts, the chief being the accusations that Scotland had invaded England first, and the Scots Commis-sioners had interfered with the English government and seduced the affections of the people from Parliament. The necessity of the war was also given a five-part defence: all amicable ways of settlement had been denied; a civil request for reparations after Hamilton's invasion had been angrily refused; without authority, Charles II had been proclaimed king of Scotland; the Scots had declared the English Parliament to be composed of sectaries, and had thus aligned it with the malignant and papist factions; and finally it was evident that Scotland herself was preparing to invade England again. On these arguments from necessity Parliament rested its main case, because it graciously admitted that offences against justice could often be overlooked.[1] Henry Parker summarized the English position when he wrote, 'There is a Justice of warre sometimes that derives it self only from necessity: but in the War that is now waged by our Parliament in *Scotland*, we may truly avow, that our Arms are just because they were necessary, and we as truly avow, that they became necessary by being so egregiously just.'[2]

[1] *A Declaration*, p. 6. The summary is of pp. 1–9.
[2] *Scotlands Holy War* (London, 1651), p. 64. On the English side, see also *A Declaration of the English Army now in Scotland, Touching the Justness and Necessity of their Present Proceedings in that Nation* (London, 1650); *A Short Reply unto a Declaration... Together with a Vindication of the Declaration of the Army of England* (London, 1650); *A Pertinent and Profitable Meditation, upon the History of Pekah* (London, 1650); *The English Banner of Truth Displayed: or, the State of this Present Engagement against Scotland* (London, 1650). The

The tone of the dispute on both sides was always self-righteous, rarely angry. Pained surprise at the hypocrisy of the opponent was mixed with protestations of the innocence of one's own cause, and, to a modern reader (and I think to Marvell), there is little to choose between the justice and necessity of England's attack (disguised as a defensive war) and the justice and necessity of Scotland's defence of herself. Against this back-ground, Marvell's plea of necessity, 'The same *Arts* that did *gain* | A *Pow'r* must it *maintain*', is a blunt refutation of all canting argument. It was known that foreign wars were often useful at the commencement of new states, and by arguing from physical rather than moral necessity, Marvell has terminated the argument before it bogged down in party wrangling. The invasion was expedient, as Marvell realized and admitted. Critics have discovered that Marvell's epigram was not peculiarly his own,[1] but in actuality it was one of the grand commonplaces. John Speed, who held that the usurper Henry VII had gained the throne with the help of divine providence and had kept it by his own wisdom, wrote that 'wee must now present unto you his actions in the person and state of a King, maintained by him with like mixture of *courage* and *skill* as it was atchieved, to the verification of that rule: *That things are kept by the same arts whereby they were gained*'. William Bridge in

English army's declaration was so well known that at least two or three writers, and *The Perfect Diurnal* for 22–29 July 1650, merely refer to its argu-ments as so familiar that they do not bear repetition. The English case gained much popular support from the publication of *Collonel Greys Portmanteau Opened* (London, 1650). The Scottish case was well put by William Prynne, *Sad and Serious Considerations Touching the Invasive War against our Presbyterian Protestant Brethren in Scotland* (n.p. 1650). That wars were just when they became necessary would appear to be an old political maxim. See e.g., Francisco Sansovino, *The Quintessence of Wit*, trans. Hitchcock ([London], 1590), Maxim 41, p. 5.

[1] E. E. Duncan-Jones, 'Notes on Marvell's Poems', *N&Q*, CXCVIII (1953), p. 431, quotes an example from Fulke Greville's *Mustapha*; Patrick Cruttwell, *The Shakespearean Moment* (New York, 1955), p. 195, quotes Clarendon's *History*; L. Proudfoot, 'Marvell: Sallust and the Horatian Ode', *N&Q*, CXCVI (1951), p. 434, finds a good 'source' in *Bellum Catilinae*, II. 3–6.

1644 refuted in the margins of a reprinted royalist tract the argument that that government which is set up with the sword would be obliged to maintain itself by the sword, but George Wither in October 1650 defended the puritans with the same principle from the charge that they had set up a military tyranny. Ascham apologized for the government with the identical excuse: 'Wherefore for these reasons [that the aftermath of a civil war is more dangerous than a foreign war] though the Usurper thought not of establishing himselfe in an absolute Jurisdiction, yet at last he will finde himselfe oblig'd to secure his conquest by the same meanes he obtained it.' More strikingly, in 1651, Clement Walker began the first chapter of the most virulent of the attacks on Cromwell with the words 'That every thing is kept and maintained by the same waies and means it was got and obtained; is a rule true both in Philosophy and Policy.'[1] In these examples it is significant that John Speed, writing long before the civil war, could quote impartially an adage which attached itself naturally to the mention of a usurper. Thereafter it appears to have been associated first with the royalist cause, as a reason for refraining from bloodshed before it was too late, then with the parliamentarians as a defence of their martial law. To the royalist Walker it epitomized all that was wrong with the Cromwellian usurpation. Marvell, however, reflecting on Cromwell's superiority to Julius, may have remembered the comment of Velleius Paterculus that 'in the light of experience due credit should

[1] References for the previous quotations are John Speed, *The Historie of Great Britaine*, 2nd ed. (London, 1623), p. 954; William Bridge, *The Loyall Convert* (London, 1644), p. 26; G[eorge] W[ither], *Respublica Anglicana* [1650] (n.p. The Spenser Society, 1883), p. 43—Wither's authorship of this pamphlet has been denied; Ascham, *Of the Confusions*, p. 98; Clement Walker, *The High Court of Justice; or Cromwells New Slaughter House in England* [*Hist. of Independency*, Part III] (n.p. 1651), p. 3. See also [Henry Parker,] *Jus Populi* (London, 1644), p. 14; [Dudley Digges,] *The Unlawfulnesse of Subjects Taking up Armes* (1643), pp. 17–18; Robert Sanderson, *Lectures on Conscience and Human Law* (1647), trans. Christopher Wordsworth (Lincoln, 1877), p. 139.

be given to the counsel of Pansa and Hirtius, who always warned Caesar that he must hold by arms the position which he had won by arms'.[1]

The forward youth who conquered Caesar has not failed to learn from Caesar's error. Like Lucan's Caesar, he thinks nought done while aught remains to do. His marching is both an imperative—the poet's endorsement of Parliament's com-mission—and a statement of fact in the present tense. Now he is about to hunt the Picts, and the ironies of the poem may be enhanced if we see in this hunter of men a reference to Nimrod, the founder of the first empire. The allusion is not a critical certainty, but may be conceded to readers who wish to emphasize Marvell's distrust of Cromwell, if they will re-member that in political controversy Nimrod was not always the villain he is reported to be, because his empire, although founded and maintained by the sword, was recognized to have prospered by God's ordinance. Walter Raleigh, with historical impartiality, weighed the evidence and concluded that Nim-rod's was a 'just authority',[2] and the Engagers, quoting Paraeus, had agreed that his power was lawful. Nedham reminded the presbyterians that the world had grown so vicious after the flood that a strong man was needed to oppose the wilfulness of the nations.[3] Nevertheless, whatever excuses were made for him, Nimrod remained a daunting figure, and Cromwell's pursuit of the Scots and their 'Caledonian Deer' blends with Marvell's contemptuous expressions into a serious menace to those who have dared to become Cromwell's

[1] Compendium of Roman History, trans. Frederick W. Shipley, Loeb Library (London, 1924), II. lvii.

[2] History of the World (London, 1677), p. 109.

[3] The Case of the Common-wealth of England Stated (London, 1650), p. 6. See also [Francis Rous,] The Lawfulnes of Obeying the Present Government (London, 1650), p. 7; Richard Saunders, Plenary Possession Makes a Lawful Power (London, 1651), p. 17; and Ascham, Of the Confusions, pp. 21, 108, Bounds & Bonds, pp. 23–4, A Combate betweene Two Seconds, p. 7; also The Exercitation Answered (London, 1650), pp. 45–7.

enemies. The 'Clymacterick' which he has already brought to England may be visited on other nations also.

The sword he carries in his hand is 'erect', not upside down as critics would have us believe when they speak of its talismanic cross-hilt, but 'besides' its power to banish the spirits, it symbolizes Cromwell's invincible force. It has a double aspect, therefore, that might be described as religious and secular, or sacred and warlike, and in the present bellicose posture of the country the second of the sword's functions is more visible. In 1650 Hobbes discussed the magistrate's sword in analogous terms: 'Now seeing that every man hath already transferred the use of his strength to him, or them, that have the sword of Justice, it followeth, that the power of defence, that is to say, the sword of war, be in the same hands wherein is the sword of justice; and consequently those two swords are but one, and that inseparable and essentially annexed to the sovereign power.'[1] And earlier James Howell had affirmed that the King's sword was not single or chymerical, but 'an aggregative compound sword' composed of all the military strengths of the kingdom.[2] As Parliament officially marched on Scotland armed with the arguments of justice and necessity, Cromwell's sword in the ode would seem to combine the two principles. With one he would banish shadowy spirits and mete out justice to tyrannies, with the other he was compelled to defend his own usurped power.

The duality of Cromwell's sword, its right against 'all States not free' and its naked might, is but a final example of the poem's reflection of an historical dilemma. Similarly, Cromwell

---

[1] *De Corpore Politico*, part II, ch. 1, in *English Works*, ed. Molesworth, IV, p. 130. E. E. Duncan-Jones, in 'The Erect Sword in Marvell's Horatian Ode', *Études Anglaises*, XV (1962), pp. 172–4, discusses the lines in a different way, but also finds that the cross-hilt is not banishing the spirits. She appears to concur with Legouis, however, that the poem is essentially classical and not Christian. It is both.

[2] *The Instruments of a King: or, a short Discourse of the Sword, the Scepter, the Crowne* (London, 1648), p. 5.

the falcon on the green bough is still the predator who drew
Walker's comment, 'Oliver is a Bird of Prey, you may
know by his Bloody Beak'.[1] The 'restless' Cromwell, the
destroyer, the usurper, and the intimidating and subtle hunter
are all unquestionable parts of the total portrait, but while they
testify to an awareness of the fearful power which has been
concentrated in one man, they are reconciled in the vision of
Cromwell's destiny.

If one seeks not for the personal and historical reasons that
render a view of Cromwell's dangerousness compatible with
the main theme but for the rhetorical procedure which permits
their unification, one must turn to the logical skill of the argu-
ment. Marvell appears, then, to have planned his ode as a public
address which would follow the rules of a deliberative oration.
Deliberative speeches generally dealt with a 'difficult' subject
(the *genus admirabile causae*) and were marked by a moderate
manner, a concern with advantage and expediency, and an
emphasis upon the benefits which would accrue in the future
from following the proposed advice. Quintilian also reckoned
the crowning of Julius Caesar a deliberative topic.[2] The ode
divides neatly into an exordium of eight lines, a *narratio* or
'statement of facts' which relates Cromwell's career until the
moment he became *de facto* master of England (lines 9–24),
and a section (lines 25–56) which it is possible to read as an
amplification of the *narratio* but which I prefer to regard as a
divisio such as the author of *Ad Herennium* recommended for the
praise of character.[3] The proof of the thesis, composed of
several different kinds of argument, extends from Charles on
the scaffold to Cromwell in the republic's hand (lines 57–96),
but this passage may be divided into a *confirmatio* (lines 57–80)
and a *refutatio* (lines 81–96) if the violence of the contemporary

---

[1] Quoted by Yule, *The Independents*, p. 64. Walker stole the metaphor from
Cleveland's *The Character of a London-Diurnall*.

[2] *Inst. Or.* III. viii. 47. The Loeb Library editions have been used for refer-
ences to the orators.

[3] III. vii. 13–viii. 15.

attacks on Cromwell is felt to be the background for the account
of Cromwell's humility. The peroration looks forward with a
controlled millenarian emotion to England's success under her
new leader. Moreover, the analysis of virtue into its four kinds
was a method commonly suggested by the orators,[1] and Cicero
discussed both positive and natural law under the heading
'Justice' when he was expanding the honourable ends of a
deliberative discourse.[2]

The disposition of Marvell's argument into an oratorical form
is not in itself one of the merits of the poem, but it may have
played a part in enabling those merits to come about. The
speech pattern is a simplifying device, the main function of
which is to insure that the theme is conveyed clearly and
persuasively. It is a structure that exists for the sake of an argu-
ment, and the expression of the rhetorician's private feelings or
reservations must be subservient to, and controlled by, the
purpose of the discourse. They may be useful because, as
Marvell wrote later, 'a great skill of whatsoever orator is, to
perswade the auditory first that he himself is an honest and fair
man',[3] but the sincerity of a rhetorician, which it is his first
duty to imply, can only be inferred by the listener and not
known categorically. One may have no doubt that one of
Marvell's real convictions is embodied in the argument itself,
but the moment he decided to cast his ode into the form of a

[1] *Ad Heren.* III. ii. 3 and vi. 10 and viii. 15; Cicero, *De Inven.* II. liii. 159 ff;
Quintilian, *Inst. Or.* III. vii. 15.
[2] *De Inven.* II. liii. 160–2. As Aristotle (*Rhetoric* I. ix. 35), Cicero (*De Or.*
II. lxxxi. 333) and Quintilian (*Inst. Or.* III. iv. 16) were agreed that delib-
erative and epideictic oratory had much in common, and that their topics
were not mutually exclusive, I would not quarrel with readers who would
prefer to read the ode as a panegyric with a deliberative intent rather than as
a deliberative discourse in which 'extensive sections are often devoted to praise
or censure' (*Ad Heren.*, trans. Harry Caplan, III. viii. 15). D. A. G. Hinks,
'Tria Genera Causarum', *Classical Quarterly*, xxx (1936), pp. 170–6,
discusses the difficulties of making distinctions between deliberative and
epideictic oratory.
[3] *The Divine in Mode*, in *Works*, ed. A. B. Grosart (n.p. 1872–5), IV, p. 79.

political oration he committed himself first to arguing a case—not to saying everything—and second to a certain order of proof. Even if he wrote sections of the ode before he determined on a rhetorical scheme, the scheme would eventually dictate the movement of the poem and limit the choice of proofs. Simplicity, however, brings its own kind of freedom, and within the limitations of a formal pattern the poet's *inventio*, *dispositio* and *elocutio* (the triad that Dryden was later to condense into the one word 'imagination') could move with a fine discrimination. On the other hand, the stronger the argument the more it compels the refractory elements of experience to take their place in a proper relation to it. Hence the usurping Cromwell, the Lucanic Caesar, the loved Charles, the bloody head, and the feared Nimrod can all be recognized as emotional factors with the potential power of destroying the thesis, but which the idea of Cromwell's dictatorship is capable of transforming into proof of its own validity. A less subtle poem could have been the only consequence of a less compelling structure. A mere panegyric on the campaign would perforce have obliterated the signs of the damage Cromwell had done in the past to his country, whereas the actual argument demands an historical consideration of his whole career.

The true analogy for the power of rhetoric to reinterpret old and often unpleasant facts is the power of providence to change the course and thus the meaning of history. No one in 1642 could have foretold that Cromwell's ambition would one day destroy the monarchy, and right-minded men would justly have resisted it; but Marvell was attempting to read history, not only taking account of later events, but writing in a time of war when great changes were still in the making and a victory in Scotland was by no means a foregone conclusion. From a limited perspective of a few years, the Protectorate was to show that Marvell had interpreted the times correctly, but the difficulty of achieving certainty of any kind in a period of duress when providence was still immediately directing England's destiny led Marvell to make his proposition some-what tentatively, as if he realized that he, like others, might later be susceptible to providential correction. Some of the important verbs in the ode are in the optative or conditional:

> What may not then our *Isle* presume
> While Victory his Crest does plume!
> What may not others fear
> If thus he crown each Year! (97–100)

A tentative suspension of final judgment would better describe the tone of the ode than the customary 'impartiality', for the poet who had been wrong before about the significance of the revolution was not about to commit himself again and so soon to any declamatory absolutes. A few years later he could be more positive, and the tone of *The First Anniversary* reflects the difference between a firm but cautious affirmation and a full confidence in Cromwell's ability to rule. Even by the end of 1650, which is the probable date of the composition of *Tom May's Death*, the battle of Dunbar had been hailed as a miracu-lous proof of God's favour to Cromwell, and Marvell could expli-citly deny that republicanism in its pure form—that is, without a single person as the head of state—was relevant to England's needs:

> Go seek the novice Statesmen, and obtrude
> On them some Romane cast similitude,
> Tell them of Liberty, the Stories fine,
> Until you all grow Consuls in your wine.
> Or thou *Dictator* of the glass bestow
> On him the *Cato*, this the *Cicero*.
> Transferring old *Rome* hither in your talk,
> As *Bethlem's* House did to *Loretto* walk.
> Foul Architect that hadst not Eye to see
> How ill the measures of these States agree.
> And who by *Romes* example *England* lay,
> Those but to *Lucan* do continue *May*. (43–54)

The alleged inconsistencies between the ode and Marvell's earlier and later political utterances disappear when the ode's theme is understood. The later panegyrical attitude towards Cromwell becomes a natural development, and the earlier laments about the degeneracy of the age and the loss of public virtue form the grounds on which a great national leader becomes a necessity:

> Our Civill Wars have lost the Civicke crowne.
> He highest builds, who with most Art destroys,
> And against others Fame his owne employs.
> I see the envious Caterpillar sit
> On the faire blossome of each growing wit.[1]

At any time, and most of all in a crisis, the political poet's duty was to squash his own envious caterpillar and to seek to know the good of the state. The apostrophe on the poet in *Tom May's Death*, spoken by Ben Jonson, distinguishes Marvell's own sense of his responsibility from what he considered to be May's timeserving, and the witty reference in his elegy on Lord Hastings (1649) to 'the *Democratick* stars' which 'all that Worth from hence did *Ostracize*' suggests his abiding contempt for popular government. England required a deliverance from its democratic masters, its rule by parliamentary committees and a Council of State, and nothing in the ode belies the implication of the other poems of 1648–50 that the overthrow of the monarchy was a successful crime, in which Cromwell himself had had a hand. In the words which echo through these poems, the arts of war have destroyed the constructive arts of peace, and the ode itself, steeped in the imagery of battle, can be read as an unfinished war-drama, from the forsaking of the peaceful muses in the first stanza to Cromwell's maintenance of his warlike '*Arts*' in the last line. Marvell appears to think that England will be at war for many years, and this one fact alone justifies his call for a *dux bellorum*. The '*Royal Actor* born' has been superseded by the royal actor self-made, who awaits only a call from the people to assume the command which the

---

[1] *To his Noble Friend Mr.* Richard Lovelace, lines 12–16.

heavens have ordained for him. His success is inexplicable on any other terms, and the unenvious arts of the poet must be employed to validate God's will, not to oppose it. Enemies of Cromwell and of the existing government were busy deriding such an opinion, contending that evil permitted by God was no justification for persisting in it, but Marvell had a stronger millenarian streak than they did, and viewed the climacteric as more final and irreversible. His millenarianism, however, was tempered by his aristocratic bias, his dislike of religious and political enthusiasm, his classical training and Horatian irony, and, perhaps above all, by his opinion of the poet's role. His function was to speak not himself but the truth, to mirror reality, not to express opinion, and the solemnity of the ode is in part derived from the effacing of personality. Neither the Engagers nor Marvell wished to add to the already strident voice of faction, but they saw that providence had ruined a great work of time, and felt, by the same token, that it could raise up another. If the party-coloured mind persisted, however, in its ignorant chatter, more chaos could be the only result. The people of England, like the poet, must learn to forget themselves and their prejudices, and to mark the signs God had given. Whatever their politics, or their past allegiance, or their religion, they ought to recognize in Cromwell the man chosen by God to lead them forward to a future which He had prepared, and which He alone could discern.

3

'He seems a King by long Succession born': 'The First Anniversary of the Government under O.C.'

As we have seen, Marvell did not identify himself with the forward youth in the ode who was instructed to put on his armour, because to have been 'forward' against Cromwell would have been presumptuous. Marvell's self-conscious modesty is one of the principal characteristics of his poetry, especially of those poems which deal with matters of state or are addressed to his social superiors, and it is balanced by an equal arrogance and feelings of natural superiority to his forward opponents in disputation who meddled without decorum in business that was above their heads. Marvell's unwillingness to publish the Horatian ode turns his public poem into a modestly private statement, as if he were holding a watching brief over Cromwell's fortunes, and he was not especially inconsistent, therefore, in retiring to Yorkshire to write the languishing numbers that the ode formally renounces.

His two years' service under Lord Fairfax was clearly an important reflective period of his life, and a master more likely to have engaged his respect would be hard to imagine. The poems Marvell addressed to him reveal a warm regard for the man in whom nature had joined dissimilar parts. 'Dissimilis Domino coiit Natura sub uno.'[1] His learning and piety, rigour and gentleness, courage and humility all enter Marvell's portrait of him, and the fact that he deplored the execution of the King while believing in the cause of the revolution is likely to have played a part in Marvell's estimate of his

[1] 'Epigramma in Duos montes Amosclivum Et Bilboreum. *Farfacio*', line 15, Margoliouth ed., p. 56.

innate nobility. Images of the civil war recur in the poems of retirement, but muted by the distance between the green world of Nunappleton and the violence of political society outside, and it was with reluctance as well as eagerness that Marvell decided that his own vocation was to enter the fray. These feelings can be discerned in *Upon Appleton House*, a discussion of which is postponed since it is not a political poem, and it is in that masterpiece that the hankering after an active life implicit in the opening lines of the ode finds its overt expression. By February 1653, as Milton's letter to Bradshaw explains, he was hoping for a minor post in the government, but his wish was frustrated and he succeeded merely in exchanging one tutorship for another. Eton was not Yorkshire, however, and William Dutton was Cromwell's ward, and the change in Marvell's attitude, his active interest in affairs of state, is immediately apparent in *The Character of Holland* and in the long Latin epistle written to Ingelo in Sweden that praised Cromwell and Queen Christina, and was probably intended to be shown to both of them. There could seem little doubt that Marvell had embarked on a course that would bring his name to the attention of the government by proving that he could be useful as a writer of impeccable Latin, and as a staunch supporter of Cromwell himself. This is probably the personal ambition that lies behind his publication of *The First Anniversary*, recorded by Thomason on 17 January 1655, but one easily forgets—so busily political does Marvell appear at this time— that he had no official connection with the government until 1657, and that *The First Anniversary*, like the ode, is the comment of a detached observer of national affairs. It is not the work of a court poet, although Marvell's praise of Cromwell has sometimes been mistaken for a sycophantic adulation, and it has been at least implicit in much criticism that the warmth of his feelings was in part responsible for the poem's seemingly loose structure and untidy technique. These strictures are misconceived, mainly because Marvell's stance was more critical and more in keeping with his unaffiliated status than the tone of the poem would suggest. A deliberative poem has been read as a straightforward panegyric on the Protector, with the consequence that the argument has gone unperceived, and the diverse parts of the poem which it holds together have seemed disconnected. Hence, for example, the very important kingship imagery that Professor Mazzeo has discussed serves to raise Cromwell to the dignity of a Protector *sui generis*—a political phenomenon whom Marvell praises almost blasphemously as a king—but at the same time increases the hyperboles of Marvell's admiration, so that we are back where we started with the poet's uncritical subservience to his new hero.[1] But if the poem is read as an argument that Cromwell should accept the English crown and institute a new dynasty of kings, then the structure and imagery of the poem can be accounted for more completely than by presupposing their merely panegyric aim. Paradoxically, this exposes not Marvell's supreme flattery of the Protector but his concern for the country's future, a concern which transcends private admiration and manifests the serious calling to which Marvell felt himself elected as a political poet.

Any critic of Marvell would admit that *The First Anniversary* does not possess the superb restraint of the ode, but it is also a longer and more ambitious poem that should be accepted as Marvell's first attempt to speak to a large public in terms that it would readily understand. Marvell was not to reach a popular audience until *The Rehearsal Transpros'd* nearly twenty years later, and *The First Anniversary* seems to have passed unnoticed in the literature of 1655, but the coherence of its argument and the farsightedness of its political purpose should exempt Marvell from the usual suspicion of having entered a poetic and intellectual decline simultaneously with his decision to engage in an active political life. The accusation is inherently im-

[1] Joseph Anthony Mazzeo, 'Cromwell as Davidic King', in his *Renaissance and Seventeenth-Century Studies* (New York, 1964), pp. 183-208.

probable, and nothing in *The First Anniversary* substantiates it. Even if a demonstration of its unity were attempted on purely imagistic grounds, a method rarely successful with seventeenth-century poems, the poem would still emerge as one of the most interesting productions of the Interregnum. Time, for instance, is an obsessive theme, and most of the parts of the poem are related to it: obliterating, useful, and useless time in the first section; hoped-for millennial time in the third; destructive time (death) in the fourth, and restored time (the extended simile of the returning sun) in the seventh and last. Were mere eulogy his aim, Marvell lost an opportunity of proving that the fulfilment of time had arrived, and that the millennium—so conspicuously unrealized but so tantalizingly near in the poem—had been ushered in by the Protector's rule. Another equally important strand of imagery constantly contrasts the downward movement of mortal things (sinking weights, dying men, heavy monarchs, tedious statesmen, and so on) with the ascending movement of Cromwell and his works. His churches rear their columns, the stones of his palace fall into place, and he himself 'cuts his way still nearer to the Skyes' (46). The constructive work of Cromwell and the destructive nature of time are in continual conflict, and their interaction in the poem generates a mood not only of excitement as one is achieved in the teeth of the other, but of apprehension lest Cromwell's works should be destroyed at his own death. The poem has considerable homogeneity viewed in these terms alone, but certain passages remain outside the main imagistic pattern and are only related to it by the thesis which makes all the parts coherent.

The thesis is the natural result of Marvell's having found himself right in his earlier prediction. The Scots had been subdued, and though Dunbar was one of Cromwell's luckiest victories it was also his greatest, which with most justice he could attribute to God's favour. The challenge from Charles Stuart in person had been met at Worcester, and there was no

danger of another royalist uprising. Cromwell's star was at its
zenith, and the evidences of the previous five years had confirmed
Marvell's belief that Cromwell ruled by God's ordinance, not
by mere permission. The first anniversary of the Protectorate
was itself a fair cause for more rejoicing, though like every other
stage of Cromwell's career it posed the question of what was to
follow. The year had been notable less for the improvement in
domestic than in foreign affairs, but here the success was
remarkable, and as a result Cromwell was at the height of his
power.[1] The Dutch war had come to an end on terms which
were to England's advantage; treaties had been concluded
with Sweden, Portugal, and Denmark, and another with
France was in preparation; minor Protestant states were being
courted with emissaries, and envoys of tiny principalities from
the North Sea to the Baltic were waiting to be heard in London.
As the head of the greatest sea-power in Europe and a diplomat
of now proven ability, it was altogether appropriate for Marvell
to terminate his poem with an address delivered by a foreign
king, and to commence it with a comparison between Crom-
well's activity and the sluggishness of ordinary monarchs.

At home, on the contrary, the difficulties had possibly
increased and Abbot records that 'it was beyond the ingenuity
of even [Cromwell's] most devoted followers to evolve a con-
stitutional argument for his assumption and exercise of supreme
power and to make him seem a *de jure* ruler by any stretch of
legal technicality'.[2] The first Parliament of the Protectorate was
preoccupied almost exclusively from its first meeting in Sep-
tember 1654, and through the new year, with the Instrument of
Government, a sign that constitutional problems were upper-
most in the thought of public men, and their solution of para-

[1] W. C. Abbott, *The Writings and Speeches of Oliver Cromwell* (Cambridge,
Mass., 1937–47), III, p. 525; henceforth cited as Abbott. His account of the
Protectorate years surpasses any other in comprehensiveness. He reports
(III, p. 523) that 'by the end of November, 1654, the Protectorate at last
seemed on the way to something like a permanent footing'.
[2] III, p. 181.

mount importance. The legality of the 'Single Person' in the constitution was a battle which had been fought and won during the first weeks, but the means of choosing a successor to the Single Person were not settled. Some favoured an elective, others an hereditary, Protectorship, while a certain number hoped Cromwell would accept the crown. A good deal of evidence concerning the vitality of the kingship issue as early as 1654 can be found in the histories of the period, though never widely aired by historians, and more is available in the pamphlet literature.

Two of the most fully reported meetings at which kingship was discussed took place even before the Protectorate began; one at Lenthall's house on 10 December 1651, the other a year later when Cromwell asked Whitelock the famous question, 'What if a Man should take upon him to be King?'.[1] Yet another year later, in December 1653, Lambert and his fellow officers, when making an outline for the Instrument, had offered Cromwell the title of king, but he had refused.[2] By January 1654 some foreigners, including Queen Christina, were inclined to think Cromwell should have accepted the crown.[3] A little later, Hyde and the Venetian resident independently reported rumours of the title of emperor.[4] In September Paulucci passed on the news that Cromwell had rejected the thought of kingship, but from 16 to 18 October there was a debate in Parliament on the motion that the

[1] Abbott, II, pp. 505–7 and 589 ff.
[2] C. H. Firth, 'Cromwell and the Crown', *EHR*, XVII (1902), p. 429, and S. R. Gardiner, *History of the Commonwealth and Protectorate* (London, 1903), II, p. 319.　　[3] Abbott, III, p. 149.
[4] Abbott, III, p. 285. John Thurloe, *A Collection of State Papers*, ed. Thomas Birch (London, 1742), II, p. 614, has a letter of intelligence from Cologne, dated 29 Sept. 1654: 'Here is a common report, of which your letters say noethinge, that the protector went into the parliament-house, and there had his peroration for an houre; and that after, the parliament with unanimous consent called his highness emperor; and his title they have written thus: *Oliver, the first emperor of Greate Britaine, and the isles thereunto belonging, allways Caesar, &c.*'

Protectorship be made hereditary.[1] The motion was lost by a heavy majority, but sixty or sixty-five members voted for it, and Bordeaux reported that Cromwell had hoped to keep the title in his family. A similar decision was passed again in December without a division, but, at the same time, Broghill and Cromwell discussed a possible compromise with the Stuarts.[2] Two days before Christmas, when Marvell's poem may have been in the press, Augustine Garland, supported by Henry Cromwell and Sir Anthony Ashley Cooper, moved to have the Protector crowned, but this motion was also dropped after a short debate.[3] Dissolving Parliament in January, Cromwell 'went out of his way to protest against the idea that the government should be made "a patrimony"',[4] but within six months a crowd was assembling at Westminster expecting to hear Cromwell announce his acceptance of the crown, and the making of the Great Seal was delayed because his title had not been fixed.[5]

Defenders of the Instrument denied Cromwell would king it, or pointed out that while kings in the past had hindered the reign of Christ, wise kings did not. The dangers of an elective system were made the excuse for demanding negotiation with Charles II, and another writer asked why, if others had made profits from the war which they expected to pass on to their sons, the Protector's acquisitions should not be hereditary also.[6] One

[1] Abbott, III, pp. 482–3; Gardiner, *History*, III, pp. 200–1.

[2] Abbott, III, pp. 524–6.

[3] Firth, 'Cromwell and the Crown', p. 429; Abbott, III, p. 549; Gardiner, *History*, III, p. 225. Abbott, pp. 476–7, also believes that it was about this time that Wither presented his 'Discourse' to the Protector, which suggested an alternative form of government to the hereditary rule Cromwell was supposed to favour.

[4] Firth, 'Cromwell and the Crown', p. 430; Abbott, III, p. 589.

[5] Gardiner, *History*, III, p. 304.

[6] See (all dates London, 1654): *An Apology for the Present Government, and Governour*, sig. A2ʳ. *The Grand Catastrophe, or the Change of Government*, esp. pp. 12–15; *An Admonition to my Lord Protector and his Council of their Danger: A Copy of a Letter Concerning the Election of a Lord Protector*, esp. pp. 6–8,

poetaster concluded a poem in a volume of tributes published at Oxford to celebrate the Dutch treaty with this suggestion:

> Rise now, by whom both *Arts and pollicy* stood,
> Thou one *Seth's Pillar* in a double *Floud*!
> To thee we prostrate *Crowne* and *Booke*: with it
> Rule *Champion* of our *State*, with *that* of *wit*.[1]

The most explicit proponents of monarchy I shall quote later. They were Samuel Hunton, who wrote at least two tracts on the subject, and John Hall of Richmond, whose *Of Government and Obedience* is one of the lengthiest works on constitutional theory to appear during the Interregnum. He refused even to consider aristocracy and democracy as viable means of government, because multitudes cannot control themselves: 'And therefore I should rather think, that the most rational course that in this case [when a government has been overthrown] can be taken to recover their former happiness and peace...[is] that they return to the same form of government and obedience under which they formerly enjoyed them.'[2]

In spite of Parliament's unwillingness at this date to alter the thirty-second article of the Instrument, the matter was once more

19–37. An important defence of the Instrument, i.e. of the status quo, was [Nedham?] *A True State of the Case of the Commonwealth*. The dissolution of the Nominated (Barebones) Parliament was defended by John Hall, *Confusion Confounded: or a Firm Way of Settlement Settled and Confirmed*. The (clearly accurate) attribution of this pamphlet to Hall occurs in John B. Shaw, 'The Life and Works of John Hall of Durham', unpub. Ph.D. dissertation at The Johns Hopkins University (1952), pp. 210–11. Defences of a strong executive are to be found in *Sedition Scourg'd*, in *Somers Tracts*, ed. Walter Scott, VI, pp. 297 ff., and *A Representation Concerning the Late Parliament, in the Year 1654. To Prevent Mistakes* (n.p. 1655), in which the author is nevertheless critical of the dissolution of the First Parliament. M[ichael] H[awke,] *The Right of Dominion* (1655) is another strongly monarchical tract.

[1] John Ailmer, in *Musarum Oxoniensium* (Oxford, 1654), p. 97.

[2] (London, 1654), p. 188; see also pp. 190–1. Arthur Barker, *Milton and the Puritan Dilemma, 1641–1660* (Toronto, 1942) in a long note on p. 382 argues that the absence of references to the disadvantage of kingship in Milton's *Defensio Secunda* (1654) and the *Pro Se Defensio* (1655) 'can only be explained by the possibility that Oliver might yet become king'.

to the forefront in May 1655, and again in July. Long before
the issue became the first item on the political agenda, and
Cromwell was begged to take the crown, the succession was
clearly a topic which would neither lie down nor, even, fail to
be the subject of a serious political discourse celebrating the
Protectorate. On the other hand, the plea for kingship would
by no means command unanimous assent, and Marvell is
cautious in making it. To a contemporary reader, however,
who was not limited to the inadequacies of an historical and
rhetorical reconstruction, the message would be plain enough.

Readers generally agree that the poem falls into seven clearly
defined sections, although the transitional passages make the
exact lines of demarcation a matter of opinion: (1) The com-
parison of Cromwell with the 'heavy Monarchs', ll. 1–48; (2)
Cromwell's building of the harmonious state, ll. 49–116; (3) The
advent of the millennium which Cromwell has brought nearer is
postponed by man's sin, ll. 117–58; (4) The coaching accident,
ll. 159–220; (5) A series of brief proofs that Cromwell has not
employed his power arbitrarily, ll. 221–92; (6) A short diatribe
against the Fifth Monarchists, ll. 293–324; (7) The tribute of
foreign monarchs to Cromwell's astounding success, ll. 325–402.

The opening sentence is also a judicial sentence, for the
irrefutable truth it contains casts its shadow over all the Pro-
tector's achievements, which appear superficially to defeat the
operations of time:

> Like the vain Curlings of the Watry maze,
> Which in smooth streams a sinking Weight does raise;
> So Man, declining alwayes, disappears
> In the weak Circles of increasing Years;
> And his short Tumults of themselves Compose,
> While flowing Time above his Head does close.　　　　(1–6)

The joyful anniversary commences with the reminder that all
such celebrations are transitory, and the lines also, as Miss
Lloyd Thomas and Miss Bradbrook have said,[1] are ethical

---

[1] *Andrew Marvell* (Cambridge, 1940), p. 78.

proof that Marvell writes in full consciousness of the passing importance of his own labours. Death, which anniversary poems often commemorate, is the brute fact against which Cromwell's 'greater Vigour runs, / (Sun-like) the Stages of succeeding Suns' (7-8). By employing the usual pun on sun/son, Marvell has called attention immediately to his real theme, besides transferring the traditional image of kingship on to the uncrowned Protector. Cromwell defies the weak circles of increasing years, while the 'heavy Monarchs make a wide Return' (15). Their ripples are infinite but useless, but Cromwell as the 'Jewel of the yearly Ring ... the force of scatter'd Time contracts' (12-13). Apocalyptically, he has turned his immense powers to the Christian task of redeeming the time and tuning 'this lower to that higher Sphere' (48). The imagery works strongly to defeat the memory of Cromwell's mortality, and to make a way for the later suggestion that time itself may be approaching its destined end; but as Cromwell 'cuts his way still nearer to the Skyes' (46) we pick up a premonition once again. Moreover, as Cromwell is contrasted with the heavy monarchs who 'neither build the Temple in their dayes, / Nor Matter for succeeding Founders raise' (33-4), he is indeed a Davidic king whose successor is England's proper concern. Cromwell has excelled David in leaving both temples and 'Matter', but the hint, later to be developed, that Cromwell may be unable to complete his mission is inescapably present. The kings do not even 'begin' to perfect the 'sacred Prophecies' (35-6), but while Cromwell has begun, the time of their perfecting has been carefully left open to the reader's speculation. Marvell has insinuated that no single ruler will be able to fulfil all the prophecies, although Cromwell alone 'in one Year the work of Ages acts' (14). Over his success are suspended two unknowns—the approaching end of the world, which his deeds seem to have hastened, and the possibility that he will not live to see the Day—and to these considerations the remainder of the poem is addressed.

The description of Cromwell as Amphion is the most strictly panegyric section of the poem. The comparison had been made before by Cromwell's eulogists,[1] and on its acceptability the subsequent argument depends. If the new state were not harmonious and constructed on sound principles, its perpetuation could be only a mistake. Rhetorically, it was necessary to describe the Protectorate, a kingdom in all but name, as a flawless pattern of a commonwealth, and in Amphion Marvell had a figure long renowned in the mythological books as the type of successful politician who by persuasive oratory could soften the hearts of the hardest men. He 'persuaded those who lived a wild and savage life before', wrote the most imitative of all mythologists in his *Pantheon*, 'to embrace the rules and manners of civil society'.[2] One admirer of Cromwell, after exclaiming that not only war but love had conquered England, wrote, 'Thus a *sweet concord* do's *He timely* raise / From th'lofty *Treble* and the humble *Base*'; and another came even nearer to describing the new state as Marvell saw it: 'Away with Concord now, since that we see, / The loudest Discords make best Harmonie.'[3] The law of *concordia discors* is the cosmological origin, as it were, of the mixed state, and the mixed state was the basic concept of the English constitution. Among political books circulating in England, Malvezzi formulated the classic expression of the idea in the ninth discourse of his *Discourses upon Cornelius Tacitus*, but Marvell's passage in this poem ranks with *Cooper's Hill* as probably the most sustained utterance on the subject in English political poetry before Pope. The cardinal fact is that the building Cromwell has constructed, 'Knit by the Roofs Protecting

[1] Fitzpayne Fisher, in *Inauguratio Oliviariana* (London, 1654), p. 15, and references to Cromwell's cithara in *Musarum Oxoniensium*, pp. 9, 16.

[2] Andrew Tooke, *Tooke's Pantheon of the Heathen Gods* (Baltimore, 1838), p. 324. Tooke, like Picinelli in *Mundus Symbolicus*, was following Boccaccio and Conti.

[3] John Ailmer, in *Musarum Oxoniensium*, p. 97, and J. Nethway, in the same work, p. 96.

weight' (98), is an essentially royalist edifice, lacking nothing but the title to distinguish it from the princely state. Without the sovereignty of the roof, the walls would collapse into 'a multitude...like a heap of stones, before they are cemented and knit together into one building',[1] or, as another royalist, Sir Francis Wortley, once commented, the true English protestant 'thinks it not fit to pull downe the Cantrell of an Arche till the key-stone be settled, and then the greater the weight is, the stronger it will be'.[2] When the time came, on 24 March 1657, to discuss once again the offer of the crown to Cromwell, Colonel Bridge wrote: 'I was somewhat confident in the morning, that we should have laid the topstone of that great and noble structure we have been so long in framing before this time. But we have not been able to bring it to an issue.'[3]

For the related imagery of the circular state with Cromwell as its centre, there is evidence also that the most monarchical of Cromwell's supporters were thinking in these terms. Samuel Hunton the kingling (as an advocate of Cromwell-for-king was later derogatorily called) exclaimed, 'Would you con-centrize all your particular ends in the generals Centre, you would there meet, whereas now you are bemet with, and it would render you powerfully defensive and offensive, so it's factions that fractions you, *and self-ends that divide and undo you*.'[4] And John Hall discoursed at some length on the subject:

---

[1] [Dudley Digges,] *The Unlawfulnesse of Subjects Taking up Armes* (1647), p. 15.
[2] 'Character of a True English Protestant' [1646], quoted in B. Boyce, *The Polemic Character, 1640–1661* (Lincoln, Nebraska, 1955), p. 19.
[3] Quoted in C. H. Firth, *The Last Years of the Protectorate, 1656–1658* (London, 1909), I, p. 147. For king as keystone of an arch, see Juan de Solorzano, *Emblemata Regio Politica* (Madrid, 1653), emblem 48, and Andres Mendo, *Principe Perfecto y Ministros Aiustados* (Leon de Franci, 1662), emblem 70. For the throne as a roof upheld by the walls of justice and mercy, see Thomas Fuller, *The Holy State and the Profane State*, ed. M. G. Walten, II, p. 352.
[4] *His Highnesse the Protector-Protected* (London, 1654), p. 7. The following year Hunton became yet more blatantly a kingling in *The King of Kings: or the Soveraignty of Salus Populi*—a pamphlet signed S. H. which can be certainly identified as Hunton's by a reference on p. 5.

For, in this respect, it [sovereignty] must be (as before said) like the Center in a circle; for there, as the singleness of the Center makes the union and meeting of the circumference, and consequently but one Circle; so two Centers, though never so like and neer, yet (having circumferences drawn from them) will make two Circles. And further, as the Center gives being to the circumference, so the circumference to it again: for until this be drawn, the center is but a point; as untill the subjects be, the King is but as another man. And as, until this Center be fixed (whereby to measure equal distances on all hands) it will remaine an uncertain round, and not a Circle: so in policy, till the body of the people are fixed upon an unity (as upon a Center) they will have no assurance of equal and certain proportions amongst themselves.[1]

The Amphion myth offered further advantages; it allowed him to glide over the troubles of that anxious year, and indeed to pretend that the quarrels and disappointments of the republicans were a concordant discord, not a real threat to the state; it afforded an excellent illustration of that speed of action which so often caused Cromwell to be compared with Caesar (a comparison conspicuously missing in the poem); and it permitted him to allude to the military operations, of which the Western design was the chief, and to the controversial new ecclesiastical settlement as elements of Cromwell's success. However, no special significance need be attributed to the 'Palace' which Amphion erected 'with a Touch more sweet' (61), although it does suggest that palaces were not of themselves evil. The section concludes by bringing to the forefront the promise of the Fifth Monarchy, which is crucial to the total argument.

The Fifth Monarchy, 'a notion', said Cromwell, 'I hope we all honour, wait, and hope for',[2] had an especially wide appeal in 1654–5, as the First Parliament was troublesome precisely on account of the large number of enthusiastic saints

---

[1] *Of Government and Obedience*, p. 57.

[2] Abbott, III, p. 437. For the conflicting hope and pessimism aroused by Fifth Monarchism, see Ernest Lee Tuveson, *Millennium and Utopia* (Berkeley, Calif. 1949), pp. 22–112, esp. 85 ff.

it contained. There was no more fruitful way of proposing still further changes in the constitution than by appealing to the hopes of the approaching millennium. Chiliasts were inclined to be precise in their demands for overturning, but vague about the kind of government they would institute. It would be a theocracy ruled by a single party, and if Christ appeared in person to reign (many doubted this) there would be no need for a temporal monarch. However, inherent in their schemes was a belief in the great captain who would lead the troops until Christ's arrival; and, until Cromwell had disappointed them, he was their natural choice.[1] Harrison in 1653 was reported to have envisaged, literally, some kind of monarchical rule, and seems to have favoured himself for the office;[2] but John Rogers declared that thousands were looking to Cromwell as 'our conqueror upon Christ's and the Commonwealth's account'; there existed also 'a prediction, which says C. shall sound within the walls of Rome',[3] and John Spittlehouse humbly requested that 'the Lord would so operate by his Spirit upon all our affections who claime an interest in the benefits that doe accrew unto us by the marvellous Acts of the same providence, as also instrumentally upon him (*viz.* our present Deliverer, Generall, and Judge), whom the Lord hath been pleased to make use of'.[4] Marvell's argument could draw directly, there-fore, on an already well-established belief that Cromwell was

[1] Louise Fargo Brown, *The Political Activities of the Baptists and Fifth Monarchy Men in England during the Interregnum* (Washington, D. C., 1912); ch. III remains standard for this year. A convenient summary of their predictions is to be found in Thomas Richards, *A History of the Puritan Movement in Wales...1639 to...1653* (London, 1920), pp. 192–6. Arthur Barker, *Milton and the Puritan Dilemma*, has a useful chapter, pp. 193–214; and, because of its full quotation, the appendix ('The Free Spirit in Cromwell's England') in Norman Cohn's *The Pursuit of the Millennium* (London, 1957) does much to show why the Ranters could be accused of all kinds of lasciviousness (to which Marvell later refers).   [2] Gardiner, *History*, II, p. 276.

[3] *Sagrir, or Doomes-Day Drawing Nigh* [1654], in Edward Rogers, *The Life and Opinions of a Fifth-Monarchy Man* (London, 1867), p. 77.

[4] *A Warning-Piece Discharged* (London, 1653), p. 24.

destined to play a part in the arrival of the millennium: few
doubted the times were approaching, and Cromwell himself
speculated in public on their nearness.[1] Yet Marvell's appeal was
not directed, as the later diatribe shows, to the lunatic fringe of
this group, but to the sober-minded Christians who were con-
tent to wait for the indisputable signs of the glorious Day. He
was voicing orthodox opinion in his statement, 'a thick Cloud
about that Morning lyes, / And intercepts the Beams of Mortal
Eyes' (141–2), for it was an abuse of providence to attempt to
hasten God's designs, as John Goodwin reminded the faithful
at this time.[2] Marvell's proposition does in effect seek to speed
the day, so the modesty with which it is made is peculiarly
important. Without more conclusive proof, neither Marvell nor
England could be positive that time's useless course was
drawing to a close, and almost every sentence carries a qualifica-
tion. No thesis was ever put more tentatively:

> O *would* they rather...
>
> How *might* they under such a Captain...
>
> *If* gracious Heaven to my Life give length...
>
> What we *might* hope, what wonderful Effect
> From such a wish'd Conjuncture *might* reflect...
>
> That *'tis the most* which we determine can,
> *If* these the Times...
>
> And well he therefore does, and well has *guest*...
>
> And *knowing not* where Heavens choice may light...
>
> But Men alas, *as if* they nothing car'd...   (105–49)

Cautious though he is, Marvell was not challenging God's
plan if he envisaged all protestants united in a war against
Anti-Christ, and the possibility of such a crusade seemed much

[1] Abbott, III, p. 436. C. A. Patrides, 'Renaissance and Modern Thought on
the Last Things: A Study in Changing Conceptions', *Harvard Theological
Review*, LI (1958), pp. 170–3, documents the belief that the times were near.

[2] *Sugkretismos, or Dis-satisfaction Satisfied* (London, 1654), p. 16. For the
moderate millenarian view, see Thomas Goodwin, *The World to Come, or,
the Kingdom of Christ Asserted* (London, 1655).

nearer in 1654 than it had in 1650, when Marvell concluded
the Horatian ode with a similar threat to 'all States not free'.
The princes, however, were 'Unhappy'—that is, 'infelix',
unblessed by fortune[1]—and Cromwell remains splendidly and
desperately 'alone' in his struggle against the forces of evil.
Kings and 'Men' co-operate to frustrate the work Cromwell
has begun. England should lead the vanguard of the Church
Militant, but something is lacking, and 'Hence landing
Nature to new Seas is tost, / And good Designes still with their
Authors lost' (157–8). Marvell claims no certainty in diagnos-
ing either the cause or the remedy for the discrepancy between
Cromwell's achievement and its perfect fruition, but he does
suggest them both in the lines which carry the most explicit
avowal of his theme:

> Hence oft I think, if in some happy Hour
> High Grace should meet in one with highest Pow'r,
> And then a seasonable People still
> Should bend to his, as he to Heavens will,
> What we might hope, what wonderful Effect
> From such a wish'd Conjuncture might reflect.
> Sure, the mysterious Work, where none withstand,
> Would forthwith finish under such a Hand:
> Fore-shortned Time its useless Course would stay,
> And soon precipitate the latest Day.
> But a thick Cloud about that Morning lyes,
> And intercepts the Beams of Mortal eyes,
> That 'tis the most which we determine can,
> If these the Times, then this must be the Man.
> And well he therefore does, and well has guest,
> Who in his Age has always forward prest:
> And knowing not where Heavens choice may light,
> Girds yet his Sword, and ready stands to fight;   (131–48)

If the poem is panegyric, then this passage can be read only as
Professor Carens reads it: 'If the vision of the reign of the saints,

[1] Suggested in another context by Patrick Cruttwell, *The Shakespearean
Moment* (New York, 1955), p. 190.

ushered in by Cromwell, is suggested as a possibility, it is withdrawn in the very act of offering it to our imaginations.'[1] God, then, permitted Cromwell as a second-best leader, but would later send an even greater man who combined grace with power. But this is absurd. Cromwell is clearly intended as the figure of 'highest Pow'r'—the whole poem so far has demonstrated that—and his eager service of the Lord must class him also among 'th'Elected' (156); he is *par excellence* the man God has elected. If grace, therefore, has been denied him, it must be either because the time of the millennial kingdom has not yet come, and God thus withholds his especial blessing, or because mankind 'all unconcerned, or unprepar'd' is frustrating God's wish to endow Cromwell with the grace necessary to finish His work. No one can know if the first alternative offers the correct explanation, but Marvell *is* certain that 'If these [are] the Times [of the millennium], then this must be the Man' whom God has chosen to complete 'the mysterious Work.' The meaning depends on the interpretation of 'High Grace', and on the knowledge of how 'Heaven's choice' would visibly 'light' on a man.

The conjuncture of High Grace with one already possessed of highest power would occur, if we read literally, 'in some happy hour', and nothing fits the demands of this formula so well as the conferring of grace in the hour of coronation. The significance of this grace had been one of the principal controversies of the civil war, with the royalists claiming that grace confirmed for ever an already hereditary sovereignty, and endued the King's person with special sanctity and healing powers. For the puritans, the balm was more nominal, and hence dispensable if the King's spirituality proved deficient. The Archbishop at Charles's coronation prayed that the King might 'joyfully receive the seat of supreme Government by the

[1] James F. Carens, 'Andrew Marvell's Cromwell Poems', *Bucknell Review*, VII (1957), p. 64. See also Lawrence Hyman, *Andrew Marvell* (New York, 1964), pp. 98–9.

gift of [God's] supernatural grace', and Robert Brown in a lamentation when the reign had ended declared, 'The holy Oyle thus employed [in the coronation] is no longer bare and common Oyl, but χαρισμα, the *gift of Grace*; which (however vilified by Enthusiastiques and Solifidians) betoken the Grace of *Christ and Kings*.'[1] The lesson of the civil war had been, however, that high grace when not allied with highest power was of no avail.

The Protectorate had been called into being by the Instrument of Government, namely, by an Act of Parliament, and no religious ceremony of anointment distinguished the Protector with divine grace. Lacking this unction, Cromwell insisted in his speech dissolving Parliament on 22 January 1655 that the terms of the Instrument must be followed if the balance between the extremes of monarchy and democracy was to be maintained:

The Government called you hither, the constitution whereof being so limited, *a single person and a Parliament*, and this was thought most agreeable to the general sense of the nation, having had experience enough by trial of other conclusions, judging this most likely to avoid the extremes of monarchy on the one hand, and democracy on the other, and yet not to found *dominium in gratia*.[2]

The essence of the Protectorate was its retention of the typical structure of the English constitution, but dispensing with the inalienable privilege inherent in *dominium in gratia*. The time had now come, Marvell believed, to return to the old form in its entirety, and to anoint Cromwell with oil. It was inconceivable Cromwell should anoint himself, and God was therefore powerless to bestow His grace until the people awakened

---

[1] *The Manner of the Coronation of King Charles the First at Westminster, 2 Feb., 1626*, edited for the Henry Bradshaw Liturgical Text Society by Christopher Wordsworth (London, 1892), p. 27; [Robert Brown,] *The Subjects Sorrow: or Lamentations upon the Death of Britains Josiah King Charles* (London, 1649), p. 10. See also Percy Ernst Schramm, *A History of the English Coronation*, trans. L. G. Wickham Legg (Oxford, 1937), pp. 125, 128-9.

[2] Abbott, III, p. 587.

from their apathy. The accepted commonplace that God no longer directly instituted kings as He had occasionally done in Jewish history left the disposal of government to human acts. Of the possible ways in which monarchies could be instituted, succession was of course ruled out for Cromwell, and conquest was no longer a plausible argument as it had been for two or three years after 1649. Election remained the only route to the throne, as Cromwell recognized. 'Heavens choice' could not finally be known until the people had consented. The views of the audience to whom *The First Anniversary* is addressed were admirably expressed in 1654 by the Smectymnuan William Spurstowe. One call to kingship, he explained, was immediately of God.

The other is mediate; which is by the designation and appointment of man. Thus *Moses* did by the advise of *Jethro*, select and chuse out of the people such persons as were endued with qualifications fit for Magistracy... And this is the Call which is usuall and constant, which being after a regular and due manner performed, becomes the Call of God. But a Call there must be, to give a title to Magistracy: or else it is not an Authority, but an usurpation; not a mission, by Gods ordinance, but a permission by his providence.[1]

'Is Magistracy Gods Ordinance?' inquired Thomas Hall, '*then none may usurp it, or enter upon it* without a Call from him. As in the Ministry no man may take that honour to himself but he that is called; so in Magistracy none may assume this office to himself, but he that is called of God, either mediately or immediately.'[2] In the puritan mind the call to the magistracy was exactly analogous with that to the ministry, and the process of authorizing a minister included the selection of the candidate, his examination for fitness, his actual election by the

[1] *The Magistrates Dignity and Duty* (London, 1654), pp. 27–8. Cf. Marvell in *The Rehearsal Transpros'd* (*Works*, ed. Grosart, III, p. 398): 'I conceive the magistrate, as in Scripture described, is the ordinance of God constituting him, and the ordinance of man assenting to his dominion.'

[2] *The Beauty of Magistracy, in an Exposition of the 82 Psalm* (London, 1660), p. 32.

people and his solemn installation.[1] Cromwell himself had always represented his authority as a call from the people, or the army officers, and his second speech to his Parliament, invoking a great cloud of witnesses in the three nations, is the best illustration of the puritan doctrine of election that I know of.[2]

These were the beliefs to which Marvell appealed, and the first hundred and thirty lines of the poem should therefore be read as the statement of Cromwell's fitness for his vocation, of his election by God. They lend force to a word in line 133: 'And then a seasonable People *still* / Should bend to his, as he to Heavens will.' Not until the people had proved once that they could act seasonably by electing Cromwell king, could they be seasonable 'still'. And if they continued to recognize Cromwell's leadership the latter days would surely be hastened, when, as Colonel Lane described them, 'not a dog shall dare to bark or wag his tail against any servant of the Lord'.[3] The same Colonel used satirically the very arguments which Marvell offered in good faith: 'Let us consider *the Policie of the man:* view his Intellectuals a little, and we shall see, that (according to the received opinion of our times, that *grace is but a secondary qualification in Rulers and Magistrates; natural gifts and accomplishments to be sought after in the first place*) he was as fit for the Magistracie as any man (of that Judgement) would fix upon.'[4] Marvell and Lane concurred in finding Cromwell disgraced, in different senses.

Marvell's disquisition for kingship, spoken, like no other section of the poem, in the first person singular, never strays beyond the confines of orthodox and millennial belief.

---

[1] James L. Ainslie, *The Doctrines of Ministerial Order in the Reformed Churches of the 16th and 17th Centuries* (Edinburgh, 1940), p. 143. The Call was supposed to hinder ambitious men. See the list of quotations from works of the reformers, pp. 140–2. Also Anon., *Stereoma, The Establishment* (London, 1654), pp. 89 ff. Election was generally held to be more important than ordination (Geoffrey Nuttall, *Visible Saints* [Oxford, 1957] pp. 88 ff.).

[2] Abbot, III, pp. 451–62.

[3] *An Image of our Reforming Times: or, Jehu in his Proper Colours* (London, 1654), p. 30.   [4] *Ibid.* p. 5.

Cromwell's works are unquestionable, his election by God secure; he himself 'ready stands to fight', but waits patiently for a call; millenarians could understand the need for a captain-general, and all moderate men would rest satisfied with the poet's humility. The creation of a monarchy by popular consent was the natural apotheosis of Cromwell's glorious works. In subsequent parts of the poem, the utilitarian reasons for king-ship are enforced by the description of the anarchy which would follow Cromwell's death, and further evidence is offered of Cromwell's suitability for the task.

The coaching accident preceded by only two weeks the debate in Parliament on the succession, which was influenced, Abbott records, 'in some degree' by Cromwell's narrow escape.[1] Wither was certainly careful to dissociate himself in his poem on the event from those who wished to style the Protector 'Emperor'.[2] One effect immediately intended by Marvell's lines was to counter the sarcasms for which the fall afforded the occasion. The Governor of Calais regretted that Cromwell did not manage his coach as well as the rest of his business, but for others the horses had shown themselves less pliable than Parliament, and the ruder sort commented that Cromwell and Thurloe in the coach were Mephistopheles and Dr Faustus 'careering it in the Air, to try how he could govern Horses, since Rational Creatures were so unruly and difficult to be reined'.[3] The passage, however, is less transiently polemical

[1] III, p. 482.

[2] *Vaticinium Causuale*, in *Miscellaneous Works, First Collection* (n.p. The Spenser Society, 1872), p. 9.

[3] Thurloe, *State Papers*, II, p. 656; James Heath, *A Chronicle of the Late Intestine War*, 2nd ed. (London, 1676), p. 363. For an anonymous 'Elogy' see Historical Manuscripts Commission, Thirteenth Report, Portland MSS (London, 1892), p. 678; also 'A Jolt on Michaelmas Day' reprinted in *Political Ballads of the Seventeenth and Eighteenth Centuries*, ed. W. Walter Wilkins (London, 1860), I, pp. 121–4. C. H. Firth points out that the contrast between horses and Parliament was heightened by Cromwell's having extracted an engagement to recognize his authority only a fortnight earlier ('Cromwell's Views on Sport', *Macmillan's Magazine*, LXX [1894], p. 404).

than this, and yet more simple than Carens's suggestion that 'the accident, of course, symbolizes the impulse to anarchy loose in the land', or Mazzeo's, which links the fall not only, quite properly, with the Fall, but with the pattern of rising and falling in the poem.[1] It is, briefly, an obituary discourse in which Marvell describes what would have happened, had Cromwell been killed: 'So with more Modesty we may be True, / And speak as of the Dead the Praises due' (187–8); and it was a fine touch to close this section with references to the ascent of Elijah, one of the favourite texts for funeral sermons in the seventeenth century.[2] The horses, those 'poor Beasts' (191) who had endangered Cromwell's life, become a metaphor for the people of England left without their driver:

> Thee proof beyond all other Force or Skill,
> Our Sins endanger, and shall one day kill.
>   How near they fail'd and in thy sudden Fall
> At once assay'd to overturn us all.
> Our brutish fury strugling to be Free,
> Hurry'd thy Horses while they hurry'd thee.   (173–8)

No less than his ancient and saintly mother, no less than his countrymen, Cromwell is subject to the effects of the Fall, and when, for the second time, Cromwell is compared with 'Nature' (204), a reader does well to remember the grace which the Protector still lacks; in fact the overthrow of nature

---

[1] Carens, p. 65; Mazzeo, p. 201.

[2] See Patrick's funeral sermon on John Smith printed in *Select Discourses* (London, 1660); also M. Sylvester's sermon on Baxter, *Elisha's Cry after Elijah's God* (1696), and the anonymous *A Call from Heaven to Gods Elisha's, to Mourn and Lament, When God Takes Away His Elijah's, either by a Natural, or by a Civil Death* (London, 1667), which begins 'I know many excellent Funeral Sermons upon this Text are in Print' and cites marginally T. Hooker, O. Sedgwick, J. Collins, J. Gauden, S. Patrick. See John Collinge, *Elisha's Lamentation for Elijah* (1657) and Cotton Mather's funeral sermon by Thomas Prince, *The Departure of Elijah Lamented* (Boston, 1728). Godfrey Davies in *The Restoration of Charles II* (San Marino, Calif., 1955), p. 11, notes that Cromwell's death and Richard's succession were in several addresses compared with Elijah and Elisha.

at Cromwell's death points back to the irony of Cromwell's position which has been gradually emerging during the course of the poem. Cromwell's power over the unyielding 'Matter' of 'the Minds of stubborn Men' (77–8) is similar to the power of grace; he is also 'Angelique' and has learned 'a Musique in the Region clear', and yet he is confined to the world of 'things', which he manipulates superbly. On the other hand, ordinary monarchs 'nor more contribute to the State of Things, / Then Wooden Heads unto the Viols strings'(43–4), yet they may reign malignantly for all platonic years. Nominally they possess the grace and the longevity which Cromwell deserves, although in their own persons they are both un-graced and as mortal as other men. The reasons of state which prevent them from acknowledging Cromwell as their natural leader are abetted by the apathy of his people, but Marvell foresees the day, if 'gracious Heaven' permits *him* sufficient life, when a host of kings will 'chase the Beast'. Until that time he can only commend Cromwell, who pursues the Monster 'alone', and the implication remains, disguised though it is, that Cromwell may in the future lead the hunt as a king.[1] The international pursuit of Anti-Christ will not begin until Cromwell's anomalous status has been rectified, until grace has been added to nature, and the effects of the Fall become in part recoverable. The 'Panique groan' (203) which greets Crom-well's/Nature's fall is the more pointed an allusion in that no Christ-like successor was born at the instant of Cromwell's death; justice, reason, courage, religion—the virtues Christ came at the original panic moment to restore—lie obstructed and disheartened. Cromwell's work is lost in a second, and the ship of state founders unsalvageably.

The indisputable proof of the poet's concern with the suc-

---

[1] The force of '*Hence* oft I think...' is enhanced by the progression from the unhappy princes waiting for a commander to 'Angelique *Cromwell*', who is at present forced to fight the beast alone. Cromwell with grace would take his proper position at the head of all the princes.

cession in these lines lies in the reference to Elijah with which the section concludes: 'We only mourn'd our selves, in thine Ascent, / Whom thou hadst left beneath with Mantle rent' (219–20). Marvell followed conventional exegesis in ascribing Elisha's anguish to his sorrow, not for Elijah, but for Israel, but neither scripture nor commentary records that the mantle which Elisha wrapped round his shoulders was a 'Mantle rent'. Elisha tore his clothes, and Elijah's were consumed, but the cloak which symbolized the succession and the double portion of his father's spirit vouchsafed to Elisha was whole and inalienably his. If England were not to be left shivering with dissension, the succession ought to be assured at once.

Elijah was the poet's *trouvaille*, because yet another aspect of the prophet's *figura* was available to serve as an apt transition to another section. In calling Elijah 'the headstrong Peoples Charioteer' (224), Marvell followed the Vulgate text of 4 Kings ii. 12, 'Pater mi, pater mi, currus Israel et auriga eius', rather than the English version which translated 'auriga' as 'horsemen'. The standard reading of the verse stated that Elijah had assisted Israel more by his prayers than an army of horses and riders could have done;[1] his unwillingness to take part in political affairs was also well known; he had been married to contemplation and solitude, and had been one of the authors of monastic life.[2] Thus he was ideally suited to be a type of Cromwell's reluctance, and hence fitness, to rule, and Lyra had even offered a political interpretation of the text which was identical with Marvell's use of it in the poem; Elijah was both chariot and charioteer because one is led while the other leads,

[1] Vatablus, in *Critici Sacri* (Amsterdam, 1698), vol. II, on 2 Kings ii. 12; Estius, *Annotationes in Praecipua ac Difficiliora S. Scripturae Loca* (Moguntiae, 1667), on 2 Kings xiii. 14; Matthew Poole, *Synopsis Criticorum* (London, 1669), I, p. 595; Grotius, *Opera Omnia Theologica* (Amsterdam, 1679), I, p. 158. Annotated editions of the Vulgate also give this interpretation.

[2] Cornelius Lapide, *Commentarius in Iosue, Iudicum, Ruth, IV Libros Regum* [etc.] (Antwerp, 1653), on 1 Kings xvii. 1.

demonstrating 'that he rules well who first is led in obedience'.[1] The origin of this *sententia* in Aristotle underlines the similarity of this entire section to the *refutatio* in the Horatian ode. The first half of Marvell's proof consists in the argument from Cromwell's death; the second, which is the concern here, refutes those enemies who have always accused Cromwell of tyranny, but also covertly argues for a monarchy as the solution to those arbitrary tendencies which Cromwell's deeds, though fully justifiable, have contained. The innuendo of 'For to be *Cromwell* was a greater thing, / Then ought below, or yet above a King' (225-6) is later sustained, for to be Protector is at once to be both inferior to, and yet 'above', that is, to command more arbitrary power than, a king.

The order of the refutation is determined approximately by the chronology of Cromwell's dominion: his part in killing the King (229-38), the erection of the republic (239-48), his dissolution of the Long Parliament (249-56), his strong measures against the levellers and sectaries (257-64), and, probably, his dissolution of the Nominated Parliament (265-78). In the first of these vignettes Marvell has conflated the punishment threatened to the house of Ahab with Elijah's overtaking of Ahab's chariot, an incident which was illustrative of Elijah's humility and spiritual power, so that Cromwell is both Elijah and storm, just as in the ode he had been scourge and deliverer; and in both roles he is of God. In constructing the commonwealth he 'walk[ed] still middle betwixt War and Peace' (244), a happy mean which is immediately destroyed when, in dissolving Parliament, 'He on the Peace extends a Warlike power' (251). Gideon's revenge on '*Succoths* Elders' had proved very difficult to justify, the commentators tending to minimize it by the comparison with

[1] Nicholas Lyra, moral commentary on 1 Samuel ix in *Bibliorum Sacrorum Tomus Secundus* (Lugduni, 1545), fol. 72^v. Quoted in Lapide, *loc. cit.* See also Martin Del Rio, *Adagialia Sacra Veteris et Novi Testamenti* (Lugduni, 1614), p. 258.

a schoolmaster chastizing little boys. Joseph Hall remarked truthfully, 'I cannot thinke of *Gideons* revenge, without horror. . . Justice is sometimes so severe, that a tender beholder can scarce discerne it from cruelty.'[1] Marvell's unscriptural reference to the silence with which the Israelites greeted Gideon's action suggests his own, or at least his rhetorically adopted, criticism of Cromwell's high-handedness, for their failure to applaud must originate in disapproval; but Marvell is careful to emphasize Cromwell's refusal to profit personally from his strength. 'No King might ever such a Force have done' (255) is not, however, a congratulation, but an exhortation. Similarly, the familiar tale of the olive and the bramble (257–64) is left open to an interpretation which differs slightly from the conventional praise of the olive for avoiding public life. The anointment Cromwell rejected is 'thine Oyl', and the plainness of the Protector's heart does not enable him to escape the responsibilities of power. Brambles will be kings if olives are not crowned instead.

In the simile of the 'lusty Mate' who wrenched the tiller from the hand of the careless helmsman, thereby saving the ship of state, Marvell paraphrased the most famous political metaphor of his day. Originally invented by the author of the *Vindiciae contra tyrannos* to exemplify Calvin's dictum that lesser magistrates had the right to resist the greater in cases of necessity, it had been modified by independents and levellers, and later by supporters of the new Commonwealth in 1649–51, so that any person whatsoever, not solely a lesser magistrate, could assume command in emergencies; in the early uses of the metaphor the drunken pilot had been asked politely to step aside for the duration, whereas after 1649 he had been cast unceremoniously into the waves.[2] Except for its application to a new event,

[1] *Contemplations upon the Principal Passages of the Holy Storie. The Ninth Book*, in *Works* (London, 1621), p. 914.

[2] The evidence for these generalizations is given in my note, 'Marvell's "lusty Mate" and the Ship of the Commonwealth', *MLN*, LXXVI (1961), pp. 106–10. Charles's version of the simile is to be found at the end of *Eikon*

Marvell's rendering appears completely conventional, but the lines on Noah which follow ('Thou, and thine House, like *Noah's* Eight did rest, / Left by the Wars Flood on the Mountains crest': etc.) contrast so sharply with the image of arbitrary but necessary power in the mate that it is easy to recall while reflecting on this passage the angry and often lengthy objections of the royalists to the puritan metaphor. At least they established the wholly temporary nature of the usurping helmsman's authority, and they inquired pertinently whether he should not be court-martialled for mutiny as soon as the ship reached port. The simile proved extraordinarily useful and adaptable so long as Parliament was seeking to justify its unconstitutional measures, and it was revived in a highly elaborate form at the Exclusion crisis,[1] but it could not serve as a good example of constitutional action in normal times. Marvell says as much:

> 'Tis not a Freedome, that where All command;
> Nor Tyranny, where One does them withstand:
> But who of both the Bounders knows to lay
> Him as their Father must the State obey. (279–82)

The first couplet glosses the preceding incident of the mate; the second introduces the ideal figure of Noah/Cromwell with which the *refutatio* concludes.

By invoking the idea of a *pater patriae* Marvell went beyond the concept of the Protector as envisaged in the Instrument, and harked back to royalist paternalism and the theory of the mixed monarchy. Except for Filmer, who had reiterated his notions during the Commonwealth period, the patriarchal origin of kingship had operated rather as a powerful analogy than as a literal fact. Practically all royalists had been willing to

Basilike, just before the prayers: 'Nor doe I wish other, than the safe bringing of the ship to shore, when they have cast me overboard; though it be very strange, that Mariners can find no other means to appease the storm themselves have raised but by drowning their Pilot.'

[1] Charles F. Mullett, 'The Popish Plot as a Ship's Mutiny', *N&Q*, CLXXIV (1938), pp. 218–23.

concede a contract or limitation somewhere along the line from Adam's kingship, but, as an analogy, paternalism was of obvious usefulness, rendered more so by the common inter
pretation of the commandment to honour one's father and mother as an order to obey princes and governors. If the king
ship of Adam was the cornerstone of patriarchal theory, the kingship of Noah was no less important, and, after the deluge of the civil war, a good deal more relevant to Marvell's poem. Although Bishop Overall's suppressed *Convocation Book* had clearly intended to settle the matter once for all,[1] Noah's patriarchy became one of the casuistical issues of the century, because it allowed the royalists to side-step the awkward truth that the tyrant Nimrod had scripturally the best claim to be called the first king. The spread of Noah's children, wrote Henry Ferne, must have occurred 'by the direction and order of Noah', and the election of rulers, which commenced with Cham, was a defection from God's original plan.[2] Charles Herle, who realized Nimrod's kingship was an embarrassment to his opponents, did not allow this opinion to go unchallenged, and Griffith Williams later conceded Nimrod's usurpation but protested that men must not fight over words: it was certain there had been kings since Adam, 'and so named ever since *Noahs* floud'.[3] Sir John Spelman also appealed to Noah, and Dudley Digges found the other loophole for avoiding Nimrod when he argued that Shem, who was often identified with Melchisedek, was the prime monarch, and Nimrod's monarchy was irregular.[4] One expects casuists to argue in this

---

[1] *Bishop Overall's Convocation Book MDCVI* (London, 1690), p. 8. For two other authoritative statements on the Noah question, see John Selden, *Titles of Honor*, 3rd ed. (London, 1672), pp. 6–10, and James Ussher, *The Power Communicated by God to the Prince*, in *Works*, ed. C. R. Elrington (Dublin, 1847), XI, p. 249.   [2] *Conscience Satisfied* (Oxford, 1643), p. 8.

[3] [Herle,] *An Answer to Doctor Fernes Reply* (London, 1643), p. 16; Williams, *Jura Majestatis, The Rights of Kings* (Oxford, 1644), p. 15.

[4] [Spelman,] *A View of a Printed Book* (Oxford, 1642), p. 13; [Digges,] *A Review of the Observations* (Oxford, 1643), p. 3.

way, and the examples are quoted to show that Noah could not have been employed in a political poem unwittingly. Marvell emphasized his intention of proposing Cromwell as a replica of Noah the king when he continued to denounce the 'Chammish issue' in the diatribe which forms the penultimate section of the poem. Noah's children who laughed at his nakedness had not infrequently been compared with rebellious subjects,[1] and Cham's descendants had been cursed by Noah as the Fifth Monarchists had been cursed by all and sundry, including Cromwell. This wild segment of the people had done much to hinder both the political and religious settle ments of the Protectorate, and Cromwell, having fought all his battles in the name of the Lord of Hosts, must have found it particularly galling to be denounced as the Little Horn. When Marvell cursed them as the locusts from the bottomless pit (311–12) he was only turning their own imagery against themselves and applying a text which had long been used to condemn heretics and schismatics.[2] The purpose of the philip pic is not to relieve feelings, however, or even to please Crom well, but to expose the Fifth Monarchists as a real danger. The sons of Cham, of whom the chief was Nimrod, are waiting to seize control of the state, and only Cromwell stands between them and the fulfilment of their designs; they are overtly con trasted with the noble family of Cromwell. If the crown is not to devolve on the Chammish issue, as it did in the Bible, it must descend to the worthy offspring.

From Noah presiding over the survivors of the deluge, the

[1] Griffith Williams, *Vindiciae Regum; or the Grand Rebellion* (Oxford, 1643), p. 34; Hall, *Of Government and Obedience*, sig. A2ʳ; L'Estrange, *An Account of the Growth of Knavery* (London, 1678), p. 15.

[2] E.g. Andrew Willett, *Sacrorum Emblematum Centuria Una* (Cambridge, n.d.), sig. 14ᵛ; Samuel Richardson, *An Answer to the London Ministers Letter* (London, 1649), who begins his tract with a page of the smoke/false learning analogy; also John Holland, *Smoke of the Bottomless Pit* (London, 1651); and John Tickell, *The Bottomless Pit Smoaking in Familisme* (London, 1651). The Simpson Marvell cites as especially noxious must be John, not Sydrach, as Grosart and Margoliouth annotate.

final scene moves back to Adam watching the first sunset of the world and wondering in despair if there would ever be another dawn.[1] At first glance, Marvell appears to be returning to Cromwell's coaching accident, and the relief which had followed its momentary terror. But duplication of that kind would be redundant, and the surprised kings could not have referred to the erasure and rebuilding of the state (352) had they been concerned with the aftermath of the fall in Hyde Park. As an account, however, of the utter blackness into which England had been thrown in 1649 and her subsequent recovery under Cromwell, the extensive simile is significant; it was with this identical sunset image that the royalists had most frequently lamented Charles's execution and foreseen the rising sun of Charles II.[2] Like the harmonious building, the sun image is inescapably royalist, as John Ailmer knew when he wrote the poem which concluded with an offer of the crown to Cromwell:

> *Benighted* was our *spheare* with all its *Glories,*
> Darke as black *Melancholies* territories,
> As th'*Hermits* vault th'inheritance of *Night*:
> *Confus'd* as *Chaos* lay ere th'*infant light*
> *Usher* to all the *Beauties* were to come
> Had issued from the *Masses* pregnant *Wombe*:
> Till our *Great Oliver* from a budding *Star*
> Full blown a *Sun*, and fixt in's golden *Sphear*,
> Beauty and warmth displaies, and with a *ray*
> Of his *own light* creates us a *new* Day.[3]

[1] On this image, see E. E. Duncan-Jones, 'Marvell, Johnson, and the First Sunset', *TLS*, 3 April 1959, p. 193, who quotes Lucretius, Statius, and Manilius.

[2] E.g. [Thomas Bayly,] *The Royal Charter Granted unto Kings* (London, 1649), sig. A2ᵛ; [John Quarles], *Regale Lectum Miseriae*, 2nd ed. (1649), p. 49; [George Wither,] *Vaticinium Votivum* (n.p. 1649), p. 79; [John Cleveland,] *Monumentum Regale* (n.p. 1649), p. 2; and esp. a cavalier ballad, 'The Royall Health to the Rising Sun', in *Cavalier and Puritan*, ed. Hyder E. Rollins (New York, 1923), pp. 247–50, and John Sadler, *Rights of the Kingdom* (London, 1649), sig. 3ʳ. Simon Ford, *Primitiae Regiminis Davidici* (London, 1654), pp. 1–2, has an implied comparison of Cromwell the Protector with the middling condition of 'Morning-Twilight' between a king and no king.

[3] *Musarum Oxoniensium*, p. 96.

Finally Cromwell is the 'Soul' of the new England—another conventional image of a king—and 'seems a King by long Succession born' (387). The praise of the foreign monarch ends in a riddling couplet which can be read only ironically, as a gloating allusion to the probable collapse of Cromwell's work at his death: 'O could I once him with our Title see, / So should I hope yet he might Dye as we' (391-2). When Marvell speaks again in his own person, as he immediately does, he addresses Cromwell for the first time as 'Prince'; he cannot resist a final reminder that the Protector is now 'venerable' (both aged and regal) and his 'End' is in sight. The 'End', however, is also the monarchy for which Cromwell is destined and the 'Prize' for which the poet has competed. Marvell's purpose may fail if he 'contends' further, and he is content to close his poem by offering in 'Love and Duty' the proposal to crown Cromwell made in 'Fear or Spight' (395-6) by the Saturnian princes. In the last simile of Cromwell as the angel of the commonweal troubling the pool and healing it, Marvell returns his audience full circle to his initial image. The elegiac overtones implicit in the poem's title rise once more, like ripples, to the surface, and Cromwell, if he had caught the allusion to *respice finem*, no doubt put down the poem feeling very old.

The First Anniversary has always seemed to lack unity: panegyric lapsed into doubt, transitions were awkward, biblical and classical allusion alternated unevenly, and the imagery, though plentiful, worked inconsistently. Yet this proves nothing except that the principles of renaissance rhetoric, our knowledge of which has grown so rapidly in the past two decades, has generally been applied only to shorter poems. Instructed by Professor Weinberg in the connections between the *Ars poetica* and deliberative oratory in *cinquecento* theory, and persuaded many times over of the logical basis of metaphysical imagery, we ought to be surprised if a long political poem was not structured, or 'disposed', according to a rhetorical plan. The least interesting aspect of Marvell's poem, because merely a framework, is the close relation the structure bears to a deliberative oration: exordium (1–48), *narratio* (statement of what Cromwell has done, 49–116), *divisio* (statement of theme, 117–58), *confirmatio* (proof of the utility of thesis, 159–220), *refutatio* (denial of frequent accusations, 221–92), digression (traditionally placed near the end of an oration, and sometimes a diatribe, 293–324), and a peroration. An adept at rhetorical analysis could probably refine considerably on the simple scheme proposed here, and would certainly be able to demonstrate from the poem a large number of the Topics of Invention (the most notable being the Testimony at the close), but Marvell's intention would remain unchanged, and it is this conception, not its disposition into rhetorical parts, which finally unifies the poem. One sees this especially clearly in the *confirmatio*, *refutatio*, and digression, each of which has distinct subjectmatters that together constitute a proof of the thesis and advance it in different ways. The coaching accident loses its point if it merely symbolizes the impulse to anarchy in England, and the attack on the Fifth Monarchists is gratuitously violent in a panegyric unless it is related to their threat to step into Cromwell's shoes. With equal skill, the series of analogues in the *refutatio* manages to accomplish its primary purpose of defending Cromwell against his accusers while advancing an alternative which will render arbitrary action less likely in the future. Rosemond Tuve said much better what I am suggesting. Quoting Wilson's statement that the orator must find out apt matter, she asks, 'To what is the matter "apt"? What does the distinction between "matter" and "purpose", made several times, mean—if not that the directing conception determines my selection of things true and likely...How can words and sentences (probably figures of words and figures of thought) confirm the cause, unless the process is one of fit incarnation of an intention?...Purposes are given body in suitable matter and made articulate through suitable form... The subject of a poem is an embodied purpose.'[1]

If one insists, however, that the reading of a political poem of this order may proceed accurately without reference to a deliberative oratorical scheme provided the intention is grasped, one tries, as an historian, to avoid the intentional fallacy. Tact is the only solution to the problem, because any thoroughly rhetorical poem develops a *persona* or attitude which may bear little relation to the author's private opinions. On *a priori* grounds, Marvell might have proposed his thesis in pure cynicism to advance his own political career, and his 'real' opinions might not be represented in the poem at all. However, Marvell appears to have taken seriously the classical precept that a good orator must also be a good man, and the argument for kingship in 1655 was sufficiently a minority opinion to make it unlikely that Marvell would have chosen it for self-seeking ends. Similarly, it would be wrong to underestimate, on the grounds that Cromwell had merely begun to perfect the sacred prophecies, the importance of the millenarianism in the poem, or to think that it was Marvell's rhetorical concession to a puritan audience.[2] The poem is so deeply imbued with it that Cromwell's fitness to govern cannot be detached from the millennial hopes he inspired. Above all, his speed in action was the miraculous quality on which the hope was based: the rebuilding of the state, like the rebuilding of the navy in the last section, was not literally performed in an hour, but imagistically the poem works to establish the instantaneousness with which Cromwell's purposes have been accomplished. Marvell also gave him a curious genealogy of righteousness, like an

[1] *Elizabethan and Metaphysical Imagery* (Chicago, 1947), pp. 389–91.
[2] As I suggested it might be in an earlier version of this chapter. This paragraph is indebted to arguments I lost with my student, Mrs Carolyn Karcher. I am grateful to her intelligent persistence for making me reconsider the importance of the millenarianism in the poem. Mrs Karcher also contrasted the circular, platonic time of the heavy monarchs and the linear, Christian time represented by Cromwell.

Old Testament leader or like Christ Himself, and his 'Saint-like Mother' is invoked to guarantee Cromwell's own status as a modern-day saint. The poem is unique in Marvell's corpus for the fervour of its millennial emphasis, but the violence of the attack on the Fifth Monarchists themselves points to the conservative and constitutional mind that is equally operative in the argument.

The dilemma of the Commonwealth is reflected in this duality of revolutionary and non-revolutionary principles. The revolution had initiated a period of constant change. One reform led to another, one failure to a second attempt, one victory to yet further and unforeseen consequences. It is also a commonplace that Pym—whom Hexter calls 'moderate' and Wormald 'violent'—and the other parliamentary managers were trapped by the events they had set in motion and were forced to continue along dangerous paths by fears for their personal safety. The execution of the King was the result more of the logic of events than of the malice and anti-monarchism of the army leaders. The breathing-space obtained for the country by the Engagers had not stopped the process, and *The First Anniversary* is itself a record of the innovations that the government could not avoid. Much of the immense amount of legislation during the Commonwealth also looks improvised, to say the least, and the insecurity of the constitution was matched by the differences in religion and the uncertainty of war. Time in such crises runs faster, and the millennial hope looks forward to the final cataclysm when time will be swallowed up and all problems will be over. It positively rejoices in the increased tempo, and approves of overturning and innovation as evidence that the end is near. It welcomes change and scorns stability, and in *The First Anniversary*, as Cromwell 'hurles e'r since the World about him round…Here shines in Peace, and thither shoots a War' (100–2), Marvell has caught the excitement of a mood that basically is unconcerned with constitutionalism and regards Cromwell's kingship as a small but significant step that would immediately be transcended by its apocalyptic result. Millenarianism in this aspect regards enthusiastically a future of foreign wars against the Beast, and is in favour of kingship not because it would assure the succession but because all successors would be unnecessary. *The First Anniversary* is remarkably reticent about the son who would actually succeed Cromwell if he were king, but the reason is that kingship held a greater possibility than the assurance of tranquillity promised to the lines of heavy monarchs. Marvell entertained this hope in the poem, and I think also as a man, but it was of course incompatible with the other reason for kingship that saw in the crown a safeguard against further disturbances, and an assurance that the wild gallop of the revolution would end in a peaceful and permanent settlement.

To achieve a Fifth Monarchy by due process of law was really a contradiction in terms, but to Marvell the possibility of a millennium was as cogent as the certainty that kingship would restore the older blessings of regular government. When the crown was offered to Cromwell in 1657, the Master of the Rolls remarked that the Instrument 'hath no limit at all', and, like him, Marvell feared a ruinous competition for power under an elective system and believed that only Cromwell's virtue saved England from abuse by an executive with dictatorial powers. The millennial hope aside, kingship seemed to provide the one means of closing the gulf between might and right that the execution of a king had opened. Power had to be turned into authority, and the transformation would occur when grace was added to nature. To the royalists of the civil war, defending their rights against Parliament's arbitrary power, grace took precedence over nature,[1] and to the puritans who looked to providence for their right to rule, 'natural gifts and accomplishments [were] to be sought after in the first place'; but in an unembattled monarchy authority would be established firmly

---

[1] Thomas Jordan, *Rules to Know a Royall King, From a Disloyall Subject* (1642), p. 1, discussed by Sirluck in *Complete Prose Works of John Milton*, II, p. 29.

in both nature and grace, and the anointing oil would confirm the dispensations of providence. In 1659 the problem was still unsolved, and Richard Baxter was perplexed by it. 'Great Disputes there are', he said, 'whether *Dominium fundatur in Gratia, vel in providentia*, or in what? Things that are co-ordinate or subordinate are faigned to be contraries, or inconsistent in causality or interest: and in that way men may quarrell as long as they live about any thing where they would have wise men see the weakness.' His own discussion first bases common domi-nion in common grace, and attributes to special grace the power of bestowing dominion 'with an *intention* to use it for some special good'. But, he continues, 'the immediate proper *Foundation of Propriety* [dominion] is the *Law*, or *Gift of God*, that giveth all the Creatures on such and such terms, directing men to the just means of acquiring and possessing'. The re-mainder of his argument proclaims the origin of political ownership to be 'in gracious Providence, common or special, and sometime in judicial Providence'.[1] True casuist that he was, Baxter preferred to discuss particular cases of the conferring and transferring of power, but his general statement on the eve of the Restoration showed that the ideal dominion remained a co-ordinated relationship between grace and nature, but that in practice it was still necessary to emphasize the natural or providential source of a ruler's authority.

Until the Restoration arrived to set all speculations straight and to return grace and providence to their ancient harmony, history may be said to have let Marvell down. History, not intelligence, was at fault for the failure of his next poem, *On the Victory obtained by Blake over the Spaniards*. The poem demonstrates the difference between the fit incarnation of an intention and an unsuccessful one, but by that time Marvell had been deprived of the only intention that was worth com-memorating. No one has missed the way in which Blake is largely a surrogate for Cromwell in the poem, and any slow

[1] *A Holy Commonwealth* (London, 1659), pp. 134–6.

reader perceives the description of the beautiful and temperate Canary Isles (24-38) to be like the numerous accounts by other poets of England's happy Garden State. The descent of the Spanish fleet on Teneriffe and its defeat thus re-enact the defeat of the Armada in 1588—an analogy Marvell made almost explicit (9-10) and which is the more likely in that Milton spelt it out at some length in the Declaration of War against Spain in 1655.[1] The conclusion which these comparisons suggest is summed up in the couplets:

> Your worth to all these Isles, a just right brings,
> The best of Lands should have the best of Kings.
> And these want nothing Heaven can afford,
> Unless it be, the having you their Lord;
> But this great want, will not a long one prove,
> Your Conquering Sword will soon that want remove.
>
> (39-44)

Marvell still had the theme of *The First Anniversary* in mind,[2] but the accidents of history frustrated his hope and his poem. The battle in the bay of Santacruze took place on 22 April 1657, Cromwell rejected the offer of the crown after much hesitation on 8 May, and the news of the victory reached London on 28 May. The poem was written before Blake died on 7 August. As a panegyric, the poem may fairly be said to sustain or incorporate its intention, but there is more in the verse than was needed or can be explained by its eulogistic end. When 'Victorious *Blake*, does from the Bay retire' (162), we may or may not be invited to read here a metaphor for Cromwell's refusal of the kingly bays, but we can reasonably ask why nothing developed from the initial metaphors, and whether the major part of the poem is not as literal as it appears to be, and not to be distinguished in kind from Waller's effusion over the preceding battle, which concludes by proposing for Cromwell 'A royal sceptre, made of Spanish gold'.

[1] Abbott, III, p. 890.
[2] Pierre Legouis, *André Marvell, Poète, Puritain, Patriote* (Paris, 1928), p. 199, caught up with Marvell's desire for Cromwell's kingship at this point.

For once Marvell could not justify the ways of providence to men, and the remaining months of the Interregnum were no less obscure. Good designs were with their author lost, and the approval of Richard's Protectorate that Marvell tacked on to his elegy on Cromwell is a rather pathetic gesture towards constitutional continuity, which implies his distrust of the army factions. 'A Cromwell in an houre a prince will grow' (312), but an hour was about all the time Richard had, and although Marvell appeared officially hopeful about the new regime (and the serenity of the transfer had amazed Europe), he had not forgotten that the 'rugged track' (306) on which Oliver had trodden so masterfully was still ahead, and that only divine guidance would see Richard safely through.

The elegy shows all the force of Marvell's sentiments for Cromwell, and is the fitting conclusion to the eight years of his conviction that Cromwell was a man of God. The sense of personal loss must have been the greater for his knowledge that the two great possibilities for which Cromwell stood, the millennium and constitutional order, were further away than they had ever been. Marvell's recollection of Cromwell's clemency, the love he bore to his family, his compassion and piety, speak much for the qualities of good government that Marvell had perceived under the martial façade, and for the peace that he had imagined would reign at home under Cromwell's rule. The great personal loyalty in Marvell's life that produced in him a more than dutiful submission was above all to Cromwell, and perhaps in a hardly lesser degree to Fairfax: that part of the usual picture of Marvell's loyalism will always be true, and should have been strengthened by the preceding chapters. Personal loyalty, however, was but a fraction of a more encompassing allegiance to destiny and the visible ways of God, because the appointed leader was himself but a detail in the total scheme. Nor did loyalty to Cromwell alter Marvell's feeling about the tragedy that had occurred in 1649. Even in *The First Anniversary* when Cromwell's glorious

sun is rising to begin a day the like of which England had
never seen, the horror of the loss of England's earlier sun is
recalled, and the men who rejoiced in its setting are execrated:

> And Owls and Ravens with their screeching noyse
> Did make the Fun'rals sadder by their Joyes.   (333–4)

By following providence, Marvell did not reject the loyalties of
former years, and there is no trace that he ever reneged on the
feelings he had had for Cromwell. He did his best to keep pace
with history, and who is to say, because the Restoration proved
he had misread the signs, that his devotion to the idea of strong
and responsible government was of no avail? We do not know,
but he may have felt with many thousands of others that the
Restoration when it came was the only possible solution.[1]
Loyalism, by accepting the present and not rejecting the past,
did not meet the future with a categorical opinion that a Stuart
monarchy must be wrong. In fact, it affirmed the need for an
English monarchy, and among the crowds who greeted
Charles so inebriately there must have been many who would
have cheered at Cromwell's coronation. I do not believe that
Marvell celebrated; but in the three years since Cromwell had
refused the crown, the Hand of God had disguised its purposes,
and Marvell's own hand had become uncertain. With the
Restoration, the divine plan was at least clear, and thereafter
Marvell employed his remarkable gifts in the cause of true
religion and true English government.

[1] Unless an historian can uncover much fuller records of Harrington's Rota
which Marvell is reported to have attended, we shall remain in the dark
about Marvell's politics during the last months of the Interregnum. His
support for Richard's Protectorate in September 1658 is the final notice of
them. In February 1659 he stated clearly to Sir George Downing that he
did not believe that 'all pow'r is in the people', and that it had reverted to
the Commons on the death of the Protector (*Letters*, p. 294).

4

'The Country is the King':
'The last Instructions to a Painter'

Preliminary Considerations

Two problems have, or should have, disturbed all students of Marvell who have followed his thought into the Restoration period. The first is the authenticity of various texts, mostly doggerel verses, that were attributed to him by contemporary and notoriously unreliable copyists and subsequently have been admitted to the canon by modern editors; the second is the question of his political sincerity. Professor Legouis in particular has detected traces of what he takes to be opportunism in Marvell's later writings, and has commented that 'too many of his biographers have taken at their face value statements lofty indeed but vague enough when scrutinized closely. They have not allowed for tactics because they have not put these statements side by side with Marvell's other utterances and his actions.'[1] This second problem is implicit at all times, growing acute as the reign progresses and party politics become increasingly a reality, until by the time Marvell wrote *The Growth*

[1] Pierre Legouis, *Andrew Marvell: Poet, Puritan, Patriot* (Oxford, 1965), p. 198; see also pp. 158, 171, 177, 179. Caroline Robbins has also taken the view that Marvell was 'essentially an opportunist' in her unpublished dissertation, 'A Critical Study of the Political Activities of Andrew Marvell', University of London, 1926, p. 303. I am grateful to Miss Robbins for permission to read her study, a microfilm of which is now in the Folger Library. I share her opinion that Marvell was never a republican in any sense, but think more highly of his whiggery than she does. Cf. Lawrence W. Hyman, *Andrew Marvell* (New York, 1964), p. 92: 'It might be simpler and ultimately less confusing if we were to concede that Marvell was an opportunist in the sense that he shifted his political position whenever he felt it necessary to do so to secure the kind of government he wanted.' If this means that he shifted his position in order to keep the balance between King and Parliament, Professor Hyman is correct.

of Popery it becomes crucial for an interpretation of that work and for the assessment of Marvell's final political position on the eve of the Exclusion crisis. Loyalism is consistent with a pre-dominantly critical attitude towards the government such as Marvell maintained, but it is not loyalty to the crown if it expires with the first breath of corruption at home or at the first hint of a French alliance or of catholic tendencies in the King. I shall argue later that, just as Marvell's loyalty to Charles I and the Commonwealth was complete until those dispensa-tions had been dissolved, so are his professions of loyalty to the monarchy at the end of his life to be taken literally. Neither his sincerity, in my opinion, nor his conviction that the King's prerogatives were sacrosanct is to be disbelieved.

The authenticity of texts is pertinent to this matter, because poems like *Upon his Majesties being made Free of the City* (1674), *The Kings Vows* (1670), or *On the Statue Erected by Sir Robert Viner* (1674) may be distinguished from *The Last Instructions* and the prose tracts not only by their wretched quality but by the coarse freedom with which they discuss the person of Charles II. None of Marvell's indisputable writings can be accused of levity on so important a subject, and granted the seriousness with which he approached his political tasks it is highly unlikely that he would have sought to encourage such mischievous attacks on the monarch. That he thought such things one may well imagine, but the high-mindedness of his acknowledged works, his letters, his recorded speeches in Parliament, and indeed his personality as a whole, are inconsistent with the debasement of a low style. At least the burden of proof that he did write most of the verse satires ascribed to him must rest with his editors, and neither Margoliouth nor Professor Lord, who has searched so diligently among the manuscripts, can be said to have been convincing in his attributions.[1] Even were most of the satires less doubtful than

---

[1] Of the fifteen satires that Margoliouth admitted to the canon in 1927, often hesitantly, he disowned Marvell's authorship of *Britannia and Rawleigh* in

they are, however, correct procedure would still permit an emphasis on his most important and authentic work, and about this there is no dispute. If he departed occasionally from his loyalist principles and from the high standards of his literary performance, one could forgive an exasperation with the King which afflicted many of his contemporaries, and which is understandable even at our distance from Restoration intrigue, but one of the most notable consistencies of *The Last In-structions* and the prose is Charles's exemption from personal abuse. The usual fiction that his ministers were wholly re-sponsible for his misrule was essential to Marvell's view of the English constitution and the nature of parliamentary government.

The seven years that intervene between the Restoration and

his second edition. George deF. Lord in his edition of *Poems on Affairs of State, Vol. I: 1660–1678* (New Haven, Conn., 1963) has rejected *The King's Vows, Nostradamus' Prophecy,* and *A Dialogue between the Two Horses. Clarendon's House-Warming* was not attributed to Marvell before Cooke's edition in 1726, and Lord's re-examination of the MSS. has produced no new acceptable evidence, as the mere inclusion of the poem in Bod. MS. Eng. Poet. d. 49 only slightly raises the possibility of its being Marvell's. Although this collection of satires is appended to a 1681 folio of Marvell's poems, and is probably Thompson's second MS. book, several poems in it are definitely not Marvell's and others are highly suspect. A similar inclusion there of *Upon his Majesties being made free of the Citty* does not alter Margoliouth's fact that it is 'not ascribed to Marvell in the MSS. or the first printed edition; the attribu-tion dates from 1697 *State Poems,* but is supported by no evidence'. Again, Margoliouth was doubtful about *The Statue at Charing Cross,* and Lord, who collated twelve texts containing no attributions, allowed it to Marvell solely on the basis of Eng. Poet. d. 49. Out of fifteen texts of *On the Statue Erected by Sir Robert Viner* (Margoliouth's *The Statue in Stocks-Market*) none ascribes the poem to Marvell, and Thompson and the Bodleian MS. remain the sole authorities. The authenticity of *Upon his House* and *Upon his Grand-children* is not discussed by Margoliouth, but the brief verses contain no references to the King in any case. Neither is my argument affected by the two Latin poems, and that leaves only *The Last Instructions, The Loyal Scot,* and *Further Advice to a Painter.* It is not known whether Marvell or another poet added the anti-prelatical sections to *The Loyal Scot. Further Advice,* which does slander the King, is attributed to Marvell in one MS. and in the 1697 *State Poems.* At least six other texts are silently anonymous.

the writing of his longest poem may be said, on the evidence of
that outburst, to have culminated in Marvell's fierce opposition
to Charles II's administration. One would like to know more
about the stages of this development, though they are not hard
to guess, but the reticence of his letters does not reveal much
until the crisis itself is reached. The letter that he and John
Ramsden wrote to the commissioners of the Hull militia on
the day of the Restoration is as silent as it could be about
their emotions on an occasion which was driving most Lon-
doners berserk with enthusiasm, but later letters contain correct
expressions of Marvell's approval for His Majesty's prudence
and moderation, and a prayer, in January 1661, that 'I
beseech God to stay his hand from further severity in that royall
family whereon the nations being and well-fare is so much
concerned'.[1] Nothing can be attributed to these sentiments
except propriety, although the quality assumes a greater im-
portance as it becomes harder to sustain, and it is in other areas
that we find the predictable expression of his private opinions.
Most of Marvell's letters merely record the debates and decisions
of Parliament, on the principle he early enunciated that 'it
becomes no private member, the resolution having passed the
house to interpose further his own judgement in a thing that
can not be remedied',[2] but on the subjects of toleration, stand-
ing armies, and the fear of popery he adopted positions which,
once again, do not distinguish him from thousands of his
countrymen, but which he never bothered to conceal. In 1661
he acted as teller for the yeas when the Commons considered
making law the Declaration of Breda, and he voiced his
approval of Calamy and 'other moderate men'.[3] His anti-
prelatical bias is equally apparent during his early parliamentary
years from his support for a bill to sell some of the bishops'
lands. On money matters it is possible to discern his growing
anxiety, shared by most of the Commons, about the administra-
tion of the King's finances, and already by 1663 he was inform-

[1] *Letters*, p. 17. [2] *Letters*, p. 1. [3] *Letters*, p. 7.

ing Mayor Wilson that 'the House is as zealous as ever for his Majesty but is sensible also of the necessityes of the Country'.[1] The danger of raising taxes, such as a general excise, which could readily be perpetuated, he observed as early as 1660. Finally, a passing remark apropos a suit in the same year could be said to summarize the legal difficulty which had beset all the constitutional experiments of the Interregnum: 'He that hath Law on his side in matters of possession hath much towards the satisfaction of his conscience. And especiallie, where as in this the possession is not peculier to a mans selfe, but the interest of a wholl corporation.'[2]

To impose a progressive scheme on these scattered reflec, tions would be imaginary, but it is quite natural to suppose that Marvell's opposition to the government was intensified by the bitter legislation against the dissenters passed during the Oxford session of Parliament in 1665 (itself a product of fears aroused by fighting a war against a protestant country), and by the obvious defects in the management and extravagance of the war. If Marvell played a more active role in Parliament after his return from Lord Carlisle's embassy, as Miss Robbins has noted,[3] it was because in January 1665 the Dutch war had already begun and lacked only the formal declaration of its commencement, and its course in the next two and a half years aroused public concern and animosity. Marvell had left the country in July 1663 when the temper of the House was more placid and the glow of the Restoration, though impaired, still lingered, and he had returned to a national scene that was intrinsically con, troversial. The ardour of the House for the Dutch war had at first known no bounds,[4] and the moderate successes of the

[1] *Letters*, p. 36.   [2] *Letters*, pp. 10–11.
[3] 'A Critical Study', p. 72.
[4] For pro-Dutch sentiment in the country, however, see *Calendar of State Papers, Domestic, 1665–1666*, pp. xxv–xxix. Charles Wilson, *Profit and Power: A Study of England and the Dutch Wars* (London, 1957), pp. 123–6, discusses nationalistic feelings at the time. For the Parliament in 1663, see D. T. Wit, combe, 'The Cavalier House of Commons: The Session of 1663', *Bull. of*

first year led by November to a flat refusal to accept the French
mediation for peace, and an eagerness on a part of the majority
of members to support a war against France, also, which the
rejection of the 'célèbre ambassade' entailed. Naturally, a
segment of opinion had always opposed these actions, but not
until 1666 did it start to drown the voices of the still belligerent.
The division of the fleet and the loss of the Four Days' Battle,
the huge expenditure on the navy, the aftermath of the plague,
and then, in September, the Great Fire decisively altered the
drift of public opinion. 'Plague, fire and war' were constantly
invoked as the three latest judgments of God on a sinful nation
—with Baxter substituting the ejection of faithful ministers
from their parishes for the scourge of war—and Marvell's own
preoccupation with fires, about which he said he had become
almost superstitious, was no doubt enhanced by his sitting on a
committee to investigate their causes, and bears witness to
jitters in which he was not alone. In November 1666 he wrote
of 'the nations extreme necessity'.[1] The decision not to put out
the fleet in 1667, and to equip small squadrons instead, caused
much shaking of heads even before its disastrous consequences
had occurred, and by February 1667 Marvell was writing, 'We
have some hope of a good alliance or of a Peace God grant it.'[2]
The same letter records without comment the French menace to
the English colonies. Everything, both in national affairs and
in Marvell's correspondence, points to 1667 as another climac-
terical year, such as in the past had led him to put pen to paper.
In April he sent Lord Wharton a bold sermon by Stillingfleet,
who had inveighed in the King's presence against the evil of
mocking sin and scoffing at religion, with the comment that

the Inst. of Hist. Research, XXXII (1959), pp. 181–91. J. R. Jones, 'Court
Dependents in 1664', in the same journal, XXXIV (1961), pp. 81–91, shows
that Marvell, by virtue of his secretaryship to Carlisle's embassy, was listed
as a court dependant, and thus could be expected to vote with Clarendon on
the repeal of the Triennial Act.
[1] Letters, p. 43.
[2] Letters, p. 54.

such polished oratory was 'suited with the delicacy of his audi-
tory rather then the notoriousnesse of the Evill. For certainly the
impiety of men is growne so ranke in this kind and all others,
that if Ministers instead of preaching and arguing could thunder
and lighten, it were all but too litle.'[1] The summer brought the
conclusion of the war and the fall of Clarendon, and the
autumn, sometime before the Chancellor's flight on 29 Novem-
ber, *The Last Instructions to a Painter*. By good fortune a letter
to Mayor Franke has survived, written 3 October, seven days
before Parliament met to impeach Clarendon and to investigate
the misconduct of the war, which reveals Marvell's motives in
writing the poem. He needs directions, he says, for his future
business, and adds:

I shall need to say one thing onely, and scarse that, for I am sure your own
observation must have prevented me: that there never appeared a fairer
season for men to obtain what their own hearts could wish either as to
redresse of any former grievances or the constituting of good order and
justice for the future. And therefore we ought neither to be wanting to
God in praising him for his good disposall of all things to this purpose;
nor to the King in celebrating his prudence and constancy by which
these things are so happily brought about; nor to our selves in taking hold
of the opportunity.[2]

The tone is exactly right, and the final clause could even have
sprung from the complacency of knowing that he had already
taken the opportunity providence offered. The time had come
again to remove his corslet from the wall, and he chose the
sharpest weapons he could find. The passage is of particular
interest because it defines the rhetorical intention of a poem
which took a satirical, and hence largely abusive, form. Yet in
fact the intensity of the letter, the gratitude to God and the King,
as well as the urgency which Marvell feels the moment demands,
are contradicted by nothing in the poem, the total seriousness of

[1] *Letters*, pp. 296–7. Stillingfleet's sermon is in his *Works* (London, 1710),
I, pp. 17–30.
[2] *Letters*, p. 56.

which becomes, with gradual acquaintance and comparison, one of its most distinctive features.

The point requires some illustration because *The Last Instructions* has received the worst Press and the least notice of any of Marvell's important productions,[1] and this illustration is provided by the literary context of the poem, which in any case has to be considered. *The Last Instructions* belongs to a series of Advice-to-a-Painter poems which began with Waller's *Instructions* in 1665 and which by the autumn of 1667 had produced five satirical imitations: the *Second*, *Third*, *Fourth* and *Fifth Advices*, and *The Last Instructions*. Waller's poem is a fair example of the panegyric art of amplification and hyperbole, and celebrates not only the leadership of the Duke of York at the battle of Lowestoft and the courage of his commanders, but the English sovereignty of the sea after the first campaign of the war. In the envoi to the King, his navy is described as the emblem of his power, with which he will 'secure our peace, / The nation's glory, and our trade's increase'.[2] The *Second Advice...for drawing the History of our naval Business* ridicules some of the same commanders, including the Duke, and casts aspersions on the management of the fleet at home—William Coventry's venality, Clarendon's incompetence, and so on. The *Third Advice* (dated in one manuscript 1 October 1666) is a continuation of the story, but is roughly divided into two parts, the first largely an account of the Four Days' Battle which tends to confirm Pepys's opinion of the English Admiral, Albemarle, as a blockhead, and the

---

[1] Exceptions must be made of Ephim G. Fogel, 'Salmons in Both, or Some Caveats for Canonical Scholars', *Bull. N.Y. Public Library*, LXIII (1959), p. 301, and Earl Miner, 'The "Poetic Picture, Painted Poetry" of *The Last Instructions to a Painter*', *MP*, LXIII (1966), pp. 288–94.

[2] The quotations from all the *Advices*, except Marvell's, and from *Divination* quoted below, are taken from Professor Lord's edition of *Poems on Affairs of State*, already cited. Mary Tom Osborne's *Advice-to-a-Painter Poems, 1633–1856* (Austin, Texas, 1949) is an annotated finding-list of the *genre* that is very useful.

second a long monologue by his duchess at home which serves as an opportunity to catalogue the maladministration that has made her George's task impossible at sea. The constructive suggestion both poems have to make about English policy is that the war be abandoned immediately. The *Second Advice* blames Clarendon, unjustly, for setting the sea on fire and concludes: 'Let justice only draw and battle cease; / Kings are in war but cards: they're gods in peace'; and the third is more emphatic, for Waller's emblematic navy is here interpreted in the envoi as the wooden horse that will betray the English Troy. 'Here needs no sword, no fleet, no foreign foe: / Only let vice be damn'd and justice flow.'

Both satirical poems have the merit of being occasionally amusing, and they must have succeeded in annoying and embarrassing their victims, but the criticism of the *Second Advice* which Christopher Wase made in his poem entitled *Divination* (1666), and which applies equally well to the third, is as cogent now as it was then. His implied charge of sedition may be ignored, but when he writes of 'Slanders at random flying', or asks 'What cares Detraction, planted in the dark... Whether it true or seeming crimes object?' (151–5) he has made a legitimate point. All the poems have to say is, 'Behold your iniquity and stop the war', and Wase was correct in assuming that such criticism could not but be frivolous, because the call for peace did not by itself constitute a respon-sible national policy.

> Since our discovering Monarch, whom he styles
> Imperial Prince, King of the Seas and Isles,
> Led by his counsel, he would but prefer
> In his own island to be prisoner.
> Great politician! Should our fleet at ease
> Ride in vain triumph o'er the Narrow Seas,
> Waiting our baffled carracks with half freight
> Return'd from India, to convoy in state?
> Or while their busses on our rifled shore

> Be fully fraught, look on, and keep the door?
> Such gilded pleasure-boats with pasteboard guns
> Neptune ne'er saw, nor of so many tons.   (249–60)

Wase's accusations are substantiated in particular by the *Third Advice*, where the point of view is so badly handled that for half the poem it remains problematical. The transparent cause of the uncertainty is the figure of the 'monkey Duchess' who is presented as so lewd and ignorant a woman that her hostile narrative about the government might appear to be discredited before it began. Only two hints, one at her introduction and another in the envoi, convey the fact that this 'Presbyterian sibyl' is to be heard as another Cassandra, and hence the reader's disbelief is part of the intended effect. The device has literary merit as an idea, and justifies the coarseness of the duchess's language, but at the same time the force of her criticism is dissipated by its origin in an irresponsible, garrulous, and selfish *persona*. The effect of public-spirited indignation, or of telling but unwitting satire by a truthful *ingénue* cannot, and could not have been, attained by this method. The irrelevance of many of her bitter couplets, as for example her complaint that the famous division of the fleet was engineered by Arlington's desire to 'break' her husband, also detracts from the credibility of her denunciation. To a lesser extent, the same fault may be found with the *Second Advice*, where the first evidence of the author's opposition to the war is put into the mouth of a cowardly gallant who dreads the approaching conflict. The vituperation of *The Last Instructions*, on the contrary, gains in power from being the product of a less ambiguous technique, and neither does the poem fall under Wase's stricture of advocating nothing better than an idle navy and peace at any price. If Marvell was the author of the *Second* and *Third Advices*, and Professor Lord has argued that he was,[1] then not

---

[1] 'The Case for Internal Evidence (4): Two New Poems by Marvell?' and 'Comments on the Canonical Caveat', *Bull. N.Y. Public Library*, LXII (1958), pp. 551–70, and LXIII (1959). Professor Lord's articles and Professor

only was his rhetoric much inferior to what it became a year later but he was guilty of an appalling error in policy. It was precisely the belief of government and people alike that the Dutch war could not continue, coupled with the lack of funds, that led to the failure to put out the fleet in 1667 and the consequent invasion of the Thames by the Dutch warships. Wase's apprehension of the dangerous unpreparedness implied in the proposals of the two *Advices* was perfectly justified. *The Last Instructions* is not a peace poem at all, as may be shown, and if a year had not passed since the writing of the two *Advices*—a year in which any putative author might have seen his error and changed his mind—one could assert categorically that all three of them could not have been the work of the same man. The treaty when it came caused widespread dissatisfaction, and the flippancy of the two *Advices* was revealed the following year by the historical result of implementing their craven demands for a cessation of the war. Nowhere had they insisted that only an honourable peace was to be sought, and the scurrility of their attacks on individuals is not exonerated, as it is in *The Last Instructions*, by a mature appraisal of the state of Europe and an awareness that peace was not a panacea.

Other reasons should emerge for considering *The Last Instructions* to be different in kind from its predecessors, but one other preliminary question about their relationship remains. The opening lines of *The Last Instructions*, 'After two sittings, now our *Lady State*, / To end her Picture, does the third time wait', apparently refer to two earlier poems, and the assumption seems generally to have been made that Marvell recalled the *Second* and *Third Advices*. He certainly had not forgotten them, and when he calls on his painter to draw Anne Hyde 'again' he can have been thinking only of these poems or of Waller's *Instructions*, as the duchess is absent from the *Fourth* and *Fifth Advices*. Similarly, there are a sufficient number of verbal

Fogel's replies have been republished in a collection of essays, *Evidence for Authorship*, ed. David Erdman and E. G. Fogel.

echoes, or near echoes, no one of which alone amounts to much, to make it at least probable that he had read both poems care-fully. However, the *Fourth* and *Fifth Advices*, as Margoliouth observed, are exactly contemporary with *The Last Instructions* and cover the same ground. They form virtually one poem cut in half, which commences with the events in the House of Commons during the fall and winter session of 1666–67 and ends with the government's trepidation during August and September 1667 as it awaited the reassembly of Parliament on 10 October. Margoliouth correctly concluded that the parallel nature of *The Last Instructions* and the two later *Advices* is evidence that Marvell was only responsible for the longest of them, but it is also the best argument for thinking that the 'two sittings' of the one painting which *The Last Instructions* is to complete must refer to the *Fourth* and *Fifth Advices*. They are exclusively about 'Lady State', the government, and the House of Commons, whereas the *Second* and *Third Advices* were mostly concerned with naval affairs and only tangentially discussed more fundamental matters. Moreover, the *Fourth Advice*, with its comments on the Irish cattle bill, the delayed treaty, the 'base submissions to our arming foe', England's reliance on the good nature of her enemies, etc., bears so close a relation to *The Last Instructions* that one author must surely have had the other in mind. To copy or rework the much fuller treatment afforded the same events in *The Last Instructions* would have been redundant, and common sense suggests that, in keeping with his intention to finish a portrait already begun, Marvell decided to tell the same story and tell it right.[1] The *Fourth* and

[1] Professor Lord believes that a passage in *The Fifth Advice*, lines 119–30, refers to Clarendon's flight in November and hence he dates the composition of the poem after *The Last Instructions*. It certainly refers to someone's escape from the wrath of Parliament, but lines 78–80 make it clear that the author is going to indulge in a 'prophetic touch'. What follows are various descriptions of terror as the government awaits the reconvening of Parliament in October, and the flight is imagined as one of the consequences of the general fear. Moreover, Clarendon's flight put him in the wrong and it would not

Fifth Advices, together with the *Second* and *Third*, were published in 1667, although unfortunately in what month is not known, so there is the further possibility that *The Last Instructions* is Marvell's response to that volume, but with particular reference to the genuinely state poems it contained. The chief significance of maintaining the lastness of *The Last Instructions* is that in it Marvell's loyalist and constructive principles are better revealed. The great difference between *The Last Instructions* and the *Fourth* and *Fifth Advices* is that the one is respectful to the King and the others are extremely rude. They, too, may be condemned as splenetic vapourings that contribute nothing to sound policy. Marvell, by retouching them, has at the same time rejected the spirit in which they were written and their manifest hostility to the crown; his polemics are thus implicitly literary as usual, as well as political, and his poem would seem to be yet another example of his desire to excel in each of the *genres* he employed.[1]

If one asks, however, what exactly were the features of the Advice-to-a-Painter *genre*—an important question if the discursive structure of the poems is to be understood—an answer is not obvious. The accepted antecedents of the *genre* in the Anacreontic odes and in the handful of English poems before Waller's *Instructions* are not very helpful, because they are for the most part lyric, sentimental, and brief. Waller's poem had an immediate forebear in Busanello's panegyric, 'Il conflitto navale', but the author of the *Second Advice* was in effect creating a new sub-*genre* of the satiric epistle, whose form he imitated. That he may have been thinking of Horace is suggested by the motto that appeared on the title-page of an edition of the *Second* and *Third Advices* in 1667: '*Pictoribus atque Poetis*, / Quidlibet Audendi semper fuit potestas. / Humano Capiti

have been possible to say afterwards, 'But if the man prove true,/Let him, with Pharaoh's butler, have his due.' M. T. Osborne also dates the poem before the meeting of Parliament.

[1] All readers of Marvell must have sensed his literary competitiveness. It is clearly advanced in Joseph Summers's introduction to Marvell's poems in the Laurel paperback selection.

cervicem pictor equinam, / Jungere si velit.'[1] This composite
quotation from the exordium of *Ars Poetica* invokes Horace's
qualified agreement with the dictum that painters and poets are
permitted to dare anything, and hence it announces the courage
of the satirical enterprise. It may also hint at the novelty of
the performance, but above all it indicates that the poems are to
be grotesques, 'monsters' as the commentators called them,
which Horace declared nobody could refrain from laughing at.
Ben Jonson's version of the opening lines is as follows:

> If to a Womans head a Painter would
> Set a Horse-neck, and divers feathers fold
> On every limbe, ta'en from a severall creature,
> Presenting upwards, a faire female feature,
> Which in some swarthie fish uncomely ends:
> Admitted to the sight, although his friends,
> Could you containe your laughter?[2]

Horace, of course, mentioned this and other examples of shoddy
workmanship in order to make his own plea for decorum, but
the motto advertises the indecorousness of the poems and implies
that the roughness and lack of uniformity are part of their comic
intention. The author would have had the excuse that the
characters his painter was portraying were themselves grotesque
and that a realistic art could have drawn them in no other way.
These deductions must remain speculative, because no certain
signs of Horace occur in the earlier *Advices* themselves, and one
of the manuscripts of the *Second Advice* has an epigraph from
Persius. The motto from Horace could well have been an
afterthought, the idea of writing a satirical version of Waller's
panegyric could have been carried out spontaneously, and
epistolary freedom or the satires of Juvenal and Persius would
have offered at least a loose foundation for a digressive form.

  Marvell, however, took the hint or decided independently

---

[1] *Poems on Affairs of State*, ed. Lord, I, p. 447.
[2] *Works*, ed. C. H. Herford and P. Simpson (Oxford, 1925–52), VIII, p. 305.
Subsequent quotations from *Ars Poetica* are also from Jonson's translation.

that the analogy between poetry and painting in Horace gave him a classical anchor for his *Instructions*. His contemptuous enquiries of his painter, 'Canst thou paint without Colours? ...Canst thou dawb a Sign-post, and that ill?...Or hast thou mark't how antique Masters limn / The Aly roof, with snuff of Candle dimm' (5–10), recall Horace's

> And, Painter, hap'ly, thou
> Know'st only well to paint a Cipresse tree.
> What's this? if he whose money hireth thee
> To paint him, hath by swimming, hopeless, scap'd,
> The whole fleet wreck'd?   (24–8)

The funereal cypress became a standard example for what Cruquius called 'irrisio pictoris inepti';[1] Marvell's questions imply a no higher view of his artist's qualifications, nor perhaps of the authors who had instructed him before; and Oldham was later to follow him in substituting a signpost for the cypress tree in his modernized translation of *Ars Poetica*: 'A common Dawber may perhaps have skill / To paint a Tavern Sign or Landskip well...'[2] Horace's first imperative command in *Ars Poetica* is, 'Take, therefore, you that write, still, matter fit / Unto your strength and long examine it,' and it is Marvell's likewise: 'But er'e thou fal'st to work, first *Painter* see / It be'nt too slight grown, or too hard for thee' (3–4). The suggestion is clear that it would be too hard if the painter's crimes were not matched by his sitters'; even Horace's 'plumas' is repeated in the advice to 'draw our Luxury in Plumes'. What *The Last Instructions* will add to the earlier admonitions, and what will differentiate the finished painting from the previously bungled sittings, is the real anger which may give the portrait distinction:

> The Painter so, long having vext his cloth,
> Of his Hound's Mouth to feign the raging froth,
> His desperate Pencil at the work did dart,

[1] Q. *Horatius Flaccus: cum commentariis...Iacobi Cruquii Messenii* (Lugduni Batavorum, 1597), p. 622.
[2] John Oldham, *Works* (London, 1686), 2nd pagination, p. 3.

His Anger reacht that rage which past his Art;
Chance finisht that which Art could but begin,
And he sat smiling how his Dog did grinn.
So may'st thou perfect, by a lucky blow,
What all thy softest touches cannot do.   (21-8)

By linking his poem to the *Ars Poetica*, Marvell obtained for himself a greater freedom for the disposition of his materials than would have been permissible in any other *genre*. The epistle was the least schematized of poems and had always maintained the closest connections with satire, because both shared what Northrop Frye has termed the 'deliberate rambling digressiveness which ...is endemic in the narrative technique of satire'.[1] The satiric mixture included dialogue, character studies, anecdotes, and invective, and the epistle was regarded as primarily satiric or elegiac. (The elegy finds its place in *The Last Instructions* in the description of the death of Douglas, and the informality of so abrupt a change of pitch need have bothered no one.) Dryden specifically remembered the *Ars Poetica* when defending one of his diffuse dedications: 'I ... write in a loose Epistolary way, somewhat tending to that Subject after the Example of Horace, in his [*Epistle to Augustus* and *Ars Poetica*]. In both of which he observes no Method that I can trace, whatever *Scaliger* the Father or *Heinsius* may have seen, or rather think they have seen. I have taken up, laid down and resum'd as often as I pleas'd the same Subject: and this loose proceeding I shall use thro' all this Prefatory Dedication.' Joseph Trapp later remarked also that 'some of Horace's [poems] which are call'd Satires are as truly Epistles; so many of his Epistles might as well be call'd Satires'.[2]

As a letter written to a presumptive artist, the *Ars Poetica* was a natural choice for a classical precedent, but Horace's tone to the Pisos, though occasionally satirical, was too mild and

[1] *Anatomy of Criticism* (Princeton, N.J., 1957), p. 234.
[2] These quotations are taken from Jay A. Levine, 'The Status of the Verse Epistle before Pope', *SP*, LIX (1962), pp. 662, 660, to which article this paragraph is indebted.

reasonable for the purpose in hand, which deserved the wrath of Juvenal. One may readily admit a general prescription from Juvenal for Marvell's style, but the most specific reference in *The Last Instructions* to another satire is to Chaucer's *Nun's Priest's Tale*, and it seems likely that Marvell realized that the series of portraits and interspersed narratives could derive another and more native dimension from Chaucerian allusion and suggestion. Critics of the poem have not overlooked the striking resemblance to Chaucer in the character of the Speaker of the House of Commons (lines 863–84) which concludes with the reference to 'Canticleer' and 'Partelott'. The analogy between Turner and the rooster was not casual, however, for it had been implied in line 837 when 'Turner gay up to his Pearch does march', and hence it is impossible not to associate the King's dream of the distressed maiden which follows the Speaker's portrait with a similar admonitory vision that plays so important a part in *The Nun's Priest's Tale*. If the Chaucerian background is unmistakable here, is it not also visible in the account of Sir Thomas Daniel?

> Paint him of Person tall, and big of bone,
> Large Limbs, like Ox, not to be kill'd but shown.
> Scarce can burnt Iv'ry feign an Hair so black,
> Or Face so red thine Oker and thy Lack.
> Mix a vain Terrour in his Martial look,
> And all those lines by which men are mistook. (633–8)

Furthermore, after the Horatian exordium, *The Last Instructions* fires its first salvo at Lord St Albans, formerly Henry Jermyn, who, as 'The new *Courts* pattern, Stallion of the old', is everything that Chaucer's knight was not. There follow pictures of the 'philosopher' duchess, and then Lady Castlemaine, who like the Wife of Bath had fallen in love with a pair of legs:

> She through her Lacquies Drawers as he ran,
> Discern'd Love's Cause, and a new Flame began.
> Her wonted joys thenceforth and *Court* she shuns,
> And still within her mind the Footman runs:

His brazen Calves, his brawny Thighs, (the Face
She slights) his Feet shapt for a smoother race.   (81-6)

A few other couplets and images can be traced to Chaucer, like
the Chancellor's 'minion Imps' (495) that are clustered like
the friars under the devil's tail in the Summoner's prologue, but
I would also suggest that the long account of the battle over the
general excise ('this new Whore of State'), with its roll-call
of the troops and the names of their captains, is a satiric inver-
sion of the great tournament in the *Knight's Tale*. Some overt
Chaucerian reflection in *The Last Instructions* cannot be denied,
and the plausibility of suspecting it everywhere is enhanced by
Chaucer's long reputation in England as a satirist, which Dryden
only confirmed in his preface to the *Fables*, and by 'The
Argument to the Prologues' that Thomas Speght supplied in
his editions:

The Authour in these Prologues to his Canterburie Tales, dooth describe
the reporters thereof for two causes: first, that the Reader seeing the
qualitie of the person, may judge of his speech accordingly: wherein
Chaucer hath most excellently kept that *decorum*, which Horace requireth
in that behalfe. Secondly to shew, how that even in our language, that
may bee perfourmed for descriptions, which the Greeke and Latine Poets
in their tongues have done at large. And surely this Poet in the judgement
of the best learned, is not inferiour to any of them in his descriptions,
whether they be of persons, times, or places. Under the Pilgrimes, being a
certaine number, and all of differing trades, he comprehendeth all the
people of the land, and the nature and disposition of them in those dayes;
namely, given to devotion rather of custome than of zeale. In the Tales is
shewed the state of the Church, the Court, and Countrey; with such Art
and cunning, that although none could denie himselfe to be touched,
yet none durst complaine that he was wronged. For the man being of
greater learning than the most, and backed by the best in the land, was
rather admired and feared, than any way disgraced. Who so shall read
these his workes without prejudice, shall find that hee was a man of
rare conceit and of great reading.[1]

The court and country were to be the theme of Marvell's poem,
and the excellence of Chaucer's descriptions, in spite of his

[1] 'The Argument to the Prologues' in *Workes* (London, 1602), sig. A. ii^r.

'low and open' style—that lewdness which the seventeenth century always remembered—provided a literary respectability for the roughness of *The Last Instructions*. Chaucer was 'our ancient Poet', inferior to none in the world, and if his outspokenness and pictorial power could be combined with the Horatian authority for a discursive epistle, Marvell was probably confident that he could defend the structure and the tone of his work against all comers.

The Politics

Politically, *The Last Instructions* makes the one explicit appeal to the King to choose his ministers from the country party, and to distrust the courtiers on whom hitherto he had relied. In an obvious way, the character sketches of the court officers, the account of their venal activities in the Commons, their cowardice in the face of the enemy, and their treachery, fear, and neglect of business culminate in the King's vision and his banishment of the Lord Chancellor, and justify the urgency of Marvell's request for a drastic change in national leadership. But by this abstract *The Last Instructions* is exclusively a partisan poem about domestic politics that differs from the other *Advices* in comprehensiveness and vehemence, but is as indifferent as they are to foreign affairs and as unaware of the crucial decisions ahead which would determine England's position among her neighbours. Such is not the case, and the main significance of the poem in the history of Marvell's political career is that it shows he had fully grasped the danger of French ambitions in Europe several months before his judgment was confirmed by the Triple Alliance—that short-lived treaty which was to remain a landmark to Marvell, to Sir William Temple (whose triumph it was), to Lord Halifax the trimmer, and to a host of loyal parliamentarians who were later to lament the growth of popery and arbitrary government.

The very first vignette of the poem is of the Earl of St Albans, a new figure in the *Advices*, whose 'Age, allaying now that

youthful heat, / Fits him in *France* to play at Cards and treat'
(37-8). They are ominous words, for they introduce a recurrent
motif which requires of a modern reader some acquaintance with
the tangled diplomacy of the period, and a recognition that the
accurate accounts of royal policy in the histories are based
mostly on papers and correspondence to which Marvell and his
public had no access. A long-continued policy could not be
disguised, and events had a habit during the later years of
Charles's reign of realizing people's worst fears, but the
impression one gets of 1667, and in particular of the diplomacy
before and after the treaty of Breda in July, is that the King was
in a real dilemma from which even his unscrupulous con-
science could not deliver him. The country needed peace, and
he needed money; if his enemies would not treat with him
separately, he would be forced to try and make private bargains
under the table; and, after the war, he knew that if he did not
make an immediate new alliance with either France or Holland
they might reunite again in a treaty of their own which
would cut him out of commercial and military booty. The
situation was fluid throughout the year, and *The Last In-
structions*, by putting the worst, and as it happens a remarkably
accurate, interpretation upon the French strands of Charles's
negotiations, sought at least to direct attention to the danger to
be expected from that quarter.

St Albans was the most gallicized member of the court, the
King himself distrusting him for being more Frenchman than
Englishman, and he was, in Firth's opinion, one of the most
effective advisers responsible for the eventual subservience of
England to France.[1] On this occasion, he had left for Paris at
the end of January 1667 with instructions in Clarendon's
handwriting—so as to bypass Lord Arlington—and he was
still corresponding with the Chancellor at the end of April.[2]

---

[1] *Dictionary of National Biography*, s.v. Henry Jermyn. Also *The Life of Edward
Earl of Clarendon...A Continuation of the Same* (Oxford, 1759), III, p. 760.

[2] T. H. Lister, *Life and Administration of Edward, First Earl of Clarendon* (London,
1838), III, pp. 443-4, 450-64.

The upshot of his secret talks was a written agreement between
the two Kings that obliged Charles to refrain from making any
alliances against Louis XIV's wishes for the space of one
year; in other words, Louis had *carte blanche* to begin his
invasion of Flanders without interference from England. The
fact, if not the evidence, of this agreement was embodied in a
rumour at the time that St Albans had full power to conclude
a treaty which would have left England and Holland at one
another's throats and powerless to resist France.[1] From the
perspective of six months later, Marvell knew that St Albans'
mission had been connected with the treaty of Breda and with
the arrangements which had been made for French mediation
between England and Holland, and his first charge was that
the unofficial nature of the embassy had been a trick to dupe
Parliament into giving money for a more prolonged war when
it could be argued that no treaty was in the offing. It was an old
complaint that the court intended to end the war as soon as it
had received supply, and Charles had vigorously denied it
from the first.[2] Marvell's second accusation was more serious
and more provable, because it rested solely on the outcome of
events:

> Nor fears he *the most Christian* should trepan
> Two Saints at once, St. *German*, St. *Alban*.
> But thought the Golden Age was now restor'd,
> When Men and Women took each others Word.   (45–8)

The reference is to the specific offence of bad faith that France
had shown in her rôle as mediator. By bringing the combatants
together, and by applying pressure at the critical moment, the
mediator could influence, and even dictate, the terms of a
treaty, but he was also expected to guarantee the peace and to
ensure that both sides had fair play. The 'profound insincerity'
of Louis XIV, as Feiling shows, was transparent to all

---

[1] Keith Feiling, *British Foreign Policy, 1660–1672* (London, 1930), pp. 215–16.
Hereafter cited as Feiling, but not all borrowings are acknowledged.
[2] William Cobbett, *Parliamentary History of England*, IV, p. 297 (24 Nov.
1664). Feiling, p. 210, accepts the justice of the accusation.

informed observers of the negotiations at Breda, and was broad-
cast to everyone a month later when the Dutch invaded the
Thames and Sir Alan Brodrick voiced the common opinion
that England 'had trusted the promises of a faithless prince, and
the credulity of my Lord St. Albans'.[1] Unnecessary proof of
Louis's connivance at the Dutch raid was supplied by some
intercepted dispatches. Marvell's rather long account later in
the poem of the express that was sent to St Albans on 15 June
with appeals for peace, and the dusty answer it received, con-
firms the importance that he attached to the revelation of
French perfidy:

> St. *Albans* writ to that he may bewail
> To Master *Lewis*, and tell Coward tale,
> How yet the *Hollanders* do make a noise,
> Threaten to beat us, and are naughty Boys.
> Now *Doleman*'s disobedient, and they still
> Uncivil: His unkindness would us kill.
> Tell him our Ships unrigg'd, our Forts unman'd,
> Our Money spent; else 'twere at his command.
> Summon him therefore of his Word, and prove
> To move him out of Pity, if not Love.
> Pray him to make *De-Witte*, and *Ruyter* cease,
> And whip the *Dutch*, unless they'l hold their peace.
> But *Lewis* was of Memory but dull,
> And to St. *Albans* too undutiful;
> Nor Word, nor near Relation did revere;
> But ask'd him bluntly for his *Character*.
> The gravell'd *Count* did with the Answer faint:
> (His *Character* was that which thou didst paint)
> And so enforc'd, like Enemy or Spy,
> Trusses his baggage, and the Camp does fly.
> Yet *Lewis* writes, and lest our Hearts should break,
> *Consoles* us morally out of *Seneque*.   (427–48)

---

[1] Feiling, p. 222. He also notes, p. 149, that if France wished to make the peace,
or to share in the making of it, she was bound to declare war on England
when she did.

As the message to St Albans is the first reaction to the approach of the Dutch,[1] the passage implies the truth that France had the making of peace in her hands, where indeed Louis had been at great pains to keep it. The Earl's lack of an official 'character' now backfires, and all Louis's promises are found wanting. Only after the failure in Paris are 'Two letters next unto *Breda...* sent' (449), containing a shameful mixture of irrelevant homiletics and complete submission to the Dutch terms (449–62).[2]

The emphasis on France is only comprehensible if we remember that her power was out of all proportion to her participation in the war. Louis had been reluctant to enter it, and, until the spring of 1667, his desire to reach an early settlement had been quite genuine, although he had worked to discountenance the separate treaties that England might have made with other European powers on the basis of a mutual fear of the French armies. His navy had barely participated in the fighting, much to the Dutch resentment, and in other ways he had purposefully refused to exacerbate his quarrel with England. When Charles wanted peace he had no option but to apply to France and accept the French price, and, as Ranke pointed out, 'this is the advantage of an overpowering might, which strives after a distinct aim, that everything which needs its co-operation must be serviceable to it'.[3] Hence all the references to treating in *The Last Instructions* expose the primacy of England's relations with France. On the disappointment of the courtiers

[1] As Marvell observes, the government mistook 'Candy' for the Isle of Crete. 'Candia' was in fact in the news at this time. See *The London Gazette*, 10–13 June 1667, no. 164.

[2] Three people are involved in the letters, not two, as Margoliouth assumed. '*Coventry the Cavalier*' (458) is Sir John Coventry, nephew of 'Harry' Coventry the ambassador. Sir John 'had all along attended the Ambassy, and omitted no expence to add to the Grandeur and honour of the Ambassy, being noble in Equipage, suitable to his quality', *A Narrative, or Journal of the Proceedings of...Lord Holles, and the Lord Coventry...at Breda* (London 1667), p. 20.

[3] Leopold von Ranke, *A History of England* (Oxford, 1875), III, p. 441. Hereafter cited as Ranke.

at the loss of the excise battle, it is St Albans who 'straight is sent to, to forbear, / Lest the sure Peace, forsooth, too soon appear' (311–12), and on Clarendon's joy at the prorogation of Parliament in February, it is to St Albans that he sends his final instructions:

> France had St. Albans promis'd (so they sing)
> St. Albans promis'd him, and he the King.
> The Count forthwith is order'd all to close,
> To play for Flanders, and the stake to lose.
> While Chain'd together two Ambassadors
> Like Slaves, shall beg for Peace at Hollands doors. (365–70)

The servility to the Dutch is here concurrent with, but again secondary to, the Earl's negotiations, and these lines show also that by the autumn Marvell had correctly interpreted St Albans' January instructions as involving the sacrifice of Flanders, a large part of which had succumbed to Louis's army during the summer. Marvell clarified his attitude in a kind of afterthought to his description of the Skimmington ride (373–96), at which the courtiers had hoped to release their 'wanton fears'. The riding of the henpecked husband and the masculine wife was a form of ridicule that Marvell found analogous to his own and his painter's, but he concluded, 'So Holland with us had the Mast'ry try'd, / And our next neigh-bours France and Flanders ride.' The Dutch war had cost England the sovereignty of the sea which rightfully belonged to her, but nevertheless England and Holland, by virtue of their ancient relationship, were man and wife, not natural enemies, and they had allowed their neighbours to make fools of them. Sir William Temple, at precisely the time the ride could be presumed to have taken place, wrote a letter to Lord Holles at Breda which perfectly describes the sense of Marvell's lines. France 'has had the skill or good luck de nous endormir, both us and Holland, in this great conjuncture, and by assuring us of peace upon good terms with the Dutch, and at the same time the Dutch of never according with us, nor treating with Spain to their [the Hollanders'] prejudice, will amuse us both in a slow treaty, till they have made so great an impression in these countries, as will give neither of us the liberty to take those measures in this affair to which either of our interests might lead us, and perhaps find means to divert the treaty at last from coming to any issue'.[1] In this connection, and recollecting the much earlier abuse of Marvell's *Character of Holland*, it is remarkable how tenderly the Dutch are treated throughout *The Last Instructions*. No hint of criticism is uttered of their exploit on the Thames, and Marvell would appear to have been of Temple's opinion that De Witt was right to pursue the war until the ratification of the treaty, as in that way it would end for him with more honour abroad and heart at home.[2] De Witt had consistently refused to agree to an armistice, so was well within his rights in attacking, and the brickbats in the poem are aimed only at the futility of the English naval preparations and the cowardice of the defenders. 'The Gods themselves do help the provident' (544), and Ruyter's dignified advance up the river is recounted in terms which would have been more fitting for a panegyric on an English victory. Nothing is said to detract from '*Ruyter*'s Triumph', unless his want of an active enemy makes the victory too facile.[3]

England's predicament is finally personified in the 'sudden Shape with Virgins Face' (891) which appears to Charles as he is lying wakefully in bed musing on 'th' uneasie Throne'. Naked, speechless, veiled, her hands bound with her own tresses, the maiden's 'Beauty greater seem'd by her distress', and

---

[1] 29 May 1667. Quoted in Thomas Peregrine Courtenay, *Memoirs of the Life, Work, and Correspondence of Sir William Temple* (London, 1836), I, p. 107. Courtenay's chapter on this period, pp. 98–142, is admirable, and Marvell's view was very close to Temple's.

[2] *Letters Written by Sir W. Temple, Bart. and Other Ministers of State* (London, 1700), I, p. 110.

[3] The most comprehensive recent account of the Dutch exploit is Alvin D. Coox, 'The Dutch Invasion of England: 1667', *Military Affairs*, XIII (1949), pp. 223–33.

Charles 'Divin'd 'twas *England* or the *Peace*'. Helplessness and disgrace are true both of England herself and of the terms which she has been forced to accept in the treaty, and Charles not unnaturally shrinks from 'her touch so cold'. The vision fails to spur him to action, and his next warning comes as an 'unusual noise' of military tumult; three times he starts up but three times returns to bed. Unlike Samuel, who on the fourth occasion got the message, Charles ignores the threatening advice he has been offered:

> Thrice did he rise, thrice the vain Tumult fled,
> But again thunders when he lyes in Bed;
> His mind secure does the known stroke repeat,
> And finds the Drums *Lewis*'s March did beat.   (911–14)

The attack on Flanders, the fanfare of Louis on the march, should have been sufficient to arouse his military and defensive instincts, but familiarity with French designs has bred a false 'security'. Only on the apocalyptic appearance of his murdered father and grandfather ('Shake then the room, and all his Curtains tear') does he rise and 'straight on *Hyde*'s Disgrace resolves'. English weakness, French power, Clarendon's dismissal: the sequence had a logic in 1667, because the Chancellor had been the strongest advocate of the *entente* with France, and St Albans was known to be his tool. He had steadily rejected during the past year other possible solutions to England's misery in favour of a 'French' peace, and had even patched up his old quarrel with Henrietta Maria. He admitted in his *Life* that France had been eager to make a separate treaty with England after the negotiations at Breda were concluded, and the Dutch were persuaded into the Triple Alliance a few months later largely out of fear of an Anglo-French agreement. The agreement had in fact been initiated by the letters St Albans had exchanged in Paris, and the spectre of decided Anglo-French co-operation had influenced most of the statesmen who were concerned for the balance of power in Europe. An intercepted letter during the prorogation had seemed to confirm this possibility, and Parliament, being helpless to oppose it, was much irritated.[1] Clarendon, though not responsible for promoting the Dutch war, could now justly be blamed for steering the ship of state by a southern wind—to use a metaphor from the *Fifth Advice*. Marvell offered numerous causes for detesting Clarendon, but Charles's dismissal of him occurs because he has been reminded of the shameful peace and France's sinister ambitions. The narrative then concludes with the hopeful aspirations of Lady Castlemaine, Arlington, and William Coventry to succeed to greater positions in the King's counsels. Their personal and political motives for wishing the Chancellor away, however, including a desire to avoid impeachment themselves, are irrelevant to the issues that made Clarendon's removal imperative, and Marvell quickly rebukes their pretensions.

Most of the evidence for thinking that the foreign policy of *The Last Instructions* would have been well understood by its first readers comes from the letters and memoirs of the period and, at second hand, from the historians who are familiar with the diplomatic papers, in which opinions were often given that could find only a more guarded expression in Parliament. Temple's pamphlet of 1666, *The London Merchant's Letter to him of Amsterdam*, which advocated a separate Anglo-Dutch treaty and no French mediation, has disappeared, and *A Free Conference Touching the Present State of England* was not published until after the Triple Alliance, 'because that Respect ought to be payed to the Secret of his Majesty's Affairs, so as nothing should anticipate the King's own Labours'.[2] The same reason may have inhibited the publication of other strongly anti-French pamphlets in 1667, just as it accounts for the slightly circuitous manner of Marvell's recommendations in his poem. The deficiency was remedied late in the year by a translation of

---

[1] Ranke, III, p. 454.
[2] *State Tracts* (London, 1692), p. 6. The title has been abbreviated to *The State of England* in this collection.

Lisola's *The Buckler of State and Justice*, which received William-
son's imprimatur on 19 September. Clarendon himself re-
called, moreover, that while the negotiations at Breda were in
progress, and when the invasion of Flanders was imminent, 'it
easily appeared the Nation [England] would gladly have en-
gaged in that War, not being willing that *Flanders* should be in
the Possession of *France*'.[1] Ruvigny wrote to his master that, if
in July it had not been immediately prorogued, 'le parlement
auroit fait une déclaration de guerre perpetuelle contre la France
et la Hollande',[2] and Arlington judged in October that the
ruling humour of the country was to succour Flanders.[3]
Temple's letters from Breda, where he was a mere observer, are
full of concern with the French power, and suggestions for
loosening English dependence on it. Both England and Hol-
land, he suggested, were exasperated with France, and some of
the people he had spoken to had accused her of deliberately
fomenting the war. The 'snarling peace' would probably lead
to another conflict.[4] Japikse concluded in his study of the war
that Louis XIV's efforts to remain on good terms with both his
ally and England had gone awry; the Dutch were angered by
the lack of substantial aid he had supplied, and the English
blamed him for depriving them of the victory they so much
desired. 'Son animosité après la guerre était plus grande à
l'égard des Français qu'à l'égard des Hollandais.'[5] *The Last
Instructions* is itself a document of some importance in the history
of the development of anti-French sentiment in England,
because it narrates so fully the events and suspicions on which
it grew. For the first time in his life, Marvell may have been
speaking for a majority of his countrymen, but the representa-

[1] *A Continuation* [of *The Life*], III, p. 807.
[2] Quoted in Ranke III, p. 454 n.
[3] *The Rt Hon the Earl of Arlington's Letters*, ed. Thomas Bebington (London,
1701), I, p. 183.
[4] *Letters*, pp. 127–8.
[5] N. Japikse, 'Louis XIV et la Guerre Anglo-Hollandaise de 1665–1667',
Revue Historique, XCVIII (1908), p. 59.

tion of his views in a long poem gives him the precedence of a public spokesman. Politically, the farsightedness of *The Last Instructions* makes *Annus Mirabilis* look myopic.

The one action of the poem to fall outside the chronology of events from February to August 1667 is the long account of the battle over the excise, for which *The Last Instructions* remains the fullest authority. As Margoliouth and Miss Robbins have decided, the dispute probably took place in October 1666, at the beginning of the sixth session of Parliament, but Milward's *Diary*, the three principal collections of parliamentary debates, and the *Journals of the House of Commons* give no prominence to any particular debate about the excise, and not the slightest idea of the dramatic nature of the encounter. Milward recorded on 12 October that 'the Court party moved for a general excise of all things, which was no way pleasing', and four days later wrote, 'It will be the great contest whether the land tax (which is the opinion of the Presbyterian party) or a general excise (which the Court party proposeth) should be resolved on as the best way to raise the £1,800,000. I wish a medium between both may be found out.' On 18 October he thought a land tax would do the trick, while some still spoke up for an excise 'which will never be endured'. On 30 October the House agreed to discuss excise the next day, but not to vote on it until the land tax had also been considered. Clifford and Sir Charles Harbord then moved for the tax, 'which was much disliked'.[1] By this date the court party seems to have lost the fight, although excise remained in the air and was one of the subjects which were thought certain to be resurrected in the July Parliament: ''Tis talked that the way of raising a good sum of money for the present necessity, and for a continuance also, will be by means of an inland excise on all that is used by the buyer, viz., for back or belly, as it is in Holland; which will be the least burden-some, and will soon raise a considerable sum, both to defend

---

[1] *The Diary of John Milward, Esq.*, ed. Caroline Robbins (Cambridge, 1938). The quotations are from pp. 21, 25, 28, 35.

ourselves and to offend our enemies, which at present we are not in a capacity of either.'[1] As excise would be the easiest and most permanent tax to establish, and England's necessities had not grown any fewer, Marvell may well have thought to dispose his readers against bringing up the matter in the future, but it is quite clear that his description of the dispute is highly rhetorical and 'arranged'. We cannot prove that there was one day when the court party came very close to victory, because the evidence suggests that excise was debated over a period of time, was expected to arouse a fierce contest, and met with determined resistance on every occasion. But whether Marvell touched up one debate or conflated several, the result is one of those crowded scenes of satire that do more than any other part of the poem to convey the extent and magnitude of the court's corruption. The court party has a 'French martyr' and a 'French Standard' (168, 214) among other marks of its iniquity, but is also distinguished from the 'Gross of English Gentry, nobly born' (287) by having an efficient organization. All the warriors for excise are gathered into troops or bands, the leaders of which are carefully named, while the heroes of the country party are alone:

> These and some more with single Valour stay
> The adverse Troops, and hold them all at Bay.
> Each thinks his Person represents the whole,
> And with that thought does multiply his Soul:
> Believes himself an Army, theirs one Man,
> As eas'ly Conquer'd, and believing can.
> With Heart of Bees so full, and Head of Mites,
> That each, tho' Duelling, a Battel fights.
> Such once Orlando, famous in Romance,
> Broach'd whole Brigades like Larks upon his Lance.
>
> (267–76)

Marvell's admiration for the excise-killers should not mask the irony from which not even the House of Commons itself is exempt. By presenting the whole debate as a game of trick-

---

[1] *Calendar of State Papers, Domestic, 1667*, p. xxxvi.

track, a gamble, Marvell has saved himself from appearing to assert the supremacy of the Commons in the government of England. There is his direct testimony in the poem that a new administration drawn from the country party would regard Parliament 'as [if] in Love' (988) but he did not wish to imply that the multitudinous Commons was the be-all and end-all of legislative rule, or that he sought to curtail the necessity of a strong executive:

> Describe the *Court* and *Country*, both set right,
> On opposite points, the black against the white.
> Those having lost the Nation at *Trick track*,
> These now adventr'ing how to win it back.
> The Dice betwixt them must the Fate divide,
> As Chance does still in Multitudes decide. (107–12)

The Commons has the disadvantages as well as the advantages of being a numerous body of advisers. 'See sudden chance of War!' is the exclamation when the battle is unexpectedly won; 'To Paint or Write, / Is longer Work, and harder than to fight' (303–4). Parliament may divide into its honest and dis-honest factions, but it remains the 'publick game' (118), which is susceptible to the cheating of a corrupt Speaker or to the vagaries of a quick manœuvre in an empty House. Maxwell also knew that an administration could be changed, but the com-position of the Commons at any particular time was a given quantity which would always contain its share of peculators. The country gentlemen lacked the leadership they needed, which could not be provided without new ministers at the top. Hence a scrutiny of the Commons, like an examination of foreign policy, produces the same request to the King. Every-where the signs are the same. Clarendon stands at the nexus of these converging criticisms, not as a scapegoat—although that is what he became—but as the minister ultimately responsible for the jugglings in the Commons and the complacency of the French alliance. His wish to dissolve the Parliament was common knowledge, and no critic of the government after the civil war ever missed an opportunity to associate a standing army, such as had been mobilized to defend the country from the Dutch, with a desire to extend the royal prerogative and abolish parliaments altogether.

The indictment was as complete as Marvell could make it, and yet on 14 October he objected, with others, to thanking the King for demanding the Chancellor's seals, as it implied 'a precondemning him before any crime was laid to his charge'. Miss Robbins, while noting Marvell's 'more than usually elaborate display of thankfulness and loyalty' to the King after Parliament met in October, believes (or believed) that his wish for no hasty action over Clarendon was to prevent his escaping without a proper impeachment.[1] This might be the correct interpretation of his speech that he 'would have the faults hunt the persons: would not have a sudden impeachment by reason of the greatness of the person or danger of escape, lord Clarendon not being likely to ride away post';[2] but it can hardly be said to account for his other sentiments on 14 October:

The raising and destroying of favourites and creatures is the sport of kings not to be meddled with by us. Kings in the choice of their ministers move in a sphere distinct from us. It is said because the people rejoiced at his fall we must thank the King. The people also rejoiced at the restoration of the Duke of Buckingham the other day obnoxious. Shall we not thank the King for that too? It is said we hate him not. Would any man in this House be willing to have such a vote pass upon him? We are to thank the King for the matter of his speech. This is not in particular any part of it and comes irregularly before us.[3]

Sir John Holland likewise declared, either on the same day or two days later:

But for this particular (brought in amongst the rest) of the removal of the Earl of Clarendon, I must say that I do not at all doubt but that his

[1] 'A Critical Study', p. 116. One reason for insisting on the impeachment was to insure that Clarendon did not keep his power behind the throne through his influence with the Duke of York.
[2] Cobbett's *Parliamentary History*, IV, pp. 376–7.
[3] Milward's *Diary*, p. 328.

Majesty have done therein like himself. That which becomes a wise and just prince. But what the causes? These his Majesty have not been pleased to reveal to us, nor ought we to seek after them until his Majesty shall be pleased to give us leave. It being an undoubted prerogative of the King to remove his officers, his council, his servants as he makes them at his good will and pleasure [etc.].[1]

To read a deep plot into these and similar asseverations would be to forget that the King's prerogatives were a reality to all believers in the constitution, and that only fanatical republicans would have thought of denying them. Neither had the civil war, nor Charles's misdemeanours, destroyed the feeling for the person of the King, and Baxter reflected of 1667 that the King had had a true experience of his subjects' loyalty, who in spite of all their grievances would do or say nothing against him; but: 'What the People said of the Parliament, and what of the Court, and what of the Bishops, and what of the Women, I shall not write: But Losers and sufferers will take leave to talk.'[2] The fact is that Marvell's reluctance to have Parliament prosecute Clarendon at once, and by so doing convince the King that it was determined to curtail his rights, reinforces, not contradicts, his attitude in the poem. Marvell had his eye on the future, and the good that might come from a fresh start, and his purpose would be defeated if the King took umbrage and became stubborn. For all the vituperation of *The Last Instructions*, the poem still manifests a considerable restraint. There is not a word to suggest who the actual men were that Marvell considered to be the best candidates for high office, because the choice was wholly the King's. Buckingham was the man of the hour, enjoying an immense popularity, and his

[1] *Ibid.* p. 313. For Clarendon's impeachment, see especially *The Proceedings in the House of Commons Touching the Impeachment of Edward, late Earl of Clarendon* (n.p. 1700), and Clayton Roberts, 'The Impeachment of the Earl of Clarendon', *Cambridge Historical Journal*, XIII (1957), pp. 1–18. Impeachments form an important part of Professor Roberts's study of *The Growth of Responsible Government in Stuart England* (Cambridge, 1966).

[2] *Reliquiae Baxterianae*, ed. Matthew Sylvester (London, 1696), Part 3, p. 21.

views on toleration make it easily conceivable that Marvell approved of his bid for power. Marvell's allusion to the 'gen'rous Conscience' of those 'born to Virtue and to Wealth' (985, 983) would support such a guess and if Baxter could call the Duke 'a defender of the Priviledges of Humanity',[1] Marvell may have overlooked his large deficiency in virtue, of which Baxter was also aware. There is no way of knowing, however, as the one complimentary reference to Buckingham in the poem (357) is too casual to be suggestive, and his French interest would count against him in Marvell's eyes. Other country peers would also be possible candidates, nor would it have set a precedent to choose new advisers from the Commons. Marvell's silence about names is deliberate and, as I have already said, his relation of French treachery can be read as a reminder to the King that falls short of specifically telling him what policy he ought to adopt.

On Charles's one appearance in the narrative he is the 'lov'd King' (327), but the envoi to Charles, personally addressed to him, contains the statement of Marvell's respect for his rights:

Would she [the muse] the unattended Throne reduce,
Banishing Love, Trust, Ornament and Use;
Better it were to live in Cloysters Lock,
Or in fair Fields to rule the easie Flock.
She blames them only who the *Court* restrain,
And, where all *England* serves, themselves would reign.

(961-6)

The lines envisage that happy unity of King and Parliament in the affections of his people that had been the theme of Restoration panegyrics and was the emotional centre for almost any elaborate praise of the English constitution. It was the same unity to which Marvell had looked forward in 1654, and Charles, like Cromwell isolated by the apathy of his subjects, is now a solitary monarch cut off from his people by the machinations of evil courtiers. To lose the 'Common *Prince*' behind the

[1] *Ibid.* p. 21.

'Fence' his ministers have constructed is, in Marvell's formula-
tion, to deprive the country of its essence or substance, and to
undermine the realm: 'But *Ceres* Corn, and *Flora* is the Spring,
/ *Bacchus* is Wine, the Country is the *King*' (973–4). By this
time the 'Country' is also identified with the country party, and
the poem ends with a eulogy on the parliamentary virtues of its
members and the suggestion that all anxiety for the King's
safety would be unnecessary if the country leaders became the
new ministers.

The envoi presents no constitutional surprises, but the
dramatic change of tone between the narrative satire and the
formal apology and obeisance to the King requires an ex-
planation that will preserve the integrity of the poem and of
Marvell's intentions. Politically, *The Last Instructions* progresses
towards a reaffirmation of the ideal constitution with the King
firmly in the centre and his prerogatives intact. Poetically, it
progresses until the loyal poet and subject is revealed. The
simultaneous revelation of King and poet is logically only
possible when the satire has been completed, and the restora-
tion of the monarch to his visible eminence restores his loyal
subjects to a heartfelt allegiance. The fence raised by the
courtiers obscured Charles until it had been demolished by the
satire, and the wrath which the poet had first claimed was the
inspiration of his attack obscured for nine hundred lines the
true nature of the writer:

> So his bold Tube, Man, to the Sun apply'd,
> And Spots unknown to the bright Star descry'd;
> Show'd they obscure him, while too near they please,
> And seem his Courtiers, are but his disease.
> Through Optick Trunk the Planet seem'd to hear,
> And hurls them off, e're since, in his Career.   (949–54)

In the ideal monarchy, panegyric would replace satire, and
indignation would give place to the prayers of grateful subjects.
The abrasive poet is required only in exceptional circumstances,
and at the end of the narrative he puts down his satirical pen with

the relief of finding that it is no longer necessary, and that the image of his King is now untarnished:

> *Painter* adieu, how well our Arts agree;
> Poetick Picture, Painted Poetry.
> But this great work is for our *Monarch* fit,
> And henceforth *Charles* only to *Charles* shall sit.
> His Master-hand the Ancients shall out-do
> Himself the *Poet* and the *Painter* too.   (943–8)

All Marvell's rhetorical poems possess ethical proof of their author's good intentions, and *The Last Instructions* differs from the others only in placing it at the end. The norm of satire, the *assiette* that modern readers have affirmed to be indispensable for the author of a destructive work, is modestly defined in the concluding paragraphs, and the crudity of the device has the merit not only of marking an interesting stage in the development of epistolary satire but of making explicit the assumptions on which a loyalist could assault the administration. The principle that ministers were responsible for the King's faults, about which more will be said in the next chapter, is built into the structure of the poem, so that the crown may emerge at the end unharmed by abuse. The two chief dangers of satire—that the good gets destroyed with the bad, and the satirist is sullied by the dirt he attacks—find in *The Last Instructions* a simple but effective antidote.[1]

---

[1] The loyal and usually equable nature of the speaker is revealed once in the course of the narrative when he recounts the bravery of the Scottish Douglas, dying to defend his king and country. Probably the elegy had a political motive. At the moment Marvell was writing, the administration of Scotland was being completely recast (William L. Mathieson, *Politics and Religion* [Glasgow 1902], II, p. 217), following widespread discontent and the Pentland Rising. Scotland was also inclined to be pro-Dutch. A policy of conciliation was initiated which was to culminate in the King's speech to the parliaments of both countries on 19 October 1669 in which he proposed union. But the subject was already alive in 1667. Sir Robert Moray wrote to Lauderdale on 14 October: 'SS. [Tweeddale] will be with you in time enough to rypen your thoughts of the union before you talk any more of it to the L. keeper' (*The Lauderdale Papers*, ed. Osmund Airy, printed for the Camden

Marvell could not have written his poem without making severe private reflections on the King's prudence, but Charles had vindicated himself by deposing his Chancellor, and the hopefulness of the moment Marvell caught in the envoi and his letter of 3 October. Historians concede that with Claren-don's downfall the King was enabled to begin his personal government,[1] and Marvell fervently hoped that the change might be for the better. His loyalty, however, did not rest on his view of the King's capacities, nor was it affected by the corrup-tion that emanated from the court and penetrated to the furthest recesses of the Commons. The dictates of providence might depend on the King's conduct, because bad kings had been punished in the past, but a good subject would continue to act as if no evil performed by the crown could shake his allegiance to the constitution. Clarendon's dismissal was itself evidence that patience was rewarded and the King had recognized what was wrong. To harm his reputation, to abuse his person, or to slight his prerogatives was to hasten popular disaffection and increase the danger of civil disturbance. It was as culpably unworthy of a loyalist as Clarendon's reputed slur on parlia-ments, and certain to make the impasse between the House and the executive still more impassable.

Unexpected hope, not rebelliousness, was the immediate cause of *The Last Instructions*, and as Charles had given a sign

Society [1885], II, p. 75; see also Louise Fargo Brown, *The First Earl of Shaftesbury* [New York, 1933], p. 140, and Alexander Robertson, *The Life of Sir Robert Moray* [London, 1922], pp. 142–43). There had also appeared *A Discourse upon the Union of England and Scotland, Addressed to King Charles II, March 19th...1664* (G. W. T. Omond, *The Early History of the Scottish Union Question* [Edinburgh and London, 1897], p. 122). Given also the fact that *The Loyal Scot* as it was later enlarged became a pro-union poem, the passage in *The Last Instructions* was probably intended to prompt English sympathies for the reconstruction of Anglo-Scots friendship. The negotiations in 1667 were primarily about the lowering of trade embargoes.

[1] Andrew Browning, *Thomas Osborne, Earl of Danby* (Glasgow, 1951), I, p. 53. Browning's account of these historically very perplexing years has been of more use to me than this one note would suggest.

that he was not oblivious, Marvell could seize the moment to outline his vision of what a new administration might achieve. Until that moment, I believe, he had publicly held his peace, waiting for the propitious hour when advice could be seasonable. He wrote to Sir John Trott in August 1667, consoling him on the death of his son, ''Tis Pride that makes a Rebel. And nothing but the overweening of our selves and our own things that raises us against divine Providence.'[1] Striking so fiercely at the court a few weeks later, he had the justification of cooperating with providence, and enforcing the lesson that Clarendon's fall had already brought home to King and people. There had been happier occasions in the past when Marvell thought he had perceived the next great political step that providence had invited, and it is notable, too, that, whereas earlier poems had called for a single leader, *The Last Instructions* calls for a body of advisers. That was history, however, and the inevitable consequence of following a providence that never gave with its right hand without depriving with its left. The constitution had been restored unimpaired, but the leadership was inadequate, while during the Interregnum the opposite conditions had pertained. The loyalist had no choice but to accept what was given and make the best of God's designs. He was in duty bound to put the best interpretation he could on the King's actions, and to seize every clear opportunity to redeem the time. For all his faults, Charles had been elected by God to kingship in a way Cromwell had missed, and the alternative to loyalty could not be contemplated without the thought of another civil war. A heavy monarch might be on the throne, but it would be treason to say so, and the perfecting of nature would have to be carried on in spite of the defects of grace. The religious rather than party basis of a political satire will seem odd only to those readers of Marvell who are unpersuaded by the Christian feeling that permeates all his political poetry.

Naturally, loyalism finds as many forms of expression, and

[1] *Letters*, p. 299.

originates in as many different personal feelings, as any of the great 'isms' of the seventeenth century—royalism and puritanism, to name only two with which loyalism has much in common. Its purer strains, nevertheless, can be traced back to the expectancy and patience with which the Engagers agreed to abide by the result of a revolution rather than institute another, and the Restoration was, in a real sense, the greatest revolution of all, since it turned the wheel full circle.[1] Marvellian loyalism is to be distinguished from mere religious acquiescence by the heat with which it rejects republican government of all kinds, and the passion of its support for a Single Person in the constitution. His satire of 1667, like his diatribe on the Fifth Monarchists in 1655, defends the ruler against his worst enemies, and supports the principle of a strong executive. The unreligious nature of Charles II must frequently have caused Marvell to despair, but as long as providence governed human affairs, a way could be found to reconstruct the happy land that, in *Upon Appleton House*, Marvell confessed had once existed. The temptation to escape from the realities of political life may have been great, and an echo of how much 'Better it were to live in Cloysters Lock, / Or in fair Fields to rule the easie Flock' enters *The Last Instructions*, but Marvell's commitment to the active life appears to have been complete, and the energy with which he pursued a political ideal never flagged until his death.

[1] See Vernon F. Snow's brief but interesting article, 'The Concept of Revolution in Seventeenth-Century England', *Historical Journal*, v (1962), pp. 167–74.

5

'God send us moderation and agreement':
The prose

The Rehearsal Transpros'd

Marvell's hopes of better ministers and a change of direction in the King's personal government after 1667 received encouragement with the signing of the Triple Alliance in 1668, but were thereafter doomed to increasingly bitter reproof. The ineluctable drift of the King's policy toward a full accommodation with France was, to use a Marvellian phrase, the price of money, and the history of his diplomacy and the excuses that can be made for it need not be retold. Although Marvell was aware of the danger to Europe and to protestantism that any dealings with Louis were bound to involve, there are no further signs of it in his correspondence until 1670–1, when the survival of four letters to William Popple illuminates his state of mind immensely. Earlier letters to the Hull Corporation contain the expression of a wish for a religious 'composure' in 1668 and a similar desire for the settlement of a violent quarrel between the Lords and Commons a few months later. 'God send us moderation and agreement', he concluded, and that prayer may stand as an epigraph to all his efforts during the last years of his life.[1]

The first hint of Marvell's concern that the relations between King and Parliament were still not as they should be is heard in his unusual frankness to his constituents at the undesired proroga-

[1] *Letters*, ed. Margoliouth, p. 91. Page numbers for quotations from the letters and the prose works have been incorporated into the text of this chapter. The texts used for the prose are in *The Complete Works*, ed. Alexander B. Grosart (n.p. 1872–5): vol. III contains both parts of *The Rehearsal Transpros'd*; vol. IV contains *Mr. Smirke* and *An Account of the Growth of Popery and Arbitrary Government in England*.

tion of Parliament in December 1669: 'God direct his Majesty further in so weighty resolutions' (94). The personal letters to Popple the following year spell out the trouble. 'It is also my Opinion that the King was never since his coming in, nay, all Things considered, no King since the Conquest, so absolutely powerful at Home, as he is at present. Nor any Parliament, or Places, so certainly and constantly supplyed with Men of the same Temper' (302). Justice demanded that not all the blame should be attributed to the King, but only Charles could be held ultimately responsible for the corruption of the court, which had reached 'the highest Pitch of Want and Luxury'; significantly, Marvell added 'and the People full of Discontent' (308). 'So bewitched a Time' was it that Charles had narrowly escaped being called to order for attending the House of Lords in person, hence breaching parliamentary privilege. 'So this Matter, of such Importance on all great Occasions, seems riveted to them, and Us, for the future, and to all Posterity' (303). Matters were worsened by the recantation of five members of the opposition, 'the Apostate Patriots', who became courtiers in the Commons, and by England's base truckling to France in all things, 'to the Prejudice of our Alliance and Honour'. Add to these woes the particularly severe persecution which the dissenters suffered whenever Parliament was sitting, and the cries of 'No popery' everywhere, and one sees the justification for Marvell's conclusion that Louis XIV had nothing to worry about. 'I believe indeed he will attempt Nothing on Us, but leave Us to dy a natural Death. For indeed never had poor Nation so many complicated, mortal, incurable, Diseases' (308–9). Absolute government, persecution, a discontented people, and 'alwayes fatal Debauchery'—the state that Marvell describes fits precisely the conditions of revolution that he was shortly to enumerate in The Rehearsal Transpros'd, and his anxiety and disgust may be detected in his letters to his nephew. Readers of Marvell's prose have nearly always done their best to find a revolutionary hidden under his correct expressions, but

the picture has never been clear and Marvell's most personal
and least rhetorical statements to Popple, at a time when he
apparently despaired of constitutional government, contain no
treasonable matter, nor indeed any excuse for reading them but
as the bitter reflections of a loyal subject. Even his criticism of the
King is merely implied, and while the odium in which Parliament
was held could be stated, a natural reserve shrouds his recognition
of the principal source of its corruption. The discontent of the
people, to which he twice refers, is recalled with detachment—
a reminder that 'discontent' was a term for political restiveness
that did not quite apply to Marvell's own dissatisfaction. The
evidence of the letters does not suggest that Marvell considered a
revolution to be likely, or that he was seriously apprehensive of
civil disturbances on behalf of catholics or dissenters, but the
combination of circumstances which he described was an in-
flammable mixture that needed only an accident or a few more
acts of bad judgment to set it alight; the letters at least affirm the
potentially dangerous conjunctions in the political firmament,
and, by his own later testimony, it would be wrong to set Marvell
above the common feeling that the series of catastrophes in the
1660s were God's judgment on an erring nation, of which the
government had still failed to take account.

A republican might have found here some fuel for his hopes,
but Marvell's image of the nation dying a natural death from a
plethora of complicated diseases suggests that his keenest im-
pression was of the complexity and stultification of parliamentary
procedure when neither Parliament nor the King could be
trusted to act reasonably. The situation can be neatly illustrated
by Marvell's comments on the passage of the Conventicle Act
through both Houses in the spring of 1670. The bill itself was
the 'most malicious' but the last triumph of the royalist
churchmen in the Commons,[1] and, in Marvell's memorable
phrase, 'the Quintessence of arbitrary Malice' (301), but the

[1] Keith Feiling, *A History of the Tory Party, 1640–1714* (Oxford, 1924),
p. 132.

measures taken by the King to obtain its amendment in the
House of Lords were not to his liking. The proviso that the
Lords sought to affix to the bill reaffirmed the King's dis-
pensing powers in religion and 'would have restored Him to all
civil or eclesiastical Prerogatives which his Ancestors had
enjoyed at any Time since the Conquest. There was never so
compendious a Piece of absolute universal Tyranny' (303).
There was nothing to choose between the evil of the Act on the
one hand and the proposed remedy on the other, because the
proviso would have enabled Charles to nullify the consequences
of the bill at his discretion. If the price of toleration was an
unwarranted extension of the King's prerogatives, then the
price was too high, although the King's wish to spare the pains
of his more protestant subjects remained an example of his
superior wisdom. Whether, at this early date, Marvell suspected
Charles's pro-catholic bias in seeking indulgence for non-
conformists, he does not reveal, but his understanding of the
basic problem would not be affected by the knowledge of
Charles's perfidy. Both sides of the constitutional structure,
King and Parliament, had forsaken their duties to the country,
one by augmenting its power beyond statutory limits, the other
by trying to impose an ecclesiastical discipline on a people
who, if left alone, would be as loyal to the crown as Marvell
himself. Marvell's hatred of the church hierarchy for insisting in
and out of Parliament on national conformity must, psycho-
logically speaking, spring largely from his own self-knowledge.
As he had made the transition from Commonwealth to
Restoration without compromising his conscience, and could
acknowledge his obligations to the crown without turning his
back on the religious convictions of the puritans, then the
dissenters as a whole could be expected to do the same. The
war-cries of the bishops or a Samuel Parker were not only
uncharitable but unnecessary—and the word occurs again and
again in his writings on toleration. Uniformity was unnecessary
because, latitudinarian that he was, Marvell was aware that his

own mild conformity with the Church of England had nothing to do with his constitutional principles, or his belief that providence had ordained a return to the traditional organization of English government, which even under Cromwell had appeared to be the best model.

The Declaration of Indulgence was issued on 15 March 1672 and war on Holland was declared two days later. The immediate political purpose of indulgence, therefore, was never in doubt, and the King's counsellors may be said to have learned from their experience of the earlier Dutch war, when puritan opinion had been agitated by a conflict with another protestant country. As a sop to the nonconformists, the Declaration never had much chance of success, because suspicions of the catholics at court and of the King's sympathies had by now been thoroughly aroused, and the more limited toleration allowed to catholics by the Declaration probably deceived no one. In the opinion of Lord Halifax and many others, the dissenters would spurn the offer made to them, and their leaders were cautious even when they welcomed it. Their fears might be called practical as well as religious, for they knew that toleration at the King's pleasure could be temporary and perhaps damaging to their cause. The Declaration, however, also posed a constitutional problem of greater magnitude than, but of the same kind as, the proviso to the Conventicle Act on which Marvell had expressed himself so emphatically. The King's dispensing power in religion had long remained one of the flowers of the crown, and only its most blatant abuse by James II was to destroy it for ever and bring about the Glorious Revolution. Many responsible and moderate politicians until that time were to swear that it was the King's inalienable privilege, and, although the Lords had failed in their Conventicle Act proviso, they succeeded in attaching a general statement to the bill that the royal supremacy was not in question. The usual method of dispensing leniency, however, was by private licence from the crown, and the licences as a rule had been given only to catholics. Charles's Declaration of Indulgence ten years earlier, which was in effect the suspension of an Act of Parliament and the abrogation of penal law, had met with such vociferous opposition that he had been forced to withdraw it. One close parallel to a far-reaching dispensation could be adduced from the reign of Elizabeth, but the Commons were within reason when they claimed that the Declaration was without precedent.[1] If a body as enthusiastic for the royal prerogative as the Parliament of 1662 could be found adamant against a Declaration of Indulgence, it was unlikely that it would be less so in 1672. Charles lost this test of strength also, and his effort was a good example of the difficulties caused for everyone by one constitutional action of doubtful legality. In the long run, the dissenters profited from their year of grace, but at the time Marvell wrote the first part of *The Rehearsal Transpros'd* the permanency of their toleration was in grave doubt and the validity of the document by which they enjoyed it highly problematic.

In the light of these familiar facts, the often repeated statement that Marvell wrote *The Rehearsal Transpros'd* to support the Declaration needs reassessment, because the probability that he was disturbed by the high-handed method the King had chosen is very high, and the possibility that he voted against it when Parliament reconvened cannot be discounted: Parker seems to imply that he did.[2] Marvell's only explicit discussion of the Declaration in part 1 of his pamphlet is diplomatic and merely preparatory to exposing Parker's hypocrisy in supporting the King's prerogatives at a time when His Majesty 'had so vigorously exerted his Ecclesiastical Power, but to a purpose quite contrary to what Mr. Bayes had always intended' (117); the King, he says,

---

[1] This paragraph is indebted to E. F. Churchill, 'The Dispensing Power of the Crown in Ecclesiastical Affairs', *Law Quarterly Review*, XXXVIII (1922), pp. 297–316, and especially 420–34; also W. S. Holdsworth, *A History of English Law* (London, 1903 ff.), VI, pp. 217–25.

[2] Pierre Legouis, *Andrew Marvell* (Oxford, 1965), p. 145; in the earlier dissertation (1928), pp. 273–4.

resolved to make some clear tryal how the Nonconformists could bear themselves under some liberty of conscience. And accordingly he issued...his gracious declaration of Indulgence, of which I wish his Majesty and the kingdom much joy, and as far as my slender judgement can divine, dare augurate and presage mutual felicity, and that whatever humane accident may happen (I fear not what Bayes foresees), they will, they can never have cause to repent this action or its consequences.

(116–17)

This passage is Marvell's sole commitment to the principle of a general indulgence, and Parker had every right to object, as he did repeatedly in his *Reproof*, that Marvell had avoided the 'Grand Thesis' of ecclesiastical policy and left unanswered the doctrine of the King's religious supremacy. Only in the second part of *The Rehearsal Transpros'd*, when the Declaration was already quashed, do we find a reasoned exposition of Marvell's view on the subject. His opinion then was that the King had some power in religion but not all (304), and this view was precisely what the arbitrariness of the Declaration itself did not at first permit him to argue. He had to assume the King's power, but to avoid, so far as possible, any statements about his right to exercise his prerogatives in so sweeping a gesture, just as it was to his advantage to play down the renewed fears of popery that the Declaration had aroused. To have defended the Indulgence more openly, an obligation from which he was relieved when he wrote part 2, would have necessitated an outright explication of absolute prerogative, which he would not and could not perform. His whole argument against Parker, he declared subsequently (339–40), was based on the premise that if the claims which Parker made for the King's ecclesiastical jurisdiction were sustained, it would be only a short time before the same claims were made for his civil autho-rity. In other words, he did not think of his tract as a defence of the Declaration, but as an attack on Parker's Hobbesian absolutism; in so far as he was defending anything, it was the idea of indulgence, not the manner by which it had been promoted; and, given the ordinary subtleties of casuistry, his points of view in the two parts of *The Rehearsal Transpros'd* were not inconsistent. Marvell must have hoped, I think, that his work would further the cause of toleration in Parliament, and hence lead to legislation that would obviate the need for the King's measures. As Bate has observed, Lyttleton obtained considerable support for toleration in the subsequent debate from those who objected to the Declaration on constitutional grounds.[1] In the autumn of 1672 he probably could not foresee the Test Act against catholics, which was Parliament's positive response in 1673 to the Declaration, but he may have had in mind something like the Bill of Ease for the dissenters that made headway in Parliament before prorogation cut it short. He had set himself a tricky task, and if Parker had not been hopelessly outclassed in this battle of wits he might have won the day. Parker could rest very smugly on his assertion that he had no objection to the King's exercising his power any way he pleased, although Marvell correctly assumed that Parker's preface to Bramhall's *Vindication* was allied to the bishops' scheme to beat the pulpit drums against popery and obtain the revocation of the indulgence; his argument had a harsh consistency that easily accepted the principle of the Declaration, and Marvell's mockery is in part a brilliant camouflage for his unwillingness to meet Parker on his own terms. Had he accepted the constitutionality of the Declaration, there would have been little difference between his position and Parker's.

A clear apprehension of Marvell's predicament helps to explain certain emphases of his work. The first part of *The Rehearsal Transpros'd* is primarily an attack *ad hominem*, where there was least danger of getting lured into constitutional pitfalls. The six reasons that he offers at the close of part 1 for having written at all contain not a single reference to the Declaration, or to the cause that he was ostensibly defending. He was offended first, he says, by the 'presumption and

[1] Frank Bate, *The Declaration of Indulgence, 1672* (London, 1908), p. 110.

arrogance' of Parker's style, then by his 'infinite tautology'; his invectives against the trading part of the nation and his irreverent treatment of kings were nauseous, his profanation of scripture and debasement of the concept of grace equally unpleasant. Finally, 'he hath spoken evil distinctly of the Father, distinctly of the Son, and distinctly of the Holy Ghost' (224-7). The literary origins of Marvell's quarrels are once again apparent, and one observes his customary distaste for immodesty or display, and his allegiance to standards of decorum on all topics. His failure to mention Parker's political theory itself in his list of reasons suggests that no theory presented in such unattractive terms could be worth considering, the manner alone being sufficient to condemn it, but it serves as a reminder that, unlike other defenders of toleration, Marvell sought to remove the discussion from the realm in which it had been habitually conducted. John Owen and William Penn, for example, in their admirable tracts of the same period, base a much larger part of their argument on the inviolability of conscience, and the magistrate's usurpation of God's prerogative by not granting a freedom of worship. The worst theorem of all, Owen declared, is

that men may lawfully act in the Worship of God, or otherwise, against the Light, Dictates, or Convictions of their own Consciences. Exempt Conscience from an absolute, immediate, entire, universal dependance on the Authority, Will, and Judgement of God, according to what Conceptions it hath of them, and you disturb the whole harmony of divine Providence in the Government of the World; and break the first link of that great chain whereon all Religion and Government in the world do depend.[1]

Penn's style is less Parkerian than Owen's, but all his arguments, including his shrewd insistence that persecution is against the spirit of the first Reformation, cluster around the central truth of the puritan experience, the inner light by which

---

[1] [John Owen,] *Truth and Innocence Vindicated* (London, 1669), p. 70; William Penn's tract is *The Great Case of Liberty of Conscience* (1670), in *Select Works* (London, 1782), III, pp. 1-51.

alone a Christian must be governed. Owen and his peers were no less absolute in their convictions than Parker, who was correct, therefore, in saying that they claimed toleration as their right. But when he pretends that Marvell is an exponent of the same adamant principles he is guilty of some distortion. Marvell is no less convinced than Owen that conscience should be beyond the reach of kings, and that to disobey it is to court disaster at the Last Judgment, but the raillery of his style and the gentlemanly good nature he assumes preclude the reaction Owen invited. He believes, but will never declaim, and the reader is defied to discover in his good manners the intolerance and self-righteousness which would reveal the stubbornness of the true dissenter. The more one contemplates the core of actual belief, however, beneath Marvell's banter, the firmer the outlines become of his moderate Calvinism, his aversion to the hierarchy of the Church of England, and his concurrence with most of the fundamental positions of nonconformity. Like his father, he was willing to conform without enthusiasm to the establishment, and his praise for Hales sounds like a total admiration for his churchmanship, but in the arguments over grace and works, church government, and ceremonies he was consistently against the official views of the bishops. His bias is more apparent in the second part of *The Rehearsal Transpros'd* when the constitutional issue had been shelved and the success of the first part had given him confidence, but what distinguishes his defence from all those written by the sufferers themselves was his emphasis on the inexpediency of persecution. In this he followed the preamble of the Declaration, which had called attention to the ineffectiveness of coercive legislation since the Restoration, but his development of the theme exceeded anything that had been attempted before, although the attitude was common and no comprehensive pamphlet would be complete without it. It was the first of the three ordinary inducements to toleration that L'Estrange had confuted in 1663.[1]

[1] Roger L'Estrange, *Toleration Discuss'd* (London, 1663), p. 14.

Expedience, practicality, safety, and discretion are the terms
that pervade his satire, and they unite in the idea of the King's
prudence, which had decreed a respite from persecution.
Parker's severity is, above all, 'unnecessary', and 'Mr. Necessity
Bayes' with his 'must, must' is exposed as the object of uni-
versal contempt. 'It is yet to me the greatest mysterie in the world
how the civil magistrate could be perswaded to interest himself
with all the severity of his power in a matter so unnecessary, so
trivial, and so pernicious to the publick quiet' (385). Kings
'are so satisfied with the abundance of their power, that they
rather think meet to abate of its exercise by their discretion'
(173); 'whereas indeed the matter is, that princes have alwayes
found that uncontroulable government over CONSCIENCE to
be both unsafe and impracticable' (147). Bramhall's hope of a
comprehension with Rome he finds 'a thing rather to be wished
and prayed for, than to be expected from these kind of
endeavours...I cannot look upon these undertaking Church-
men, however otherwise of excellent prudence and learning,
but as men struck with a notion, and craz'd on that side of
their head' (24–6). The foil throughout the book to the
prudence he recommends is naturally the insane Mr Bayes, a
raving Indian running amok, a man dizzy with his own
self-importance, frothing at the mouth and railing contentedly
to his own muses like an idiot. Madness is always the opposite
to the moderate course the King has decided upon, and Parker
the 'insana laurus' which if eaten would drive the people out of
their minds. Madness in Parker's case is recognized by his
'hyperboles and impossibilities', his 'allegorical eloquence', his
impertinence and vain 'imaginations'; his style is composed of
extremes, dogmatism on one hand and railing on the other, and
nowhere is Marvell's criticism more just than in his perception
that Parker thinks in antitheses and would make anyone who
disagreed with him a fanatic (32–62). 'The miseries of Tyranny
are less, than those of Anarchy; and therefore 'tis better to
submit to the unreasonable Impositions of *Nero*, or *Caligula*,

than to hazard the dissolution of the State.'[1] The alternatives that Parker offers his reader are always of this order, who must choose between a magistrate armed with his galleys, rods, and axes, and another civil war, or the loss of religion. For Parker, political prudence admits no middle ground between severity and licence, no liberty of worship, and no freedom to disagree except in the privacy of one's own mind. His hyperboles are as excessive as Marvell paints them, and an exact representation of the extremism of his thought.

Even if the arrogance of Parker's style were not, as he said it was, the first cause of Marvell's decision to reply, Marvell's own style, between jest and earnest, can be seen now as the direct result of his concern with the middle ground where moderation would prevail. Earlier tracts in the controversy, and particularly Simon Patrick's *The Friendly Debate* with its continuations, had exhibited a formal interest in the stylistics of dispute, and the dialogue or, as Marvell calls it, the 'dramatick and scenical way of scribling' (262), was felt to have the advantage over mere casuistry in rendering opponents contemptible. Marvell's style may owe a little to Martin Marprelate and to other practitioners of the art of scoffing, but it springs immediately from his command of an area of common sense of which Parker was ignorant. Marvell's most typical rhetorical device is the surmise or conjecture, when he seizes one of Parker's statements, which may in itself be quite harmless (like the bramble on the southern side of Lake Geneva), and discourses on it at length until it has exfoliated into a preposterous piece of nonsense. Parker's 'galleys', for example, are pictured literally as manned by nonconformists, or his education is recounted as the long growth of a quixotic delusion. By 'imagining' Parker's meanings or his intentions, Marvell has conferred upon him the flights of his own fancy until Parker is no less an absentee from the real world than his *alter ego*

[1] Samuel Parker, *A Discourse of Ecclesiastical Politie*, 3rd ed. (London, 1671), p. 215.

Bayes. As every new supposition is introduced, Parker's raving becomes more patent, and the practical wisdom of toleration is more clearly defined.[1]

Marvell's pragmatism has attracted the attention of other readers of *The Rehearsal Transpros'd*—it could hardly fail to be noticed—but it has been generally misunderstood as a good illustration of his opportunism. Professor Legouis assumes it throughout his discussion of the work, and Dean Morgan Schmitter, contrasting Marvell with Locke, comments that 'neither Marvell's interest nor his purpose in writing moved him to so comprehensive a system based solidly on fundamental right and wrong'. He later develops the inference: 'He thought in terms of workable solutions, not of systems that covered all eventualities' and was 'a weather-vane in the winds of seventeenth-century ideas, [catching] those breezes that blew in the direction of individual liberties—the right to find salvation, the right to self-government'.[2] Common sense and moderation, however, although emphatic about policy that is 'seasonable' or 'unseasonable', are not enemies to fundamental right and wrong or to a constitutional orthodoxy. They tend, on the contrary, to assume these things and to seek for the most equitable application of general principles to individual circumstance. In other words, they are the handmaidens of the best casuistry, which without them becomes scholastic and wiredrawn. Before retreating to the country to write the second part of *The Rehearsal Transpros'd*, Marvell wrote to Sir Edward Harley: 'I am (if I may say it with reverence) drawn in, I hope by a good Providence, to intermeddle in a noble and high argument which therefore by how much it is above my capacity I shall use the more industry not to disparage it' (312). By his terms, Marvell

---

[1] With some justice, Parker called Marvell's work 'my book of Aphorisms and Similitudes', *A Reproof to the Rehearsal Transprosed* (London, 1673), p. 523.

[2] 'Andrew Marvell: Member from Hull; a Study in the Ecclesiastical and Political Thought of the Restoration', unpublished Columbia Univ. Ph.D. dissertation, 1955, pp. 257, 264.

might have been writing an epic, and it would be a pity if the laughter he evoked were to disguise the seriousness with which he regarded his enterprise. It remains to paraphrase some of Marvell's deepest political convictions as they emerge in the work in order to explain his preoccupation with practical matters.

Fortunately, some of the impressive statements in *The Rehearsal Transpros'd*, passages that no reader could miss, clarify the belief that had been implicit in all his political poetry, and which the experience of the civil war and the Restoration had both taught him and confirmed:

I say, with submission still to better judgments, and especially to superiors, that I conceive the magistrate, as in Scripture described, is the ordinance of God constituting him and the ordinance of man assenting to his dominion. For there is not now any express revelation, no inspiration of a prophet, nor unction of that nature as to the declaring of that particular person that is to govern. Only God hath in general commanded and disposed men to be governed. And the particular person reigns according to that right, more or less respectively, which under God's providence he or his predecessors have lawfully acquired over the subject. Therefore I take the magistrate's power to be from God, only in a providential constitution; and the nature of which is very well and reverently expressed by princes themselves, 'By the grace of God King of &c.'; but I do not understand that God has thereby imparted and devolved to the magistrate His Divine jurisdiction. (398)

Kings also, but for the grace of God, are deposed, and what Marvell means by 'a providential constitution' is illuminated by an earlier dry mock against Mr Bayes: 'Let us see therefore what success the whole contrivance met with, or what it deserved. For, after things have been laid with all the depth of humane Policy, there happens lightly some ugly little contrary accident from some quarter or other of heaven, that frustrates and renders all ridiculous' (77). Reverent princes, as opposed to the Caligulas, acknowledge their dependence on God and hence accept the tenuousness of their authority which could at any time be revoked by providential intervention. God never

abdicates 'His Divine jurisdiction', although in modern times
He has chosen to operate through natural causes. To a reader
like Parker the implications of these remarks could be read as
thinly veiled threats to the King to mind his step, but that was
the risk that Marvell ran, as he certainly knew, and he was care-
ful to balance them with other features of the providential
constitution which exonerated him from bearing any particular
animus against the crown. Parliamentarians and lawyers could,
if they chose, have taken amiss another statement: 'And indeed
all laws however are but probationers of Time; and though
meant for perpetuity, yet, when unprofitable, do as they were
made by common consent, so expire by universal neglect, and
without repeal grow obsolete' (401). By failing to come to
terms with these obvious facts, Parker, Marvell concludes, does

hereby seem to imagine, that Providence should have contrived all things
according to the utmost perfection, or that which you conceive would
have been most to your purpose. Whereas in the shape of man's body, and
in the frame of the world, there are many things indeed lyable to objection,
and which might have been better, if we should give ear to proud and
curious spirits. But we must nevertheless be content with such bodies,
and to inhabit such an earth as it has pleased God to allot us (367–8).

The bitter truth, which not all readers of his poetry have
adequately appreciated, is that for Marvell 'nature' was
always fallen, and could not be relied upon as a guide to either
man's reason or his happiness. Parker based the absoluteness of
the King's authority on a gift of nature, antecedent to Christ,
and implicitly confirmed by Him because He did not retract it.
If nature was fallen, however, this was to found absolutism on a
quicksand, and Parker's imperative divinity was beside the
point. The remainder of a long quotation already begun must
suffice to confirm Marvell's fundamental belief that kings were
no less subject to the frustrations of their 'natural' inheritance
than the rest of the world, and that their government, being of
human ordinance and postlapsarian in origin, could lay no
claims to infallibility or perpetuity:

And so also in the government of the world, it were desirable that men might live in perpetual peace, in a state of good nature, without law or magistrate, because by the universal equity and rectitude of manners they would be superfluous. And had God intended it so, it would so have succeeded, and He would have sway'd and temper'd the mind and affec tions of mankind, so that their innocence should have expressed that of the Angels, and the tranquillity of His dominion here below should have resembled that in Heaven. But, alas, that state of perfection was dissolv'd in the first instance and was shorter liv'd than anarchy, scarce of one day's continuance. And ever since the first brother sacrificed the other to revenge, because his offering was better accepted, slaughter and war has made up half the business in the world, and oftentimes upon the same quarrel, and with like success. So that, as God has hitherto, instead of an eternal Spring, a standing serenity, and perpetual sunshine, subjected mankind to the dismal influence of comets from above, to thunder, and lightning, and tempests from the middle region, and from the lower surface to the raging of the seas and the tottering of earthquakes, beside all other the innumerable calamities to which humane life is exposed, He has in like manner distinguish'd the government of the world by the intermitting seasons of discord, war, and publick disturbance. Neither has He so order'd it only (as men endeavour to express it) by meer permission, but sometimes out of complacency.   (368–9)

In this context, Marvell's distinctive contribution to the con troversy should appear more plainly. His fellow defenders of toleration sound the most familiar when they are denying that the King's prerogative can be extended to include absolute rights over the private conscience, but Marvell's case rests on the historically provable fact that absolutism *of any kind* is impossible in the fallen state of nature. Kings and priests share man's proclivity to repeat the errors of his first parents, and only the handful of clearly revealed truths in the Bible can pretend to infallibility. God, moreover, has given no more promise 'that grace is given in committing the ecclesiastical office then...in committing the civil', and the first apostles were careful to disclaim any rights of 'supremacy, impery, or dominion' over the people (464). Kings and bishops are not deities but the chief graziers of their flocks, and the laws they make are human laws, which impose a human, not a divine, obligation on their subjects to keep them. An infraction of a good law will generally infringe the divine law also, but men will have no certain knowledge of their sins against God until they reach the Seat of Judgment. While all men, kings included, are liable to be wrong, intransigence is the attitude that least becomes them, and Marvell's best hatred is reserved for the prelates of the civil war who led Charles by stages to 'that imaginary absolute government, upon which rock we all ruined' (212). Parker would lead Charles II along the same path with potentially similar results, but Marvell's warning to his antagonist to beware of 'hooking things up to heaven' (407) should not be misunderstood. It has been taken to mean that 'Marvell was coming to accept as inevitable the separation of the providential universe from the naturalistic world of seventeenth-century philosophy and science',[1] but he intends simply to reassert that Parker 'would do well and wisely not to stretch, gold-beat, and wier-draw humane laws thus to heaven' (408), that is, to insist that every ecclesiastical or civil ordinance carries with it the pains of damnation for disobedience. Marvell's whole argument depends not on unhooking the earthly life from heaven, but on hitching the two together as closely as any casuist had done during the civil war. There might be no revelation, no unction, nor any voice to speak from a burning bush, but God still shook up His universe from time to time not 'by meer permission, but sometimes out of complacency'. The absence of revelation might deceive the unwary into the supposition that their absolutism, whether in government or opinion, would pass unnoticed, but God had ordained natural political laws which would come into play if oppression were ever to grow insufferable to His people.

In a memorable exposition of these laws, Marvell compares the ecclesiastical wisdom with the attempt after the Deluge 'to

[1] Harold E. Toliver, *Marvell's Ironic Vision* (New Haven, Conn., 1965), p. 191.

erect an impregnable Babel of power' which, however, like 'all such vain attempts are still by the Divine Providence turn'd into confusion' (380). History, he continues, has continually shown that all primitive institutions become overlaid with errors, defects, and excesses, which it should be the business of political prudence to reform. Nothing exists to prevent society from amending its own manners, but should it neglect to do so, it becomes the duty of the magistrate to redress the corrupt innovations; should society and the prince fail in their responsibility, 'this work, being on both sides neglected, falls to the people's share, from which God defend every good government! For though all commotions be unlawful, yet by this means they prove unavoidable. In all things that are insensible there is nevertheless a natural force alwayes operating to expel and reject whatsoever is contrary to their subsistence' (382). Even animals can be emboldened by their common inconveniences to mutiny against man, their lord and master, 'and the "common people" in all places partake so much of sense and nature, that, could they be imagined and contrived to be irrational, yet they would ferment and tumultuate at last for their own preservation' (382). The words echo the familiar puritan excuse for resistance in the 1640s, self-preservation, but Marvell has dissociated himself from it by implying that the actions of an undifferentiated 'people' are not wholly rational, and are motivated by a blind instinct, which, accurate enough as a response to oppression and inevitable by the operation of natural law, is nevertheless too thoughtless a reaction for an educated man or an instructed parliament. The people, conscious only of their sufferings, are careless of consequences and indifferent to 'the Civicke crown' which will be lost in their overturnings.

This paraphrase will appear less selective if it is set beside the passage which has been quoted more than any other lines of Marvell's prose:

I think the cause was too good to have been fought for. Men ought to have trusted God; they ought and might have trusted the King with that whole matter. 'The arms of the Church are prayers and tears'; the arms of the subjects are patience and petitions. The King himself, being of so accurate and piercing a judgment, would soon have felt where it stuck. For men may spare their pains where nature is at work, and the world will not go the faster for our driving. Even as his present Majestie's happy Restauration did it self, so all things else happen in their best and proper time, without any need of our officiousness.   (212–13)

Few of Marvell's enemies lost an opportunity for sarcasm; the 'cause too good' was the good old cause in a poor disguise, and the passage offered them one of their best occasions for refusing to believe that there was any difference between Marvell and a rebellious dissenter. The difference, indeed, is not in their understanding of the causes of the war, because the quotation occurs at the end of Marvell's long diatribe against the anglican bishops which any nonconformist would have seconded; neither is Marvell less inclined to attribute the outcome to providence. A distinction can be maintained only with respect to the King, who Marvell believes might have been trusted, together with the natural laws which sooner or later would peacefully have accomplished the revolution. From a biographical point of view, and even allowing something to rhetoric and to the experience of twenty-five years, it is conceivable that Marvell's statement may describe his true sentiments during the civil war. Everyone has inferred his loyalty to the crown until 1649, and all we lack is any contemporary evidence that he believed then that the puritans had a true cause. The evidence of the Interregnum years is in favour of such a belief. The complexity of his assertion in 1672, however, rests on his full awareness that nature was at work in the struggle on the side of the oppressed dissenters, but that the eventual issue, which was the Restoration, had shown that men ought and might have trusted the King. Without the insidious influence of the bishops, Marvell is saying, providence might have spared England the worst of her afflictions, and the restoration of a moderate and mixed monarchy might have occurred earlier without bloodshed. Marvell knew, of course, that he could not argue with God; and, if all things happen in their best and proper time, then what actually happened cannot be laid solely at the door of men's officiousness. There is perhaps a logical flaw in Marvell's famous declaration, but it captures like no other not only his recognition of a deformed nature through which God still works, but a rare regret that providence had not been more kind, and men more conscious of the slow, but generally even, tenor of its way.

Again, the mere suggestion that all thrones are slippery and subjects occasionally revolt could be twisted into a confession that Marvell's own loyalty was shaky and potentially alienable from his sovereign; but not only would the deduction contradict the history of his various allegiances, it would ignore his often stated dread of the passionate rabble, under both Cromwell and Charles, and his refusal to identify himself with the non-conformists. The latter insisted endlessly that they were peaceable, but their role in the civil war made it virtually impossible for them to discuss the past with any frankness. Marvell's readiness to defend them and at the same time to write intrepidly about the war was linked to the different nature of his argument and to his detachment from the rights they claimed. Writing explicitly as a private man, not as a member of parliament, and as an English subject, not as a dissenter, he is able to assume in every sentence that his first duty is towards the King, and his one aim the stability of the state. He can examine the causes of the war because his overriding concern is not the right of free worship but the horror with which he contemplates a possible recurrence of strife. His assurance that no one is 'more desirous or more sensible of the necessity of publick obedience' is not hollow, and, as he adds, his emphasis on the 'aptitude and convenience' of laws, not their inviolability, 'proceeds rather from an honorable apprehension concerning God, that He could not institute government to the prejudice of mankind, or exact obedience to laws that are destructive to society' (399–400). Because the dissenters are members both of mankind and of society, Marvell does not affirm categorically that they can continue suffering indefinitely—'some think it impossible' that they should (177)—but is content to observe the unlikelihood of their starting another war on the same pretext as before. The preceding list of examples of the misfortunes which have happened to kings from their unwillingness to condescend to their people suggests that he thought the danger remained.

By grasping firmly Marvell's commitment to the providential constitution of the universe, by which all human constitutions were necessarily regulated and conditioned, one is in a better position to understand Marvell's emphasis on expedient government, and not to confuse it with expedient principles. In a world from which absolutism had been abolished by the Fall, temperance, moderation, and prudence had been left as the virtues which man must incorporate in all his institutions, or omit at his peril. The longevity of his empires, as of his body, must depend on steering a humble course between the extremes to which his pride will inevitably draw him. Such a belief does not deny the operations of the spirit that may at times especially grace a country or the person of its leader, but it does affirm that stability is normally the result of a balanced system in which no element predominates absolutely. States cannot will their perpetuity, since, like laws, they are probationers of time, but they can try to insure that their constitutions are so constructed that no one faction can claim authority at the expense of all the others. England had been blessed by its mixed or limited monarchy and, humanly speaking, the equitable distribution of power among the estates of the realm afforded her a strength that probably could not be bettered, and which could only be endangered by the failure of the components to keep their proper place.

The orthodoxy of these platitudes needs no elaboration,

because, as many historians have shown, they persist as a broad current throughout the vicissitudes of the century. Charles I had sanctioned them; and the casuistry of the civil war, the defences of the Protectorate, and the humble addresses at the Restoration had never lost sight of their importance. Marvell could hardly have appealed to a body of ideas which was more likely to command general assent, and his originality (if it may be so called) consists in the literalness and the tenacity of his grasp of first principles. Parker and L'Estrange, as well as their nonconformist opponents, would have conceded that the fallen state of nature precluded certainty in human affairs, and they explicitly admitted that government was of human ordinance, but they did not draw the conclusion from these facts that moderation in opinion and a system of scrupulously balanced powers in government were therefore the only possible means by which national stability could be hoped for. By 1659 Milton had come to recognize that immutability was not a providential gift but 'a natural consequence of a well-balanced system',[1] and most Englishmen paid lip-service at least to the principle; Marvell was among the few, only later to be known as trim-mers, who believed that moderation was the very essence of government and tried to embody their convictions in political maxims that emphasized both their adherence to the ideal of balance and the flexibility of policy which would be necessary to achieve it. Among earlier writers, Philip Hunton most clearly foreshadows Marvell's position. Hunton has been rightly credited with having perceived as early as 1643 that the pure theory of a mixed monarchy was difficult to apply in a crisis, because, in an equal allotment of powers, no single member of the mixture could claim sovereignty over the other. If the powers quarrelled, every man would be obliged to follow his own judgment, as there could be no appeal to a final and arbitrary will. The problem was not to be solved until 1688, and not conclusively even then, and all Marvell's writing after the

[1] Michael Fixler, *Milton and the Kingdoms of God* (London, 1964), p. 205.

Restoration demonstrates that he was aware of it. His attention to expediency is, in a true analysis, derived from his determination to support equally (one of his favourite words) the prerogatives of the King and the privileges of Parliament. Given the structure of the constitution, it was impossible to exalt one above the other, and the writer could only throw his weight into the side of the balance that needed correcting at the moment, without relinquishing his allegiance to the opposite factor. Under a good king, as Marvell saw, 'the dispute concerning the magistrate's power ought to be superfluous', and under three good kings in succession 'the very memory or thoughts of any such thing as publick liberty would, as it were by consent, expire and be for ever extinguish'd' (370, 373).

Parker caught the drift of Marvell's argument very well when he complained that 'though you are always excusing your self from medling with State affairs...yet are you always too prescribing to [kings] Rules of Wisdome and Discretion, teaching them when it is requisite to screw up, and when to let down their Prerogative, how to humour their Subjects, to condescend to their Infirmities, and bid them to be cover'd in their presence, and sometimes (as here) to be content with having their Power without exercising it'.[1] Given the circumstances that produced *The Rehearsal Transpros'd*, Marvell's concern with expediency centres on the discretion of the King. If Charles had resorted to 'an extraordinary...way of government' (373) in publishing the Declaration instead of relying on more parliamentary measures, it was at least an indication that, unlike his father, he had recognized in time 'where it stuck', and the sign of his wisdom could be applauded. Kings could not fail 'but by a mistaken choice betwixt rigour or moderation' (372), and Charles had shown his unwillingness 'to be trepann'd into another kind of tenure of dominion to be held at Mr. Bayes his pleasure' (81): Marvell might have substituted 'at Mr. Hobbes his pleasure', as the 'presumption'

[1] *Reproof*, p. 440.

of *Leviathan*, which is all he could find to say for it, was another term for its absolutism (75, 340). The King's royal and generous mind was a happy subject, no doubt made happier by the rarity of an occasion for praising it, and if Marvell made a mistake it was in imagining, even for a moment, that the experiment had begun 'how happy a prince and people might be under a plain and true Christian administration' (393). Charles, unfortunately, did not share with John Hales 'the native simplicity of a Christian Spirit' (132), so the Christian administration was doomed to failure, and the vices which were the cause of all disturbances were to rage unchecked. Divine and human laws were to continue to be confused, church and state were to remain virtually indivisible, and the controversy about ceremonies was interminable. The 'un-controulable principle' that had been introduced under pretence of divinity was to swell on the fodder of French subsidies, and Samuel Parker, as Marvell prophesied (429), was to be among the first to comply with James's catholic designs. Marvell himself was to grow disillusioned, but what is striking about his attitude in *The Rehearsal Transpros'd* is not his opportunism or insincerity but, on the contrary, the naïveté with which he assumed that the King's clemency could be relied upon and the Christian administration achieved in practice. He knew well enough that perfection was not to be expected, but the limited hopefulness with which he looked forward to a significant improvement in the state is as patent in 1672 as it was at all the earlier and crucial moments of English history of which he has left his recorded opinion.

An Account of the Growth of Popery and Arbitrary Government

The next five years brought not a single reassurance on any of the topics that were closest to Marvell's heart. There was no marked improvement in the cause of toleration, in spite of a growing preoccupation with popery, and the relations between King and Parliament merely deteriorated. The secret *entente* with France became a public certainty, the peace with Holland led to no confederacy of allies against the French menace, and if Marvell was indeed a member of William's 'Fifth Column' in England working to influence public opinion,[1] there was no indication that royal policy could be changed by such means. As Parliament met for a total of only eight months from April 1671 to the end of 1676, Marvell's letters are scarce, but their contents would justify the presumption that these years saw the slow attrition of his hopes, and a growing disillusion with the spectacle of public life. In one frank moment to William Popple, he commented, 'Nor is there any Philosophical Difference betwixt the Ignorance or Knowledge of these publick Matters' (319), and the same letter records the predominance of Danby, Lauderdale, and the Duke of York in the King's counsels, and a senseless uproar in the House of Commons when 'all Order was lost'. Two months earlier he could imagine only a providential intervention as a solution to the dispute between the two Houses over Shirley and Fagg (152). He implied that the King had lied in Parliament (320), and Lauderdale had been reported as willing to invade England with a Scots army (144, 321). The mischief presumably being hatched by a conclave of bishops and royal counsellors at the end of 1674 gave him much concern (313–17), and the Lords' Test Act of 1675 was an anathema which was to become vital evidence of the government's intentions when he came to write *The Growth of Popery*. Yet at the time, with uncommon good sense, he was hoping that its instigator, Danby, would not be impeached, so that 'more usefull and publick businesse may be resumed' (147). The first phase of his resentment during this final period of his life culminates in his 'reasonable transport' against the bellicose clergy in *Mr. Smirke; Or, the*

---

[1] A possibility advanced by K. H. D. Haley, *William of Orange and the English Opposition, 1672–4* (Oxford, 1953), pp. 57–9; and see index.

Divine in Mode (1676), which summarizes the main argument of that work and confirms that the violence practised in religious and political affairs was still the great enemy to the moderation for which the country craved (10):

I speak with some emotion, but not without good reason…Have they not already, *ipso facto*, renounced their Christianity, by avowing this principle [of forcing belief], so contrary to the Gospel? Why do not they Peter Hermite it, and stir up our Prince to an Holy War abroad, to propagate the Protestant religion, or at least our discipline and ceremonies, and they take the front of the battel? No, 'tis much better lurking in a fat benefice here, and to domineer in their own parishes above their spiritual vassals, and raise a kind of civil war at home but that none will oppose them. Why may they not, as well force men to Church, cram the Holy Supper too, down their throats (have they not done something not much unlike it?) and drive them into the rivers by thousands to be baptized or drowned?.... What can be the end of these things but to multiply force with force, as one absurdity is the consequence of another, till they may again have debased the reason and spirit of the Nation, to make them fit for ignorance and bondage? (81)

History can create its own metaphors, and the Popish Plot in the autumn of 1678 was the climax to the events which are the subject of *An Account of the Growth of Popery and Arbitrary Government*. It is fitting that the mystery of the plot has never been satisfactorily unravelled, as it therefore remains a symbol of the violence, the secrecy, and the tangled diplomacy of Charles's reign. Above all, it was an expression of the fear which these methods had engendered in the country, and the posthumous attribution to Marvell of complicity in it may be read as a left-handed compliment to his prescience a year earlier. If the combination of events when he wrote *The Rehearsal Transpros'd* was inflammable, the mixture in 1677 was explosive, and it was Marvell's intention, I think, to write a pamphlet which, by its own controlled vehemence, might light a train of events that would obviate a greater combustion. Written in all likelihood during the fall and winter of 1677, and appearing, Marvell said, 'about Christmass' (*Letters*, 331), it was almost certainly

planned to be ready for the reassembly of Parliament in January
and to influence its debates—a common practice among politi-
cal writers, to which Marvell refers in his letters. *The Growth of
Popery* steals the thunder from other pamphlets that appeared
before the breaking of the plot, but it is, less than any of Marvell's
other works, a commentary on hidden dangers and the voicing
of a minority opinion. The facts with which he deals and the
accusations he makes were common property, and his merit is
in recording them all at once. Louis XIV's uninterrupted
successes in Flanders during 1677 had openly dismayed many
members of Parliament during the debates, and formed the
chief cohesive factor in the House of Commons. Powle's
comment there that they lived 'in an age of so much design'
was but a polite way of referring to the conspiracy of which
Marvell accused the executive, and the sense that a deception
was being practised on the nation was widespread.[1] In March
1677, Lord Cavendish said in the House that 'he has heard it
formerly said "that there were Pensioners to the King of *France*
in the King's Council"', and he thought they were still
present, implying Lauderdale in particular.[2] The suspicion
that the French league had been formed at Dover was first
aired in 1677,[3] and the need to keep the balance of power in
Europe was an argument which nobody dared gainsay in
public. The other themes of *The Growth of Popery*—the pen-
sioners in Parliament, land armies, the fear of invasion, the
imprisonment of the four lords, and England's shabby treatment
of Holland—were equally in the public domain and the subject
of uninhibited remark. The adjournment of Parliament from
16 July to 3 December 1677 was correctly interpreted as a
decision in favour of France, and a meeting of opposition leaders

---

[1] Anchitell Grey, *Debates of the House of Commons, From the Year 1667 to the
Year 1694* (London, 1769), IV, p. 15; Andrew Browning, *Thomas Osborne,
Earl of Danby* (Glasgow, 1951), I, p. 261.

[2] Grey's *Debates*, IV, p. 200.

[3] E. S. de Beer, 'Charles II and Louis XIV in 1683', *EHR*, XXXIX (1924),
p. 87.

in April had arrived at the conclusion that Charles had no intention of going to war.[1] As Charles drew the curtains on the wedding night of William and Mary he was reputed to have said 'Now, Nephew, to your work. St. George for England', but Marvell was not alone in suspecting that the marriage was part of a catholic plot, and that St George had nothing to do with it.

What the country needed was not fuel for its anxieties, but a spokesman for its convictions, and *The Growth of Popery* is first and foremost a speaking-out, an attempt to be completely explicit about the dangers and suspicions that had already been canvassed individually. All the people desired was 'that his Majesty and his people unanimously, truly, sincerely and thoroughly declare and engage in this business, with a mutual confidence speaking out on both sides, and this, and nothing but this, would discharge and extinguish all jealousies... We hope his Majesty will declare himself in earnest, and we are in earnest; having his Majestie's heart with us, *let his hand rot off that is not stretcht out for this affair*; we will not stick at this or that sum or thing, but we will go with his Majesty to all extremities' (366–7). Earnestness, not to say a passionate intensity, is written into every paragraph of Marvell's argument; it marks the end of his raillery, and virtually the end of his patience. The jokes and the wit have disappeared, and in place of satire is a total seriousness. Things must be said in such a way that there could be no possibility of misunderstanding them, and only the anonymity of the pamphlet, which Marvell knew could not remain anonymous for long, stands between the author and the consequences of his views. There is no mincing language behind which he could take shelter later, only emphatic accusations and documented facts. In keeping with his intention to clear the air and force Charles to answer with equal honesty, Marvell published many of the messages that had passed between the Commons and the King, and one of the principal functions of his work is to give this private but factual evidence

[1] Browning, *Earl of Danby*, I, p. 228.

of the true state of affairs. *The Growth of Popery* describes the breakdown of the relations between court and country, King and Parliament, over the previous twelve years, and the documents with which its last third is interspersed give an irrefutable account of the impasse that government had reached. From this position the only deliverance was war with France, a new Parliament, and a return to former alliances. There are signs in Marvell's work of one or two prudent omissions, and his rhetoric does not fail him, but the whole tone of *The Growth of Popery* bespeaks Marvell's openness, not his devious political manœuvring, and the way to read the pamphlet is to read it straight, as his own personal vindication and advice. Its value to the whigs who followed lay in the cogency of a constitutional position which they increasingly adopted, and to the modern historian it offers a sincere and personal view of the times, unadulterated by merely party aims. In consequence, Marvell's famous impartiality, which still lingers in his evident amusement at the stupidity of Mr Smirke, would appear to have deserted him, to be replaced by an angry bias against the court. Certainly a definition of impartiality that accords an equal rightness to both sides, or which attempts a balanced and diplomatic appraisal suitable to a modern critic or historian, has to be abandoned, just as it has to be modified when discussing Marvell's position in the Horatian ode; but there is another kind of impartiality that springs from a commitment to principles and to what Professor Williamson has called 'the standards of decency' that, in his opinion and mine, always seemed to guide Marvell's judgments.[1] Such standards made him distrustful of the machinations of party politics, even when the party had similar objectives to his own, so that he could refer critically to Buckingham's leading 'the usuall life' (329), or in November 1677 to 'my Lord Shaftsbury and all his gang' (330). He could argue that Parliament ought to be dissolved and that the long prorogation was 'unprecedentedly illegal' while privately

[1] George Williamson, *Milton & Others* (Chicago, 1965), p. 135.

objecting to the tactics of the opposition in trying to carry
Parliament with them (332c–d). Similarly the Pope-burnings
that were encouraged by Shaftesbury in November 1677 drew
from him the remark, 'I am afraid they burne Popes to night'
(330).[1] The impartiality that Marvell claimed for himself, in
words which must be those of either an honest man or a
consummate hypocrite, is shown in his solemn asseveration to
Mayor Foxley on 18 January 1677. If, he said, Foxley had any
private business he wished him to perform, 'I shall strive to
promote it according to the best of my duty: and in the more
generall concerns of the nation shall God willing maintaine the
same incorrupt mind and cleare Conscience, free from Faction
or any selfe-ends, which I have by his Grace hitherto preserved'
(172).

One mark of his 'cleare Conscience' in writing *The Growth
of Popery* is in his publication of relevant documents and his
determination to be specific in his charges, but there are other
signs also that, within the limits of his conviction that the govern-
ment was corrupt, he tried to support his contention with a fair
presentation of evidence. In the first place, he never shuffled off
all the responsibility for the mess onto the executive, but was
equally ready to blame a Parliament that in large part had cor-
rupted itself without outside help. Both Houses, too, were
reprehensible in their conduct over the Shirley–Fagg dispute.
More significantly, however, Marvell's handling of some of the
main issues proceeds by stating fully the arguments with which
he disagrees, a method that expands considerably the usual
style of animadversions, where snippets from an opponent's
book are quoted briefly and then refuted at length. For example,
in the long concluding discussion of the King's reluctance to
make his alliances known to Parliament, we constantly learn
the opinion of the court party, so that in one place eleven of
their contentions are listed, before eighteen answers are listed

[1] Marvell also disapproved of a reckless speech of Shaftesbury's to Lord
Stafford about the Duke of York, *Letters*, pp. 329–30.

likewise (356–60). Elsewhere the formula 'Others said...
To this it was answered' is used with monotonous regularity.
It is possible in fact to obtain a clear picture of the whole debate
from Marvell's 'biased' account of it. He has also been accused
of less than candour in his censure of the Declaration of In-
dulgence, 'so highly praised by him at the time'.[1] Yet originally,
as we have seen, his enthusiasm was for indulgence rather than
the Declaration itself, and his recantation in *The Growth of
Popery* amounts to a categorical statement that the Declaration
had been aimed at the relief of catholics, and two pages of
reasons why the original law of Christianity which provided
against all severity to private conscience could not be upheld at
the present time (279–81). Christianity could only be pre-
served by 'humility, meekness, love, forbearance and patience',
and Marvell had nothing but contempt for the way in which
human and divine things had been bungled together 'to frame
an irregular figure of political incongruity'. Toleration would
be a necessity in a well-governed state, but, until the balance of
the English constitution had been restored, all parties must
abide by the existing rules of law:

Nevertheless because mankind must be governed some way and be held
up to one law or other, either of Christ's or their own making, the
vigour of such humaine constitutions is to be preserved untill the same
authority shall upon better reason revoke them; and as in the mean time no
private man may without the guilt of sedition or rebellion resist, so
neither by the nature of the English foundation can any publick person
suspend them without committing an errour which is not the less for
wanting a legal name to express it.   (281–2)

His attitude towards indulgence was consistent with his earlier
views because his explanation preserves his loyalty to the cause
while rejecting any wish to see it promulgated by unconstitu-
tional means.

A more surprising passage in which he is guilty, not of a
recantation, but of a rhetorical silence, is to be found in the

[1] Legouis, *Andrew Marvell*, p. 159.

brevity of his comments on 'An act for further securing the Protestant Religion, by educating the Children of the Royal Family therein', the longest document quoted in the book (340–52). It is the text of a bill in 1677 that sought to preserve the protestant church in England in the event of a line of catholic kings. Apart from calling it a cockatrice's egg and a monstrous birth, Marvell refused to draw out the implications of a proposal to commit a great deal of power to the bishops, and attributed the malice of the bill wholly to the 'conspirators'. That the bishops were either the contrivers or promoters of the bill, he declared, was a 'scandalous falsehood' and 'a sufficient warning to the clergy, how to be intrigued with the statesmen for the future' (340). Marvell's earlier speech on the bill in the House of Commons, the most fully recorded of his speeches, is perfectly clear about the danger he foresaw in allowing the bishops to present a Test to the King, and as undisguised as parliamentary procedure would allow in suggesting that they might be more inclined to fall in with a catholic king's wishes than compel him to follow theirs.[1] His silence in *The Growth of Popery* does much to confirm the merely constitutional aims of the work, because if Marvell passed up an opportunity to castigate the bishops—the bench he had described in an earlier letter as 'odiously ridiculous' (321)—he must have deliberately refrained from antagonizing anglican and clerical sentiment. By accusing the bishops only of folly, and avoiding ecclesiastical quarrels, Marvell at the same time sought the widest support for his criticism of foreign policy and his call for a new parliament. He also rejected the other possibility the bill offered of arguing that it was an offence against the royal prerogative, and this omission requires a comment.

The bill passed a second reading in the House of Commons in March 1677 and then died in committee. Historians have professed to find it strange that the opposition on this occasion

[1] William Cobbett, *Parliamentary History of England* (London, 1808), IV, pp. 855–7.

suddenly developed an unusual concern for the prerogative, like Sir Harbottle Grimstone, who argued that 'he would not, under pretence of providing against Popery do things against the legal and monarchical power of the kings of England', or like Vaughan, demanded, 'Shall the king give this power away, and lodge it in the ecclesiastics ?' Mallet declared that the bill would 'blow up the government, it states an interregnum and an oligarchy'.[1] Yet, although it was an obvious political manœuvre in the House for the opposition to uphold the pre-rogative, it was also a logical response to the bill, which, as Grimstone said, was 'a Test provided for the king' no less heinous than the Test for the people that had miscarried in the previous session. The opposition had succeeded in defeating the earlier bill, partly by stratagems and partly because it was un-mistakably Danby's attempt to reform a high-church, cavalier party, and they were not now about to see the anglican establish-ment favoured by more devious means. They distrusted the bishops as much as they suspected the King, and the opportunity to play one off against the other must have seemed irresistible. Marvell, however, had always hated the bishops, to whom he had attributed the cause of the civil war, and habitually preferred the King's prerogatives to theirs, and his speech in Parliament carries the usual ring of sincerity. The bill, he said, was 'unseasonable; it may be proper some other time, but not now'. Neither ought it to be supposed easily that the crown might devolve on a popish government, nor was it fit for a subject to imagine the death of the King. Above all, he would

cast as little umbrage on the successor, as might be. There is none yet in sight, but whose minds are in the hands of God, 'who turns them like the rivers of water'. Whilst there is time there is life, and whilst life, time for information, and the nearer the prospect is to the crown, information of judgment will be much easier. When God 'takes him on high and shows him the glory of the world', and tells him, 'All these things will I give thee, if thou wilt fall down and worship me', he thinks these will be no

[1] *Ibid.* pp. 853–5.

leaders who organized a party and carried the issue to the country through the heated years after the Popish Plot, and it was, I suggest, even more true of Marvell, who was writing before the storm broke and while there was still a chance that Charles's dependence on France could be broken by less violent parliamentary pressure.

One complication in 1677 which disappeared later was the fact that the leading 'conspirator' and Lord Treasurer, the Earl of Danby, was for the most part doing his best to hinder the King's French alliance and to build up an anglican following in both Houses. He was mainly responsible for the marriage of William and Mary that temporarily gave the opposition pause, and he may personally be exempted from some of the more serious charges that Marvell levelled at him and the other counsellors. As Marvell and all his readers knew, the 'conspirator' who was most to blame for the royal policy was Charles himself, and in any case, as head of his council, the King was logically most responsible for its decisions. As long as the King continued to rule and was not a figurehead, it was impossible to criticize his council without deeply implicating him, and good grounds existed, therefore, for taking as a personal affront any attacks on the administration. Hence the entire structure of *The Growth of Popery* is built on a rhetorical and legal fiction which permitted Marvell's original readers, as it permits readers today, to discount his professed respect for the King and to see his work as a giant subterfuge to deprive Charles of his most cherished prerogatives of making war and peace and calling parliaments when he pleased. If one may continue to be obvious, however—and a failure to take account of what should be familiar has resulted in some of the misguided versions of Marvell's later career—no parliamentary criticism of the government was conceivable during the seventeenth century without running this risk, or without distinguishing between the personal and official capacities of the King. Officially the King could do no wrong, and to his person all subjects were loyal. The legal fiction that the King was the Law, which he was therefore unable to break, and that his counsellors alone were responsible for bad advice was absolutely essential if the constitution was to function as a mixture at all. Hence fiction became truth, because subjects were obliged to speak and act at all times as if it were true, and parliaments would have been pointless without a working understanding that their conflicts with the administration did not involve a desertion of their loyalty from the crown. As a further consequence, Marvell's unusually emphatic resort to the fiction does not inevitably brand him as a rebel who sought to save his respectability and his neck by employing it. As a means of saying what dissidents wished to say, the fiction was open both to genuine republicans who might have joined a revolution and to genuine loyalists who desired only the correction of an abuse. Judgment has to be passed in individual cases, preferably in the light of subsequent deeds, without assuming in the first place either the sincerity or insincerity of the speaker. The problem is most acute during the civil war, when the execution of Charles casts a doubt retrospectively on the good faith of every casuist who was willing to do battle againt the royal forces while declaring eternal loyalty to the monarchy and the King's person. In fact, the issue of the war virtually outlawed the fiction during the first years of the Restoration, and members of the court party throughout Charles's reign registered their disapproval of it, often apparently with little conviction. They could not, however, stop its recrudescence as soon as Charles's policy became a matter of urgent disapproval, since no other means was available of making public the national sentiment.

The fiction had been in considerable demand since the struggle over the Test Bill in 1675. On that occasion Shaftesbury had argued that 'the King's authority is nothing but the law in other words', and if the King's commission were to be granted the status of law, then a standing army granted by his commission would be law. 'The King's Commission was never thought to protect or justify any man in any proceeding, when it was against his authority, which is the law.'[1] Five months later, Shaftesbury was to use the same reasons in the dispute of Shirley vs. Fagg: 'My principle is, "that the King is king by law, and by the same law that the poor man enjoys his cottage"'; but the House of Lords (whose prerogatives were being usurped in the quarrel) was also an 'essential part of the Government' by the same law. 'The King, governing and administering justice by his House of Lords, and advising with both his Houses of Parliament in all important matters, is the Government I own, I was born under, and am obliged to. If ever there should happen in future ages (which God forbid!) a King governing by an army without his Parliament, it is a Government I own not, am not obliged to, nor was born under.'[2] Shaftesbury escaped without official censure for this speech, but similar remarks by the Duke of Buckingham in 1677 when he claimed that the long prorogation had legally dissolved the Parliament landed him in the Tower: 'And, my Lords, with all the Duty we owe to his Majesty, it is no Disrespect to him to say, that his Majesty is bound up by the Laws of *England*; for the great King of Heaven and Earth, God Almighty himself, is bound by his own Decrees.' In a syllogism he was reputed to have written during the debate, he argued: 'It is a Maxim in the Law of *England*, that the Kings of *England* are bound up by all the Statutes made *pro bono publico*; that every Order or Direction of theirs, contrary to the Scope and full intent of any such Statute, is void and null in Law: But the last Prorogation of the Parliament was an order of the King's contrary to an Act of King *Edward III*...Ergo, the last Prorogation of Parliament is void and null in Law.'[3]

[1] W. D. Christie, *A Life of Anthony Ashley Cooper, First Earl of Shaftesbury, 1621–1683* (London, 1871), vol. II, appendix VI, p. lxxvii.

[2] *Ibid.* p. xcii.

[3] *The History and Proceedings of the House of Lords, from the Restoration in 1660 to the Present Time* (London, 1742), I, pp. 194–5.

The prorogation dispute produced other similar conclusions, including one by an anonymous writer who may stand for all: 'I would neither disobey any lawfull command of his Majesty, nor diminish the just *English* regall Power. I would not crop a leaf of any flower of the Crown, yet I make as much conscience not to betray my Country, or easily yeeld up the Ancient lawes and Government of *England*, by parliament, to the kings Will, to make *English* freemen tenants at will to the king, of their lawes, their parliaments, their liberties and lives.'[1]

As these passages suggest, it is ultimately misleading to speak of the 'fiction' of the King's identity with the law, since the mixed constitution depended upon the maintenance of it. Insofar as nature had not endowed the King with the God-like ability always to keep his own laws (nature was fallen), it was an invented construction open to abuses, which did not correspond with the literal facts. But without the fiction, the constitution would become a fiction, and the acceptance of one as a fact granted the other a factual existence too. Marvell's account of them both acknowledges the invented quality of the King's exemption from criticism but declares the complete adherence of his belief to it. The passage is remarkable for the frankness with which he implies at the threshold of his book that he is proceeding on an assumption, but an assumption that is necessary for everyone. 'Without that distinction [between the natural and political capacities of the King] there would be no law nor reason of law left in England' (307). Marvell succeeds, in a way which to my knowledge is unparalleled during this period, in being elaborately specific about the limitations on the King's power while sustaining a real enthusiasm for the system and a genuine respect for the sovereign's prerogatives. The passage is unduly long, but must be quoted in full in a study of Marvell's loyalism because it offers the best

[1] *A Seasonable Question, and a Usefull Answer, Contained in an Exchange of a Letter Between a Parliament-Man in Cornwell, and a Bencher of the Temple, London* (n.p. 1676), p. 5.

statement we have of the constitutional position that he upheld and defended:

For if first we consider the State, the kings of England rule not upon the same terms with those of our neighbour nations, who, having by force or by address usurped that due share which their people had in the government, are now for some ages in the possession of an arbitrary power (which yet no prescription can make legal) and exercise it over their persons and estates in a most tyrannical manner. But here the subjects retain their proportion in the Legislature; the very meanest commoner of England is represented in Parliament, and is a party to those laws by which the Prince is sworn to govern himself and his people. No money is to be levied but by the common consent. No man is for life, limb, goods, or liberty, at the Sovereign's discretion: but we have the same right (modestly understood) in our propriety that the prince hath in his regality; and in all cases where the King is concerned, we have our just remedy as against any private person of the neighbourhood, in the Courts of Westminster Hall or in the High Court of Parliament. His very Prerogative is no more than what the Law has determined. His Broad Seal, which is the legitimate stamp of his pleasure, yet is no longer currant, than upon the trial it is found to be legal. He cannot commit any person by his particular warrant. He cannot himself be witness in any cause: the balance of publick justice being so delicate, that not the hand only but even the breath of the Prince would turn the scale. Nothing is left to the King's will, but all is subjected to his authority: by which means it follows that he can do no wrong, nor can he receive wrong; and a King of England keeping to these measures, may without arrogance, be said to remain the onely intelligent Ruler over a rational People. In recompense therefore and acknowledgment of so good a Government under his influence, his person is most sacred and inviolable; and whatsoever excesses are committed against so high a trust, nothing of them is imputed to him, as being free from the necessity or temptation; but his ministers only are accountable for all, and must answer it at their perils. He hath a vast revenue constantly arising from the hearth of the Householder, the sweat of the Labourer, the rent of the Farmer, the industry of the Merchant, and consequently out of the estate of the Gentleman: a large competence to defray the ordinary expense of the Crown, and maintain its lustre. And if any extraordinary occasion happen, or be but with any probable decency pretended, the whole Land at whatsoever season of the year does yield him a plentiful harvest. So forward are his people's affections to give even to superfluity, that a forainer (or Englishman that hath been long abroad) would think they could neither will nor chuse, but that the asking of a supply were a meer formality, it is so readily granted. He is the fountain of all honours, and has moreover the distribution of so many profitable offices of the Household, of the Revenue, of State, of Law, of Religion, of the Navy and (since his present Majestie's time) of the Army, that it seems as if the Nation could scarce furnish honest men enow to supply all those imployments. So that the Kings of England are in nothing inferiour to other Princes, save in being more abridged from injuring their own subjects: but have as large a field as any of external felicity, wherein to exercise their own virtue, and so reward and incourage it in others. In short, there is nothing that comes nearer in Government to the Divine Perfection, than where the Monarch, as with us, injoys a capacity of doing all the good imaginable to mankind, under a disability to all that is evil.

(248–50)

The court might well have thought the generosity of Parliament had recently been open to question, and it would have had private reservations about the limitations on the King's will but, as Miss Robbins has said, Marvell's prolegomena would have been acceptable to all but eccentrics during a period of three centuries.[1] It is distinguished, like the rest of the pamphlet, by the high-mindedness of Marvell's tone and his undisguised determination to state both sides of the constitutional bargain as explicitly as he could. His declaration stands like an open challenge to every reader to find fault with his orthodoxy and defies the implication of disrespect to the King.

Perhaps more remarkable than what it contains, however, is what it omits, because Marvell was naturally aware that the theory of the mixed constitution, when argued by the opposition, generally included a right of resistance to a ruler who had become tyrannical. Such a right is implied in Shaftesbury's comment, quoted earlier, that he was 'not obliged to' a govern-ment which ruled by an army without a parliament, but,

[1] Caroline Robbins, *The Eighteenth-Century Commonwealthman* (Cambridge, Mass., 1959), pp. 53–4. See also Holdsworth, *History of English Law*, VI, pp. 203–17, for a discussion of the prerogative with special reference to Sir Matthew Hale, whom Marvell praised highly.

throughout the whole of Marvell's attack on arbitrary government, he made but one reference to the right of resistance and then only because he thought the administration had insisted by its Test Act on disturbing matters which were better left alone. 'But as to the *quieta movere*, or stirring of those things or questions which are and ought to be in peace, was not this so, of taking arms against the King upon any pretence whatsoever?' Had not the Acts against the dissenters sufficiently quieted the 'traiterous position of taking arms by his authority against his person'? It was nevertheless in the laws of all countries that a private man might defend himself if assaulted by any king in Christendom, but 'if this matter as to a particular man be dubious, it was not so prudent to stir it in the general, being so well settled' (307). Given the strength of his conviction that a tyranny was well on the way to being established, Marvell's restraint is extraordinary, and offers the best evidence that he desired reform without disturbance, and sought to achieve his end without raising thoughts of 1641. In effect, he eschewed the arguments from 'reason' that were so soon to become the mainstay of whig resistance. Marvell wrote not a word about contract, nothing about the state of nature, or the derivation of the King's power. He nowhere implied that the King's will should be subservient to Parliament's, and even in his final marshalling of all the arguments for and against the advice that Parliament insisted on offering the King about his alliances, Marvell emphasized the advantages of the advice and minimized Parliament's right to demand such specific terms for its money. Similarly, *The Growth of Popery* is singularly devoid of the history and pseudo-history on which the other half of whig theory depended. Marvell refers in general terms to 'precedents' and occasionally lists a few of them in passing, but his argument is not based on a manipulation of historical examples, just as his thesis in *The Rehearsal Transpros'd* had kept clear of the most common grounds for defending toleration. In his *A Short Historical Essay Touching General*

Councils, appended to *Mr. Smirke*, Marvell had shown that he could handle an historical argument with great skill, and he could if he pleased have filled *The Growth of Popery* with immemorial parliaments, the statutes of Edward III, and allusions to earlier abuses of the prerogative.

Marvell's choosing to avoid both 'reason' and history as the basis of his attack results in the same practical and pragmatic emphasis that he adopted in *The Rehearsal Transpros'd*. His argument rests simply on the opening constitutional declaration and the following assertion that a conspiracy exists to subvert its propositions. One is as eloquent and orthodox as he could make it, the other is documented in detail. By refusing to resort to the usual whig scholarship, Marvell has preserved himself from its inherent contradictions and its inescapable tendency to imply a theory of resistance. In her very lucid exposition of whig theory twenty-five years ago, Miss Behrens demonstrated that the ideals of the mixed constitution and the rule of law, to which nearly all whigs officially subscribed, were gradually undermined during the Exclusion crisis by the qualifications that were attached to them, and when history could not constrict the prerogative tightly enough, 'reason' could supply the omissions. History, as the whigs employed it, reinforced the belief in the actual, traditional English liberties, while 'reason' constituted an idea of liberty that defined freedom as the expression of the people's will.[1]

As Miss Behrens has shown, the whigs gradually realized that they had gone too far and, after the crisis, they slowly returned to the unqualified assertion of their belief in the mixed monarchy. The ultimate position they maintained is to be identified with that of the trimmers, to whom the future of whig constitutionalism belonged. The trimmers did not acquire their name until 1682 and cannot even then be identified with an organized bloc in Parliament. They did, however, stand for the fundamental principles on which the revolution of 1688 was

[1] *Camb. Hist. Journ.* VII, p. 70.

based and they represented the core of moderate opinion from which the radicalism of a Sidney was eventually seen to be a deviation. To quote Miss Behrens again, 'the Trimmer's idea of the constitution was expressed to a smaller degree in terms of first principles than that of either of the other parties to the dispute. Trimmer writings insisted on the necessity of compromise and reasonableness; they were concerned neither with the ultimate purpose of the state nor with its origins; instead they emphasized the value, assumed rather than explained, of certain specific institutions and conditions of political life. In them appears primarily a deep attachment to the religion of the Church of England, to the distinguishing features of English government, and to the ideas of liberty and the rule of law, neither of which they defined at all precisely, but which, in Halifax's words, they saw enshrined "in our blessed constitution if rightly understood and properly preserved".'[1] Apart from the clause about a love for the Church of England, this admirable summary defines the aim and emphasis of Marvell's work. *The Growth of Popery* is uncompromisingly critical, but recognizes that 'a form of government which is itself a compromise can only be made to work by people who are prepared to compromise'.[2] Marvell's pamphlet was the first great manifesto to proclaim the future whig doctrine in its entirety and it upheld the position which his successors and the country eventually adopted. The trimmers themselves were naturally accused of hypocrisy, of being amphibious creatures with tory wings and whig teeth, but L'Estrange's first picture of the trimmers, intended to be satirical, describes Marvell as he was. The trimmer, he said, was in favour of lenity, indulgence, and moderate councils; he was against violence on both sides and upheld the right of King and people. He had no wish to inflame differences and beget heats, and declared that his prince was gracious but might employ bad advisers: he prayed for peace and quietness, the government of law, and tranquillity

[1] *Ibid.* p. 70.   [2] *Ibid.* p. 71.

among protestants.[1] It is no wonder that L'Estrange and Ned‑ham called Marvell the record‑keeper of the faction and that *The Growth of Popery* became to later generations of tories the standard libel of the age. In spite of the lack of any actual evi‑dence, it is psychologically possible that the success of Marvell's work drew him into closer co‑operation with the leaders of the opposition and, for the same reason, I see a similar possibility that Marvell wrote *A Seasonable Argument* to discredit the pensioners in the House of Commons. Neither of these possi‑bilities, and they are not more than that, affects the integrity of his opposition to Charles and his wish to spare him personal abuse. As Marvell said on the last page,

some will represent this discourse (as they do all books that tend to detect their conspiracy) against his Majesty and the kingdom, as if it too were written against the government. For now of late, as soon as any man is gotten into publick imployment by ill acts, and by worse continues it, he, if it please the fates, is thenceforward the government, and by being criminal, pretends to be sacred...But this book, though of an extra‑ordinary nature, as the case required, and however it may be calumniated by interested persons, was written with no other intent than of meer fidelity and service to his Majesty, and God forbid that it should have any other effect, than that '*the mouth of all inquity and of flatterers may be stopped*', and that his Majesty, having discerned the disease, may with his healing touch apply the remedy; for so far is the relator himself from any sinister surmise of his Majesty, or from suggesting it to others, that he acknow‑ledges, if it were fit for Caesar's wife to be free, much more is Caesar himself from all crime and suspicion. Let us therefore conclude with our own common devotions, 'From all privy conspiracy, &c. Good Lord deliver us'. (413–14)

To follow Marvell's political career is to trace his allegiance to the providential constitution. In his youth he gave moral support to Charles I, while probably sympathizing with the

[1] Donald R. Benson, 'Halifax and the Trimmers', *HLQ*, xxvii (1964), p. 119. This article analyses most of the references to trimmers in the early 1680s. A trimmer, said L'Estrange, 'is a man of Latitude, as well in Politiques as Divinity' (H. C. Foxcroft, *The Life and Letters of Sir George Saville, Bart.* [London, 1898], ii, p. 273).

religious aims of the more moderate revolutionaries. In 1650 he decided that Cromwell bore the marks of an elected leader and that providence, 'not out of meer permission but...complacency', had irrevocably doomed the old dispensation. For the next nine years he looked forward to, and sought to promote, the establishment of a Christian policy that would incorporate the traditional features of English law. In so doing he was spurred by a personal respect and perhaps affection for Cromwell, and by a sober millenarian hopefulness that rejected the democratic excesses of fervent chiliasts. In 1660 he must have reflected with considerable bitterness that men ought and might have trusted the King. Like virtually a whole nation, he had been proved wrong, and the Interregnum had proved to be no more than an interlude in the Inscrutable Design. Providence had declared its hand, but it was clear also that the Last Days would not be ushered in by a Stuart. The hope for better days revived, but the millenarian possibility had disappeared forever. Any further change in the state was an eventuality that could inspire only horror. Thereafter Marvell toiled with all the patience he could muster to preserve the constitution from collapse. What Miss Robbins has noticed of the Restoration period—Marvell's stability amidst the fluctuations of two decades—would be true also of his whole career.[1] His fundamental convictions, his Christianity and his constitutionalism, did not change but were consistently applied to circumstances over which he had no control. Because of his intelligence and honesty, he emerges from history as an exceptionally valuable witness to a large body of moderate men who do not fit the old categories of royalist and puritan.

Beneath the clear-cut divisions of a battlefield or a debate in parliament there are a thousand ways in which the antagonists can be alike. A decision for one side or the other would seem often to depend on a man's last analysis of 'where it stuck'—that is, on the conviction that remains singular after all

[1] 'A Critical Study', p. 343.

similarities have been explored. During the civil war, not all
the casuists were like Hunton, but again and again one has the
impression that only an arbitrary and even unarguable difference
of feeling determines the cause for which they were prepared to
fight. Marvell stuck at drawing his sword against his sovereign,
whatever his hatred might be of the bishops, and the same
loyalty is to be perceived to Charles II even when there was
least reason to trust him. To read *The Growth of Popery* as a
popular work that tried to capture the imagination of the people
or to threaten the King is to suppose that Marvell had learned
nothing from the civil war and the Commonwealth. From the
perspective of 1677, the Interregnum and Cromwell himself had
produced nothing of constitutional value, and nothing but
more hardship for the cause too good to have been fought for.
The revolution which had once raised a great hope of a true
Christian administration had in its turn been condemned by
providence, and its accomplishments were lost in the sand.
But the natural political laws that had come into play when
men forsook moderate courses would always operate if the
same causes reoccurred. Marvell watched their wheels turning
again during the last years of his life, and in 1688 he was to be
proved a true prophet. I suspect that the bloodlessness of 1688
would have persuaded him, had he been alive, of another
divine intervention in English history, but it is impossible to
say if he would have voted earlier for Exclusion. He might well,
like Halifax, have thought it unseasonable and unwise; or,
on the other hand, he might have been willing to accept
the excuses that the whigs invented for its constitutionality.
Whatever the verdict on these speculations, it must be granted
that he died holding a view of the constitution that was an
uncontaminated and accurate distillation of the experience of
seventeenth-century Englishmen, which they embodied in
their final settlement. The Glorious Revolution showed also
that 'the way to be a constant Royalist, is to be a constant
Loyalist; not to respect the power or place for the persons

sake, but the person for the place and power[s] sake'. Allegiance would still be given to a usurping power which could show plain evidence of God's approval. Furthermore, Marvell's account of the chicanery practised by the court from the time of the Triple Alliance entered the whig histories of the eighteenth century, and its general reliability has been confirmed by the researches of contemporary historians. Both Marvell's changes and his opinions make him in fact one of the most representative men of his age. Yet for all his rightness, and his uncanny knack of standing up for attitudes that only later were to be incorporated into the common will, the final spectacle is of his defeat and resignation. The letters that survive from the last months of his life form a kind of coda to *The Growth of Popery*. Nothing had changed, the book had not achieved its aim, a new Parliament was nowhere in sight, the ministers were still in office, and the war with France was now imminent, now receding, until it finally faded away. It is a dying, disappointed, but Christian fall, captured best in a letter written on 14 May 1678: 'I doubt not but many will reflect upon this Prorogation for other reasons. But they that discourse the lest and thinke the best of it will be the wisest men and the best Subjects. God in mercy direct his Majesty always to that which may most conduce to his own and the Kingdomes happinesse' (225). And, on 23 May, 'God in his mercy direct all to the best.'

6

'Destiny their Choice':
'Upon Appleton House, to my Lord Fairfax'

Upon Appleton House is Marvell's most original and ambitious poem, the complexities of which will always elude any single reading of it. Like many of his other poems it is often bafflingly private, and one may suspect that it contains personal allusions only Lord Fairfax would have understood. Among other things, it is also a poem about Marvell himself and his calling to an active life, and explains why he chose a public career. Philosophical rather than political, and addressed to one man rather than many, it deliberately avoids oratorical schemes and polemical positions, although its argument, as I hope to show, rises with a serene finality on the ruins of an opposite point of view. More literally than any other poem it holds up the mirror to nature, and as the reader stares at the images in the glass the configurations of Marvell's deepest convictions become apparent. Hence it can offer another perspective on the more narrowly political aims that he followed for twenty-five years after his service with Lord Fairfax had ended.

Among the English predecessors of the kind of poem that *Upon Appleton House* is, Drayton's *Poly-Olbion*, Waller's poem on the restoration of St Paul's, and Denham's *Cooper's Hill* are the most important. Each of them presupposes a man looking at a local scene and finding it to be a microcosm of the larger world; the scene itself is a small mirror in which 'things greater are in less contain'd' (44).[1] As Professor Wasserman has said of *Cooper's Hill*, the poetic procedure is the 'act of transforming the physical world into values and meanings by way of

[1] Line numbers have been incorporated in the text; or reference to stanzas, in roman numerals, has been made when more convenient.

metaphor', or it may be described as the contest between the poet's thought and vision for possession of the scene, until it becomes symbolic.[1] Denham called some of his scenes 'emblems', and the objects he saw before him often 'seemed' to be rather different from their usual selves, but about the solidity and actuality of the scenes there is no doubt. One of the most curious features of *Upon Appleton House* is that Marvell has carried the 'as if' process much further, so that the objects of his vision enjoy an uncertain status in the real world. We cannot actually believe that he saw an oak felled by a woodpecker, or that the heron dropped its young purposefully on his head, nor do we believe in the destruction of the monastery by Fairfax's ancestor, or the woods dividing to form a guard. Even in the first and most objective part of the survey, we are asked to see the house literally swelling to receive its lord, and in the last section nature physically responds to Maria's entrance. Similarly, as Marvell looks at nature, a very large number of the objects he sees only 'seem' to him to be what he says they are, or to do what he says they do. The oak seems to fall content, the mowers seem like Israelites, the villagers seem, the meadow seems. The leaves in the garden seem to be ensigns, the sight seems to point the battery of its beams. The women tossing hay 'represent' the pillaging; the nunnery disappears like an enchantment, and the mowers vanish equally suddenly. The poet's own vantage point is also insecure and his personal pronoun varies between 'I' and 'we'. In the wood he 'thinks' he is safe, but he is also in a constant process of becoming, either a bird, or a plant, or a Druid, or a prisoner, and in one case even a book with bookworms (LXXIV).

The explanation of this slipperiness is that Marvell is looking not at things but at images, which are themselves reflections either of an outside reality or of the qualities of their owner, Lord Fairfax. In fact each of the poem's sections is introduced by a leading metaphor, not by a discursive description. The

[1] Earl R. Wasserman, *The Subtler Language* (Baltimore, 1959), pp. 48–9.

meadow is an abyss, the wood an ark, the garden the just figure of a fort. In the first section the house has a double meaning, and the convent section is chiefly a monologue by an imaginary nun. The poem is constituted not only by images but about images, because an art which is a mirror reflecting a microcosm must be at two removes from a macrocosmic or ideal reality. This is particularly clear in the meadow scene where the accident that 'grass' rhymes with 'glass' brings the idea into the open.

> And now to the Abbyss I pass
> Of that unfathomable Grass,
> Where Men like Grashoppers appear   (XLVII)

and later

> They seem within the polisht Grass
> A Landskip drawn in Looking-Glass.   (LVIII)

But this section is not different in kind from the others, because the changing scenes in the meadow are only more obviously temporary than the scenes elsewhere, and all of them together are transformed by the miraculous entry of Maria Fairfax at the end of the poem:

> But by her *Flames*, in *Heaven* try'd,
> *Nature* is wholly *vitrifi'd*.   (LXXXVI)

Before Maria's appearance nature was but imperfectly vitrified and gave off distorted or partial images, which the mirror of art could only 'deface' more (77).

The poetic theory behind *Upon Appleton House* would thus appear to be platonic, since the removes of art from reality are emphasized, and the rationale of Marvell's view of nature can also be found in the platonic theology in which both he and Fairfax are known to have been interested. Commenting on the shadows of Plato's cave, Ficino wrote, 'Quare non subito, sed paulatim convenientibus gradibus ab umbris rerum ad res ipsas, item a luminis imagine ad lumen ipsum est perducendus, ita ut quae in spelunca sunt apud illos, prius illic in aqua videat, quam ibidem in seipsis inspiciat', and he then illustrated this proposition with the example of the sun's reflection viewed in the water which occurred in a famous crux in the *Aeneid* and was paraphrased by Fairfax in one of his own poems.[1] In Tasso's imaginary dialogue between Ficino and Landino, Ficino explains that 'le forme corruttibile de le cose inferiori sono quasi imagini e figure: laonde in comperazione de le idee possono esser dette imagini ch'appaiono ne l'acque, ne le quali non è alcuna stabilità o fermezza'.[2] The imaginary and figurative quality of natural things precisely defines the evanescence of Marvell's nature in the poem, where the same images reoccur in different facets of the mirror in different forms. Isabella Thwaites, for example, becomes the young female rail which is killed in the grass, who becomes Maria Fairfax in her human role at the end of the poem. Images of imprisonment appear and disappear, and military metaphors undergo sea-changes. To adopt a famous metaphor of Hobbes's that Marvell had certainly read, the glass reflects the 'picture' at which it is directed, and the picture is itself a scattered representation of the true reality. Hobbes wrote to Davenant,

I beleeve, Sir, you have seen a curious kinde of perspective, where he that looks through a short hollow pipe upon a picture containing divers figures sees none of those that are there painted, but some one person made up of their parts, conveyed to the eie by the artificial cutting of a glass. I finde in my imagination an effect not unlike it from your Poem. The vertues you distribute there amongst so many noble Persons represent in the reading the image but of one mans vertue to my fancy, which is your own...[3]

In less platonic terms, however, Marvell's nature, like Ficino's, is the 'glass' into which St Paul said that all men darkly peer.

[1] Ficino, *Theologia Platonica*, VI. ii, in *Opera Omnia* (Torino, 1959), I(i), 160, misnumbered 144. The crux in the *Aeneid* is VIII. 22–5, and Fairfax's poem is *The Solitude* in *The Poems of Thomas, Third Lord Fairfax*, ed. Edward Bliss Reed (New Haven, Conn., 1909), p. 269.

[2] Torquato Tasso, *Dialoghi*, ed. Ezio Raimondi (Firenze, 1958), II, p. 894.

[3] 'The Answer of Mr Hobbes to Sr. Will. D'Avenant's Preface Before *Gondibert*' in *Critical Essays of the Seventeenth Century*, ed. J. E. Spingarn (Oxford, 1908), II, pp. 66–7. Hereafter this volume is cited as Spingarn.

The insubstantiality of all earthly things is intrinsic to almost
every discussion of St Paul's text since the glass was commonly
held to be the nature that man would leave behind when he
met God face to face.[1] Marvell on good authority, therefore,
could assume that to write a poem was but to turn one meta-
phor into another, and that the 'lesser *World*...in more
decent Order tame' of the Nunappleton estate (765–6) could
be imaged in the yet smaller microcosm of the poem. The
advantage of microcosmic mirrors, whether in poetry or land-
scape, was that all the world's dangerous actions, reflected like
Gorgons' heads in the polished shield, were rendered harmless
and pleasing. At Nunappleton the wicked Nile flows by in
'wanton harmless folds' (633), and the bloody scenes in the
meadow are pointedly referred to as 'these pleasant Acts'
(465).[2] Art thus delights while it teaches, whereas in the macro-
cosm there would have been only real parents mourning their
dead children instead of rails creaking sorrowfully in the grass.
On the other hand, the frivolity of imitating mere images was
also a platonic tradition, and when at the end of his poem
Marvell throws down his useless pen he is modestly admitting
that Maria has perfected the art he copied, and reminded him
that he is a 'trifling Youth':

[1] An interesting discussion of 1 Corinthians xiii. 12 is to be found in Gordon
Worth O'Brien's *Renaissance Poetics and the Problem of Power* (Chicago, 1956),
chapter 1. He is more concerned with other interpretations of the text than the
one given here. Donne's sermon on the text, in *Sermons*, ed. Evelyn M.
Simpson and George R. Potter (Berkeley, Calif., 1953–62), VIII, pp. 219–36
externalizes the glass as 'nature' and is full of ideas that suggest analogies with
Upon Appleton House.

[2] The idea that art is a 'harmless' image is fairly common. Davenant expressed
it neatly in his *Poem to the Kings most Sacred Majesty*, in *Works* (London, 1673),
1st pagination, pp. 268–9:

> The *Theatre* (the Poets Magick-Glass
> In which the Dead in vision by us pass;
> Where what the *Great* have done we do again,
> But with less loss of time and with less pain).

But now away my Hooks, my Quills,
And Angles, idle Utensils.
The *young Maria* walks to night:
Hide trifling Youth thy Pleasures slight.
'Twere shame that such judicious Eyes
Should with such Toyes a Man surprize;
She that already is the *Law*
Of all her *Sex*, her *Ages Aw*. (LXXXII)

Art mirrors the nature with which it is confronted, and the poem naturally defines itself first as the building which is the primary object of its vision. The poem as monument was one of the most ancient of the numerous analogies for poetry, but when George Herbert built his temple, and Crashaw constructed the steps to it, Ralph Knevet its gallery, and Christopher Harvey an adjoining synagogue, a new kind of building became naturalized in England. The Caroline poets cultivated a tradition of modest, Christian, poetic architecture, in which the expression was natural, the meaning plain, and the scale humble and unpretentious. Theirs was a style which contrasted with what George Chapman called 'the monstrous *Babels* of our Modern Barbarisme'.[1] To this company *Upon Appleton House* also belongs, for its 'sober Frame', its 'short but admirable Lines', its 'orderly and near' composition clearly initiate a working analogy between the building and the poem (1, 42, 26). The simple Christianity which Fairfax adopts in his dwelling is to be mirrored by the poet in his poem, so flawlessly indeed that the very stanza form itself is an image of Fairfacian virtue.

Let others vainly strive t'immure
The *Circle* in the *Quadrature*!
These *holy Mathematicks* can
In ev'ry Figure equal Man. (VI)

According to Puttenham, who is the main source in English poetic theory for ideas concerning the shapes and proportions

[1] Dedication to Inigo Jones of *Musaeus*, quoted in Per Palme, *Triumph of Peace: A Study of the Whitehall Banqueting House* (Uppsala, 1956), p. 315.

of different poems, Marvell's stanza of eight lines with eight syllables in each was known as 'the square or quadrangle equilater'. 'The square', he says, is 'for his inconcussable steadinesse likened to the earth, which perchaunce might be the reason that the Prince of Philosophers in his first booke of the *Ethicks*, termeth a constant-minded man, even egal and direct on all sides, and not easily overthrowne by every little adversitie, *hominem quadratum*, a square man.'[1] Elsewhere, Puttenham declared that the quadrangle was a noble stanza suited to epic verse, so Fairfax, the 'equal Man', was doubly complimented by the poem.

By the holy mathematics of Christian architecture, Appleton House could also fulfil two of the three requirements for classical buildings. '*Commoditie, Firmnes*, and *Delight*' were the invariable criteria,[2] but Nunappleton lacked firmness and was not destined to 'remain' for a long time (72), because no true Christian built for eternity in this life, and to have done so would have been presumptuous. But Appleton House was useful and delightful to its owner (56, 62), and Alberti could have commended it because 'we ought to imitate the Modesty of nature...the World never commends a Moderation, so much as it blames an extravagant Intemperance in Building'.[3] All neo-classical architects, however, would have condemned Appleton House for not conforming to the dignity of its owner. Although they might grant that the private edifices of great men could fall 'a little short in Ornament, [rather] than they should be condemned for Luxury and Profusion',[4] it would have been

---

[1] *The Arte of English Poesie*, ed. G. D. Willcock and Alice Walker (Cambridge, 1936), p. 100. 'The fift proportion is of eight verses very stately and *Heroicke*...,' p. 65. Miss Jane Vogel of Cornell University first drew my attention to Puttenham's square poems.

[2] Henry Wotton, *The Elements of Architecture* (London, 1626), p. 1. Acts passed by Parliament for the rebuilding of London after the Great Fire incorporated the same three Vitruvian principles.

[3] *Ten Books on Architecture*, trans. Leoni, ed. Joseph Rykwert (London, 1955), p. 13.   [4] *Ibid.* p. 187.

incomprehensible to them that Fairfax preferred the 'lowness' of his present residence to his more stately houses elsewhere (x). Yet Fairfax's offence is no breach of Christian decorum, because his 'Bee-like Cell' is to him 'ungirt and unconstrain'd' (40, 43), and his skimpy doorway opens on to the narrow path to heaven. Likewise, the poetic house appears by secular standards only to be insufficiently majestic for a heroic theme, and its style lacking in the elevation proper to the praise of its noble patron.

The eulogy of such a man would normally demand one of the superior forms of panegyric, and Ben Jonson, expanding a metaphor from Heinsius, had a good deal to say about the decorum of poetic architecture, and pointed out that epic was a palace by comparison with other poems.[1] One of the sons of Ben, Sir William Davenant, borrowed the idea and in his preface to *Gondibert* (a poem to which Marvell refers [456]) frequently compares his epic with a building and closes the defence of his art with a reference to his 'long continued' allegory as he finally ushers Hobbes into his poem by the 'Backdore'.[2] The presumption of Davenant's claim to have constructed an epic palace is patent and did not escape his rivals, who issued a volume of satirical verses forthwith. Davenant himself confessed in a later postcript that he had been taxed with vanity, and Marvell was to recall contemptuously twenty years later the 'presumption...of Gondibert or Leviathan'.[3] Hence it was no accident that the foreign palace with which Appleton House is contrasted in the opening stanzas, with its great size, vast columns, vain grandeur, and a hollowness 'Where Winds as he themselves may lose' (20) was copied directly from *Gondibert*. Tybalt, sent by Hurgonil, comes

[1] *Discoveries*, in *Works*, ed. Herford and Simpson (Oxford, 1925–52), VIII, p. 645.

[2] Spingarn, p. 53. The building metaphor also occurs on pp. 1, 7, 17, 20, 23, 25.

[3] *Rehearsal Transpros'd*, in *Works*, ed. Grosart, III, p. 75. Marvell also states contemptuously here, p. 226, that 'Indeed all Astragen appeared to me the better "scheme of religion"' [than Samuel Parker's].

> To that Proud Palace which once low did lie
> In *Parian* Quarries, now on Columes stands:
> *Ionique* Props that bear their Arches high,
> Which conquer'd treasure rais'd with *Tuscan* Hands.
>
> So vast of heighth, to which such space did fit
> As if it were o're⁄cyz'd for Modern Men;
> The ancient Giants might inhabit it;
> And there walk free as winds that pass unseen.[1]

Apart from the verbal parallels, even the quarries, Marvell seems to have derived from these stanzas the contrast between the modern giant, Fairfax, and the pigmies who would live after him.

It is a short step from this observation to an understanding of the many ways in which *Upon Appleton House* is an answer to *Gondibert* and its famous preface. Like *Gondibert* it is a Christian epic. '*Humility* alone designs / Those short but admirable Lines' (41-2): the lines are admirable because they arouse the epic emotion of admiration, but they are short, by two syllables, of the usual epic pentameter. Marvell does retain, however, the epic couplet which Davenant rejected, and silently doubles the length of the stanza which Davenant had argued was necessary to give the reader breath. In keeping with the modesty of his own pretensions, Marvell declares his poem has been 'built upon the Place / Only as for *a Mark of Grace*; / And for an *Inn* to entertain / Its *Lord* a while, but not remain' (69-72), and this contrasts sharply with Davenant's bold statement (which he refused to retract) that the love of fame first made him a poet.[2] Marvell scornfully dismisses the foreign architect 'Who of his great Design in pain / Did for a Model vault his Brain' (5-6), and derides thereby the 'paines' of writing to which Davenant had several times called attention in his preface.[3] Furthermore, in one of the most gracefully implicit compli⁄ments to Fairfax, Marvell has praised a heroic virtue existing

---

[1] *Gondibert: An Heroick Poem*, octavo ed. (London, 1651), bk. II, canto ii, stanzas 6-7, p. 83.   [2] Spingarn, pp. 29-31.
[3] *Ibid.* pp. 24-9.

both in the present and in England, while Davenant, like many of his predecessors in epic theory, believed that the action of an epic should be set abroad and at a distant time.

Hard though it is to understand the attention accorded to *Gondibert*, it was historically by far the most important poem of the Interregnum, and it is impossible not to believe that Marvell and his poetasting employer discussed Davenant's preface, where they are likely to have been struck by Davenant's insistence on an active rather than a contemplative virtue. He rudely stated that

good men are guilty of too little appetite to greatness, and it either proceeds from that they call contentednesse (but contentednesse when examin'd doth mean something of Lasynesse as well as moderation) or from some melancholy precept of the Cloyster, where they would make life, for which the world was only made, more unpleasant then Death.[1]

Upon Appleton House is a refutation of such ignorance, but Marvell apparently conceded Davenant's good sense in banishing all epic machinery and invocations of the muse, and approved of his wish to confine himself to a witty and natural language. Further evidence of his epic intentions can be found in the negative proposition with which the poem modestly begins, the prophecies, the narration of family history, the massacre, the siege, and the funeral triumphs over the slaughtered rails. There is also an epic tag, 'Thrice happy he' (583), a falling oak tree like the ash in one of Virgil's famous similes, and the series of dramatic 'scenes' in the meadow which correspond to the sculptures Aeneas saw in the temple at Carthage and to the pictures in the temple of Astragon in *Gondibert*. Finally, the poem has a hero who derives immediately from the *Aeneid*.

With the possible exception of Cromwell, no man in England was better qualified than Fairfax to be the warriorhero. Marvell's account of his military prowess occurs in a probably earlier poem *Upon the Hill and Grove at Billborow*:

[1] *Ibid.* pp. 14–15.

Much other Groves, say they, then these
And other Hills him once did please.
Through Groves of Pikes he thunder'd then,
And Mountains rais'd of dying Men.   (IX)

Yet Fairfax had retired to practise the better fortitude of patience, and it is this version of Christian heroism that the poem cele-brates, without denigrating the active life which Davenant held to be the only subject of epic verse.[1] Aeneas was educated in both schools, and it was to Book VIII that Marvell turned for the prototype of Fairfax's humility. In recalling 'that more sober Age and Mind, / When larger sized Men did stoop / To enter at a narrow loop' (28-30), Marvell specifically evoked the huge Aeneas ('ingentem Aenean') stooping to enter the humble cottage of Evander, who instructed him in the godlike virtue of poverty:

So talking, each with each, they drew nigh the house of the poor Evander and saw cattle all about, lowing in the Roman Forum and the brilliant Carinae. When they reached his dwelling: 'These portals', he cries, 'victorious Alcides stooped to enter; this mansion welcomed him. Dare, my guest, to scorn riches; fashion thyself also to be worthy of deity, and come not disdainful of our poverty'.[2]

As the commentators on this passage remarked, Evander's 'daring' Aeneas to despise riches implied not only the diffi-culty of such a renunciation, but its heroism too. The 'after Age' which would troop in pilgrimage 'these sacred Places to adore, / By *Vere* and *Fairfax* trod before' (35-6) would but re-enact the piety of those who in classical times had paid tribute to Hercules and Aeneas. *Aeneid* VIII has a wider relevance for *Upon Appleton House* in that Evander's guided tour of his Arcadian kingdom, with its river, its woods, and its

---

[1] The background of this Christian heroism has been outlined by Merritt Y. Hughes, 'The Christ of *Paradise Regain'd* and the Renaissance Heroic Tradi-tion', *SP*, XXXV (1938), pp. 254-77, and by Frank Kermode, 'Milton's Hero', *RES*, new series IV (1953), pp. 317-30.

[2] *Aeneid*, trans. H. R. Fairclough, Loeb Library (Cambridge, Mass., 1954). p. 85 (VIII. 359-69).

humble palace, provides a classical precedent for the sequential survey and descriptive mode of Marvell's poem.[1] With some certainty we may recognize Evander's forest 'asylum' in Marvell's 'Sanctuary in the Wood' (482), and the tawny mowers who 'Massacre the Grass along' (394) are surely the race of 'worse sort and duller hue' whom Evander describes as having shattered the peace and order of the Saturnian age.[2] Evander's lengthy historical explanation of the ruined cave of Cacus accounts also for the disproportionately long narration of the 'Neighbour-Ruine' (87) at Nunappleton. Both episodes record the craft of the building's former inhabitants, and its defeat by lawful violence. As Fairfax's ancestor has already been implicitly compared with Hercules (36), the similarity of his attack on the nunnery with Evander's story of the precipitous exposure of the cave is the more marked.

> But, waving these aside like Flyes,
> Young *Fairfax* through the Wall does rise.
> Then th'unfrequented Vault appear'd,
> And superstitions vainly fear'd. (XXXIII)

Evander had assured Aeneas that the rites for Hercules were no 'vana superstitio',[3] and as the stolen child was the cause of the young man's instant dispossession of the offending vault, so were the stolen oxen at the centre of Evander's tale.

The temptation simply to annotate Marvell's poem is irresistible. Miss Bradbrook has traced the influence of Saint-Amant, Miss Røstvig the echoes from Benlowes. Leishman has annotated from Cleveland and Waller, Ruth Wallerstein from neo-platonism and the church fathers, and Miss Scoular from

---

[1] De Segrais, *Traduction de l'Eneïde de Virgile* (Paris, 1668), in an appendix on the eighth book in vol. II notes that 'ce livre ne sera composé que d'Episodes ...tout ce qui se passe dans ce livre, est entierement Episodique'. An episode, he says, is a digression made to ornament the poem, and the good epic poet digresses from and returns to his subject so artfully that the reader doesn't notice it.

[2] VIII. 326–27.

[3] VIII. 187.

a wide variety of sources.[1] Many of their suggestions are convincing, and they add to the impression that *Upon Appleton House* is one of the most eclectic poems of the seventeenth century, a net in which are entangled the impressions of Marvell's wide reading and classical scholarship. A few more annotations of my own will be forthcoming, but the important structural forces at work in the poem have now been mentioned. Marvell's platonized Christianity establishes the kind of halfserious nature that undergoes so many transformations in the different scenes, and Virgil affords the classical support for a 'survey' poem with heroic pretensions. Without Davenant, however, the idea of such a poem would probably never have occurred to Marvell, and the structure of a poem called *Upon Appleton House* would have been very different. Although all the features of the Fairfax estate may be found in Virgil, they are not arranged to form a series of alternating panels, nor are the descriptions themselves related to a consistent ethical standard.

The 'sober Frame' of the first line is the sign that the *vita sobria* or temperance is to exercise a control over the action, and the frame itself acquires further definition by the comparison between Davenant's proud palace and the Christian humility of Fairfax's place of retirement. Bounded by a nutshell, Fairfax is ungirt and unconstrained because the discipline of his life affords him the perfect freedom promised to all God's servants. Liberty is not a place but a state of mind, and when the nun in the next section says that 'These Walls restrain the World without, / But hedge our Liberty about' (99–100) there would be nothing wrong with her argument if Fairfax were the speaker. The sublety of her seduction of Isabella consists in

[1] M. C. Bradbrook, 'Marvell and the Poetry of Rural Solitude', *RES*, XVII (1941), pp. 37–46; MarenSofie Røstvig, '*Upon Appleton House* and the Universal History of Man', *ES*, XLII (1961), pp. 337–51; J. B. Leishman, *The Art of Marvell's Poetry* (London, 1966), pp. 221–91; Ruth Wallerstein, *SeventeenthCentury Poetic* (Madison, Wis., 1950), pp. 295 ff.; K. W. Scoular, *Natural Magic* (Oxford, 1965), pp. 163–90.

misapplying the truth about Christian retirement to a bad cause. The faint overtones of sexual perversity, the self-indulgent sanctity, and the appeals to Isabella's emotions and vanity undermine the reader's belief in 'this holy leisure' (97), and it comes as no surprise to learn that Isabella had been illegally detained in the convent. Her stay there was as intrinsically lawless as her rescue was formally lawful (XXX), so everything which is true about Fairfax's retirement was false about hers. The convent represents Davenant's 'melancholy precept of the Cloyster' and the contentedness which 'when examin'd doth mean something of Lasynesse as well as moderation'. Already Marvell has condemned Davenant for failing to distinguish good retirement from bad, and for allowing his own appetite to greatness to blind him to the virtue of genuine moderation. In the garden section which follows, the theme of Fairfax's house is repeated, and the discipline of his private life is elaborated in the extended metaphors of the military plants. Gardens in epics, as Thomas Greene has remarked, are 'where heroic activity is interrupted or forgotten',[1] but Fairfax's garden is an exception which proves the rule. Marvell regrets that Fairfax has refused to emerge to make 'our Gardens spring / Fresh as his own and flourishing' (347–8) but acknowledges that retirement was pleasing not only to him but to God (346). His victory over ambition and his cultivation of conscience number him among the saints (XLV).

The garden is totally metaphorical, because the real flower-beds are seen solely as reflectors of Fairfax's generalship, and are animated by his commands. As the poet's 'sight' passes from the garden mirror, it glances with disapproval at 'proud *Cawood Castle*... As if it quarrell'd in the Seat / Th'Ambition of its *Prelate* great', and then 'ore the Meads below it plays, / Or innocently seems to gaze' (XLVI). The 'unfathomable Grass' below has seemed one of the most perplexing sections of the poem, because it bears signs of being a political allegory about

---

[1] *The Descent from Heaven* (New Haven, Conn., 1963), p. 403.

the civil war, and the difficulty of interpretation is enhanced by the nature of the images themselves. The looking-glass meadow is a deliberately distorting mirror, one of those 'frightfull looking-glasses made for sport' that Marvell told Samuel Parker he was guilty of making for Bishop Bramhall, wherein he had 'represented him in such bloated lineaments, as, I am confident, if he could see his face in it, he would break the glass'.[1] 'No Scene that turns with Engines strange / Does oftner then these Meadows change' (385–6), and one crazed image after another deflects our comprehension. 'Men like Grashoppers appear, / But Grashoppers are Gyants there' (371–2), and the 'tawny Mowers...seem like Israalites to be' (388–9). There is a kind of turbulence in the quick succession of events, and the critic who wishes to read the allegory does better to concentrate first on the general impression of the scenes than on the meaning of the individual images. The actions in the grass form together a picture of Davenant's world of 'courts and camps' which he believed was the only topic for an epic poem. The meadow represents the active life, not the contemplative order of retirement, but its activity, though harm-less like all the events in the microcosm, lacks the discipline that Fairfax brings to his garden. Just as retirement could be either a holy leisure or a self-indulgence, so the active life either conforms to good government or becomes an un-governable fury. The principal figures in the meadow, the mowers, belong to the latter category, and their tawniness gives them away. 'Tawny' was a word almost invariably used to describe the colour of the inhabitants of North Africa and Egypt.[2] The mowers 'seem' like Israelites, but they are in fact

[1] *The Rehearsal Transpros'd*, in *Works*, ed. Grosart, III, p. 21.

[2] E.g. *A Description of Africa*, in John Harris, *Navigantium atque Itinerantium Bibliotheca* (London, 1705), I, p. 307; George Sandys, *A Relation of a Journey Begun An. Dom. 1610* (London, 1615), pp. 108–9; Thomas Fuller, *A Pisgah-Sight of Palestine* (London, 1650), second pagination, p. 77; Peter Heylyn, *Cosmographie*, 3rd ed. (London, 1670), p. 922. For tawny moors and Egyp-tians in Shakespeare, see *Works*, ed. Hardin Craig (New York, 1951):

'moors'—tawny moors from Egypt rather than black moors from hotter climates. One of them is justly indignant when she seizes a rail and cries out, 'he call'd us *Israelites*' (406).

'But now, to make his saying true, / Rails rain for Quails, for Manna Dew' (407–8). The image has changed again, and the mowers/moors become temporarily true Israelites because the rails have fallen on them. They are not, however, less law-less for having become Israelites, because the biblical episode that Marvell recalls is the occasion, not in Exodus but in Numbers, when the quails rained on the Israelites as a punish-ment for lusting after the cucumbers and leeks in Egypt. 'The wish'd for Blessing from Heaven sent / Became their curse and punishment.'[1] The Authorized Version does not distinguish between the quails of Exodus and the rails of Numbers, but the Vulgate calls the first 'coturnices' and the second 'ortygometra'. The ortygometra were the rails which, according to Pliny, led their smaller cousins on migrations. The bodies of the dead rails which quilted Marvell's meadow were, in the Bible, 'two cubits high upon the face of the earth', and the black fate feared by one of the mowers (400) is the fate which smote the Israelites 'even while the flesh was in their teeth'. In the biblical phrase, the mowers were 'the people that lusted', and Calvin's comment on the original incident can serve equally well as a judgment on the mowers: 'For we knowe, that excepte mens myndes holde them selves within the boundes of reason and stayednesse: they are un-satiable, and therefore that the heat of theyr wicked appetite is not quenched with suffizance.'[2] In the topsy-turvy world of the

---

Ant. and Cleo. I. i. 6; *Tit. Andr.* v. i. 27; *MND* III. ii. 263; Eldred Jones, *Othello's Countrymen: The African in English Renaissance Drama* (London, 1965) has now discussed the matter more fully.

[1] 'The History of Insipids', in *Bibliotheca Curiosa: Some Political Satires of the Seventeenth Century*, ed. Edmund Goldsmid (Edinburgh, 1885), I, p. 7. The biblical story is contained in Numbers xi.

[2] *The Psalmes of David and others* (n.p. 1571), second pagination p. 12ᵛ (on lxxviii. 26–31).

meadow, references to political events are obscure. Certainly the levellers are condemned as the worst kind of mower, but it is doubtful if the young, unfeathered, and female rail carved by the scythe is Charles I, as several critics have said. Potentially the meadow is as allegorical as the other sections of the poem, and identifying the rail as fair a sport as giving names to the bee in the garden or the stock-doves in the wood. Where all objects have become images, as in dreams, it is legitimate to continue the search for the specific meanings they may have held for Marvell and Fairfax, but it must not be forgotten that each scene plays a part in the dialectic of Marvell's theme and that the main function of the meadow is to contrast a disordered, brutal, and military activity with the true military discipline of Fairfax's estate. His retirement is more active in a Christian sense than many superficially more heroic deeds in the active life.

With the commencement of the woodland section Marvell himself becomes the main image in his own mirror, and a crucial distinction is introduced into the argument. In so far as the wood is part of Fairfax's domain, it shares the Christian restraints of his house and garden, and is the ark-like 'Trunk' in which both he and Marvell have taken refuge from the deluge in the meadow. 'Dark all without it knits', like the pitch which caulked Noah's ark; inside, 'It opens passable and thin' (505–6). The ark had long been a symbol of the temperate life, and the unusual chastity and brotherhood of Noah's animals are reproduced in the behaviour of the trees and the birds. In its ark-like aspect, the wood is a green temple of religious devotion in which the nightingale chooses gladly to sing her melancholy song, and the corrupt oak tree willingly accepts its punishment. The birds and trees are not confined by their confinement, and to Lord Fairfax the woods divide freely to form a guard. As far as he is concerned, the wood is no more a prison than his house, and repeats the motifs of the earlier scenes. Marvell, however, takes 'Sanctuary' in the wood, as if flying from persecution or the scene of a crime, and 'The

double Wood of ancient Stocks' in which he finds himself
carries overtones of the village stocks in which he might have
expected punishment. The wood to him is Evander's asylum.
He loves his prison, and the longer he stays there the more he
craves to be bound with woodbines, and prays that his
'silken Bondage' will not break (LXXVII). The sensuousness
of his response to nature in the wood is greater than in any of
his other poems, but as we watch him—or he watches himself—
'languishing with ease...On Pallets swoln of Velvet Moss'
or lying 'carless on the Bed / Of gelid *Straw-berryes*' (LXXV,
LXVII), we should remember that the same accents have been
heard before in the nuns' justification of their solitude:

> Thus I, *easie Philosopher*,
> Among the *Birds* and *Trees* confer:
> And little now to make me, wants
> Or of the *Fowles*, or of the *Plants*.
> Give me but Wings as they, and I
> Streight floting on the Air shall fly:
> Or turn me but, and you shall see
> I was but an inverted Tree. (LXXI)

The '*easie Philosopher*' is perhaps Epicurus, and the ugly
sequence of adverbs suggests the imminence of Marvell's con-
version into a bird or a plant, and the loss of his status as a
human being—or, in platonic terms, his properly inverted tree
is in danger of turning the right way up. He is oblivious to
'Beauty, aiming at the Heart', and takes pleasure in sniping
at the world outside which cannot reach him to return his
attack (LXXVI). The wood that is for Fairfax an extension of
his freedom and discipline is for Marvell the scene of his
debauch and imprisonment. He has become a 'great *Prelate
of the Grove*' in an '*antick Cope*' (591–2), but as he practically
merges into the landscape he remains conscious enough to read
one lesson in '*Natures mystick Book*':

> Out of these scatter'd *Sibyls* Leaves
> Strange *Prophecies* my Phancy weaves:

And in one History consumes,
Like *Mexique Paintings*, all the *Plumes*.
What *Rome*, *Greece*, *Palestine*, ere said
I in this light *Mosaick* read.
Thrice happy he who, not mistook,
Hath read in *Natures mystick Book*.   (LXXIII)

His lesson can only be inferred from the poem, but Davenant
had been explicit about 'What *Rome*, *Greece*, *Palestine*, ere
said' and his remarks are so appropriate to Marvell in the wood
that they are probably the source of his line. Gondibert is on his
tour of instruction in the House of Astragon, and, having been
shown the monuments of vanished minds, is taken to see the
wiser writers whose position is only less honourable than the
Bible's:

Now they the *Hebrew*, *Greek*, and *Roman* spie;
Who for the Peoples ease, yoak'd them with Law;
Whom else, ungovern'd lusts would drive awrie;
And each his own way frowardly would draw.[1]

That law is the condition of true 'ease' and appetite a silken
bondage form one of the conclusions to which the progress
of *Upon Appleton House* has been driving. In the wood Marvell
has lost the law of self-government and given himself over to
the delicious appetites of idleness, and the scene almost im-
perceptibly changes back to the meadows by the stream which
had been the place of the mowers' carelessness. The stream has
become 'our little *Nile*...Among these Meads the only
Snake' (630–2), and looking into its '*Chrystal Mirrour*' Marvell
finds himself as mentally confused as he had been when he
stared into the unfathomable grass:

To see Men through this Meadow Dive,
We wonder how they rise alive.
As, under Water, none does know
Whether he fall through it or go.   (XLVIII)

[1] *Gondibert* II. v. 45, p. 122.

> See in what wanton harmless folds
> It ev'ry where the Meadow holds;
> And its yet muddy back doth lick,
> Till as a *Chrystal Mirrour* slick;
> Where all things gaze themselves, and doubt
> If they be in it or without.
> And for his shade which therein shines,
> *Narcissus* like, the *Sun* too pines.   (LXXX)

The final image of Marvell abandoning his lazy side on the river bank, suspending his sliding foot 'on the Osiers under-mined Root', fishing and writing poetry (LXXXI) possibly recalls Mark Antony in Egypt, but certainly marks a stage of complete debilitation in Marvell's moral fibre. The Virgilian *exemplum* would be the picture of Aeneas wasting his time in Carthage while his destiny hung fire, and the analogy is not entirely fortuitous because the approach of Maria Fairfax, who enters now to bring Marvell to his senses, is overtly reminiscent of the descent of the heavenly messenger in the *Aeneid* and other epics. A long simile of the halcyon makes her seem to fly, and the hush which greets her arrival can be paralleled by other accounts of Mercury's descent.[1] Hence Professor Allen was right when he sought to trace Maria's associations with heavenly wisdom,[2] for she comes at last to settle the debate between retirement and action that the poem has conducted:

> Mean time ye Fields, Springs, Bushes, Flow'rs,
> Where yet She leads her studious Hours,
> (Till Fate her worthily translates,
> And find a *Fairfax* for our *Thwaites*)
> Employ the means you have by Her,
> And in your kind your selves preferr;
> That, as all *Virgins* She preceds,
> So you all Woods, Streams, Gardens, Meads. (LXXXXIV)

[1] See Greene, *The Descent from Heaven*, pp. 366–7 (Cowley); pp. 340–2 (Saint-Amant); pp. 195–6 (Tasso), etc.

[2] D. C. Allen, *Image and Meaning* (Baltimore, 1960), pp. 149–53. Professor Allen also emphasizes the ways in which Maria seems to be a goddess.

Gardens cannot be meads, nor bushes flowers, and all nature recognizes its duty to fulfil the law of its own kind. Only man has a choice of destinies, and his vocation may change with circumstance. As Maria now precedes all virgins she will soon precede all wives, and her parents instead of grieving for the loss of their only child, as the nuns had grieved for theirs, will embrace the alteration that they would not prevent if they could.

> Whence, for some universal good,
> The Priest shall cut the sacred Bud;
> While her *glad Parents* most rejoice,
> And make their *Destiny* their *Choice*.　　(LXXXXIII)

For all the complexity of imagery and privacy of allusion, the theme of *Upon Appleton House* is simplicity itself. Retirement and action, like Maria's present virginity and future marriage, are only virtuous in their proper seasons and for the right people. Marvell would have received small thanks from Fairfax had he belittled the heroic deeds of his ancestors or condemned his own earlier military victories; but his vocation had changed, and Marvell could praise him best by showing that he had accepted his determination to absent himself from public life. His piety remained the same and his decision to live in the country was a matter between himself and God. Man, the rational amphibian (774), 'passeth through the degrees of all creations',[1] and in any one of them he could be at home. All that mattered was that he should choose his destiny at the same time that his destiny chose him, and then dedicate his will to the perfecting of his calling.

The rectitude of Marvell's position, especially by comparison with Davenant's, derived from a long tradition of stoic and Christian thought, and since the publication of Richard Douglas's 'Ideas of Work and Vocation in Humanist and Protestant Usage' it is unnecessary to document it in great detail.[2]

---

[1] James Howell, *The Vision: or a Dialog between the Soul and the Bodie. Fancied in a Morning Dream* (London, 1651), p. 15.

[2] Compté International des Sciences Historiques, XIIᵉ Congrès International des Sciences Historiques, *Rapports*—III. *Commissions* (1965), pp. 75-86.

Plutarch in his essay on *Tranquillity and Contentment* might prophetically have been glossing Marvell's poem: 'We may well conclude that every man is not fit for everything... and therefore ought every man to chuse that course of life which sorteth best with his own nature, and wholly apply and set his mind thereto; leaving unto others that which pertaineth to them.'[1] Cicero believed that even if some careers were better and nobler than others 'we may still regulate our own pursuits by the standard of our own nature'.[2] Macrobius commented that 'some men become blessed by the exercise of virtues at leisure and others by virtues exercised in active careers',[3] and Seneca held the same opinion in his essay *On Tranquillity of Mind*.[4] In the Renaissance, Charron's wisdom was the fullest and most traditional:

Behold here another difference of men, drawn from the diversitie of their professions, conditions and kinds of life. Some follow the civil and sociable life, others flie it, thinking to save themselves in the solitary wildernes: some love arms, others hate them: some live in common, others in private: it pleaseth some best to have charge, and to lead a publick life; others to hide and keep themselves private: some are Courtiers, attending wholly upon others, others court none but themselves: some delight to live in the Citie, others in the fields, affecting a countrey life [;] whose choise is the better, and which life is to be preferred, it is a difficult thing simply to determine, and it may be impertinent. They have all their advantages and disadvantages, their good and their ill. That which is most to be looked into and considered herein, as shall be said, is, That every man know how to choose that which best befits his own nature, that he might live the more easily and the more happily.[5]

[1] *Moralia*, trans. Holland, Everyman's Library (London, n.d.), pp. 173-4.
[2] *De Officiis* I. xxxi. 110, trans. Walter Miller, Loeb Library (London, 1961), p. 113.
[3] *Commentary on the Dream of Scipio*, trans. and ed. W. H. Stahl (New York, 1952), pp. 123-4.
[4] VII. 2 in *Moral Essays*, trans. John W. Basore, Loeb Library (London, 1958), II, p. 237.
[5] *Of Wisdome*, trans. Samson Lennard (London, 1651), pp. 189-90. This is the preface to Book I, ch. 53 (ch. 49 in Elzevir ed. [Leyden, 1659]).

Charron later discussed the difficulties of the choice, and argued that men must know both their own natures and the nature of their professions before they could reach a correct decision. Finally, quoting Cicero, he declared that '*so ought we to carry our selves, as we contend not against universal nature, but that being kept, follow our own*'.[1] The fates led their willing followers and dragged the reluctant, as Seneca had said in a celebrated maxim,[2] and the freedom of choosing was limited by one's obedience to the general law. The early reformers, as Douglas has shown, allowed nothing to man's choice in the following of his vocation, but possibly he has exaggerated a little the differences between stoic and protestant, because though the stoic might speak of choice he never divorced the human will from 'universal nature', and believed that only an eager co-operation with destiny, not a mere submission to it, was worthy of a philosopher.[3] By the seventeenth century the amalgam of stoic and Christian was complete, and choosing and being chosen were reconciled under a benign providence. Certainly in *Upon Appleton House* there is no conflict, for the 'universal good' which is to be served by the parents' personal loss is also the object of their desires. In their '*Domestick Heaven*' the 'Discipline severe / Of *Fairfax* and the starry *Vere*' (722–4) is a pattern of Christian virtue that blends perfectly with the Virgilian background, since Aeneas too had been 'the willing tool of fate', and Fairfax could legitimately be made to feel that he was Aeneas' successor.[4] The mutable nature that surrounds him, conforming to the example he sets, is not only St Paul's

---

[1] *Ibid.* II, 4, p. 257.

[2] 'Ducunt volentem fata, nolentem trahunt.' The *sententia* is the last of five lines of verse, the first four of which are attributed to Cleanthes. 'On Obedience to the Universal Will' in *Ad Lucilium Epistulae Morales*, trans. Richard M. Gummere, Loeb Library (London, 1925), III, pp. 228–9.

[3] R. D. Hicks, *Stoic and Epicurean* (New York, 1910), p. 77.

[4] *Aeneid* VIII. 133: 'fatis egere volentem'. Aeneas' words to Evander were conventionally glossed to bring out the voluntariness of his submission to destiny.

glass but the external world of a true stoic, wholly subservient to the inner will.

Yet if the woods, streams, gardens, meads each in their kind themselves prefer, the poet himself has deteriorated in his solitude and can no longer excuse his idleness. Maria, for whose sake he had been employed as a tutor of languages, now speaks 'In all the Languages as *hers*' (708) and had become an object lesson to her own master. Retirement worked for Fairfax, but not for Marvell, and as the poet turns at the end of the poem to re-enter the house, symbolically it is for the last time. *Upon Appleton House* is his parting gesture, a courteous goodbye to an employer whom he loved and respected, but who by the very terms of his virtue would not deny Marvell's wish to seek a more active life. The dialectic of the theme allows no other conclusion, but in an atmosphere where decorum counted for everything it would have been immodest to say more, or to have spoken directly of his own ambitions. It was enough to make a reluctant farewell, and to carry away the image of Fairfax's garden as a model of what life should be like in 'that dear and happy Isle / The Garden of the World ere while' (321-2).

It has been the thesis of this book that Marvell followed the great design of Christian virtue with unfaltering allegiance during his years in public life, and that Lord Fairfax's high standards and his own were identical, like the house and poem. Decorum, modesty, and moderation were the qualities that excited his life-long regard, and which he consistently sought to apply to the inflammations of the times. They were the only virtues suited to man's precariousness in his transient state, and when he forgot them the downfall of his society was sooner or later inevitable. Debauchery was 'always fatal', and political debauchery was the worst of all since its consequences affected everyone. Although *Upon Appleton House* is a poem about vocations, not politics, it contains all the principal ingredients of Marvell's political thought. Temporality, the never-to-be-forgotten context of all political schemes, is the essence of the poem's kaleidoscopic imagery, and is especially noticeable in the scenes from active life reflected in the meadow; moderation, which should be man's response to the knowledge of his shortcomings, is characteristic not only of every aspect of Fairfax's discipline but of Marvell's attitude towards his own poem and the exaggerated finalities of Davenant's preface; and Marvell's admiration for the great leader untainted with pride is a sign of the kind of admiration that he developed for Cromwell. Fairfax now ruled the lesser world 'in more decent Order tame', Cromwell the greater, and in changing from one service to another Marvell sacrificed neither his principles nor his habit of obedience, but realized that each estate must own its natural lord.

All Marvell's transferences of allegiance were of the same order, because as destiny could call an individual to forsake one good master and cleave to another, so it could alter the vocations of countries and demand that the people surrender their nostalgia and accept the new realities of a different order. As Lipsius said in a treatise that unironically he called *Of Constancie*, 'But if thou see by certain and infallible tokens that the fatall alteration of the State is come, with mee this saying shall prevaile, *Not to fight against God*. And in such a case I would alleadge the example of *Solon*...And if thou be a good citizen or common-wealths-man preserve thy selfe to a better and happier end. The liberty which now is lost, may be recovered againe hereafter; and thy decayed country may flourish in another age: why doest thou loose al courage & fal into despair?'[1] Fighting with God was the sin above all others to be avoided, and to many pious men who thought of themselves as moderates the catastrophic violence of 1649, the miracle of 1660, and the similar benevolence of 1688 were too God-like in their decisiveness to admit of any question of their ultimate origin. Like Thomas Nashe in plague time, their

[1] *Two Books of Constancie*, trans. Stradling, ed. Rudolph Kirk (New Brunswick, N. J., 1939), p. 127. This is the conclusion of the chapters on destiny.

exhortation was to 'Haste, therefore, each degree, / To wel-come destiny. / Heaven is our heritage, / Earth but a player's Stage'—a series of flickering shadows in a dark glass, and the penalties for disobedience were as grave as the rewards were glorious for faithful service. The vicissitudes of the seventeenth century enhanced rather than weakened the providential view of politics, and the rise of more rationalistic explanations of government and more modern interpretations of history should never be allowed to obscure the religious view. Marvell is one of the better examples of his kind, because it proves impossible to spend a few years in the company of his works and not to feel convinced of the integrity of the man as well as the sophisti-cation of his mind. Fairfax, I like to think, was of the same opinion, for his translation of Saint-Amant's *La Solitude* is in many ways a complement to *Upon Appleton House*, and by omitting the last two stanzas and adding the personal name he achieved a graceful tribute to his departing friend:

> Thus Alcidon whose loue inioynes
> To thinke for thee noe labor paine
> Receaue these Rustick Shepheards lines
> That's from ther liuinge obiects ta'ine
> Sence I seeke only desart places
> Wher all alone my thoughts doe use
> Noe entertainment but what pleases
> The genius of my Rural Muse
> But noe thoughts more delighteth mee
> Then sweet Remembrances of thee.

Index

Abbot, W. C., 91, 92 n., 110, 111n.,
    112 n., 118 n., 123 n., 125 n., 126
Ailmer, John, 113, 116, 135
Ainslie, James L., 125 n.
Albemarle, George Monck, first
    Duke of, 152–4
Alberti, Leone Battista, 238
Allen, D. C., 251
Allen, J. W., 19 n.
Andrewes, Lancelot, 20
Answer to the Nineteen Propositions, 13, 15
Aristotle, 101 n.
Arlington, Henry Bennet, first Earl of,
    154, 164, 171–2
Armies Modest Intelligencer, The, 28
Arnobius of Sicca, 84 n.
Ascham, Anthony, 6, 30–41, 43,
    45–8, 53–8, 63–4, 66–7, 71, 76,
    78–9, 83–4, 97, 98 n.

Ball, William, 9, 14, 24
Barker, Arthur, 113 n., 119 n.
Bate, Frank, 191
Batten, Minton, 52 n.
Baxter, Richard, 34 n., 62 n., 68,
    84 n., 141, 150, 177–8
Bayly, Thomas, 135 n.
Behrens, B., 218, 226–7
Benlowes, Edward, 243
Benson, Donald R., 228 n.
Bodin, Jean, 14, 19, 26, 82
Bordeaux–Neufville, Antoine de, 112
Bowles, Edward, 27
Bradbrook, M. C., 114–15, 243,
    244 n.
Bradshaw, John, 66
Bramhall, John, 18–19, 23–4, 191,
    194, 246
Bray, Vicar of, 8
Bridge, John, 117
Bridge, William, 9, 27, 96
*Briefe Resolution of that Grand Case of
    Conscience, A*, 82

Brosnahan, Timothy, 10 n.
Brown, Louise Fargo, 119 n., 181 n.
Brown, Robert, 123
Browning, Andrew, 181 n., 210 n.,
    211 n., 228 n.
Buckingham, George Villiers, second
    Duke of, 5, 177–8, 221
Burges, Cornelius, 51
Burroughes, Jeremiah, 9
Busanello, Giovanni Francesco, 157
Butterfield, Herbert, 3 n.

Caesar, Augustus, 73, 93 n.
Caesar, Julius, 71–4, 93–4, 97–8, 100,
    118
Calvin, John, 44, 247
Camden, William, 26
Carens, James F., 121–2, 127
Carlisle, Charles Howard, first Earl
    of, 5, 149, 150 n.
Caryl, Joseph, 53
Cassius Dio, 84 n.
Castlemaine, Barbara Palmer, Coun-
    tess of, 161–2, 171
Chapman, George, 237
Charles I, 1, 3, 9–43 *passim*, 71, 78–85,
    93, 131 n., 146, 200, 202, 205, 248
Charles II, 8, 42, 50, 60, 68, 84, 88,
    95, 109, 145–231 *passim*
Charron, Pierre, 88, 253–4
Chaucer, Geoffrey, 161–3
Christie, W. D., 221 n.
Christina, Queen of Sweden, 107,
    111
Churchill, E. F., 189 n.
Cicero, 88, 101, 253
Clarendon, Edward Hyde, first Earl
    of, 1–3, 6–7, 64–5, 67–8, 70, 81,
    111, 151–2, 156 n., 163–4, 168,
    170–2, 175–7, 181–2
Cleveland, John, 100 n., 135 n., 243
Clifford, Sir Thomas, first Baron,
    173

Cobbett, William, *Parliamentary History*, 165 n., 176 n., 215 n., 216 n.
Coffin for King Charles, A, 91
Cohn, Norman, 119 n.
Coke, Sir Edward, 20
Collins (or Collinge), John, 127 n.
Collonel Grey's Portmanteau Opened, 96 n.
Coltman, Irene, 31 n., 37
Cook, John, 90
Coolidge, John C., 93 n.
Coox, Alvin D., 169 n.
Cotton, Sir Robert, 26–7
Courtenay, Thomas Peregrine, 169 n.
Coventry, Sir John, 167 n.
Coventry, Sir William, 152, 171
Cowley, Abraham, 5
Crashaw, Richard, 237
Cromwell, Henry, 112
Cromwell, Oliver, 2–3, 7, 28, 30, 65, 67, 69–144 *passim*, 182, 188, 203, 256
Cromwell, Richard, 143, 144 n.
Croullé, M. de, 92
Cruquius, Jacobus, 159
Crutwell, Patrick, 96 n., 121 n.

Danby, Thomas Osborne, first Earl of, 208, 216, 219
Daniel, Sir Thomas, 161
Davenant, Sir William, 235, 236 n., 239–41, 244–6, 250, 252, 256
Davies, Godfrey, 127 n.
de Beer, E. S., 210 n.
Declaration of the English Army, A, 95 n.
Declaration of the Parliament, A (22 March 1649), 44–5
Declaration of the Parliament, A (26 June 1650), 95
Del Rio, Martin, 130 n.
Denham, Sir John, 232–3
De Witt, Jan, 169
Digby, George, second Earl of Bristol, 2
Digges, Sir Dudley, 18, 25–6, 97 n., 117, 133
Discourse Concerning the Engagement, A, 64

Discourse upon the Union of England and Scotland, A, 181 n.
Donne, John, 236 n.
Douglas, Archibald, 160, 180 n.
Douglas, Richard, 252
Downing, George, 5
Drayton, Michael, 232
Dryden, John, 5, 88, 102, 160, 162, 173
Duncan-Jones, E. E., 96 n., 99 n., 135 n.
Duppa, Brian, 39
Dury, John, 6, 44, 51–3, 58, 61, 79
Dutton, William, 107
Dymock, Thomas, 24

Eaton, Samuel, 53
Elizabeth I, Queen, 8, 13
English, Peter, 63
English Banner of Truth Displayed, The, 95 n.
Erasmus, Desiderius, 88
Erdman, David, 155 n.
Estius, Gulielmus, 129 n.

Fairfax, Thomas, third Baron, 30, 42, 79, 92, 94, 106–7, 143, 232–57 *passim*
Farrar, Richard, 38
Feiling, Sir Keith, 165, 166 n., 186 n.
Ferne, Henry, 9, 12–14, 24, 40–1, 133
Ficino, Marsilio, 234–5
Fifth Advice to a Painter, The, 152, 155–7, 171
Figgis, J. Neville, 15
Filmer, Sir Robert, 14–15, 22, 39, 54, 64, 132
Fink, Zera S., 89
Firth, C. H., 49 n., 111 n., 112 n., 117 n., 126 n., 164
Fixler, Michael, 205
Fletcher, R., 63
Florio, John, 88
Fogel, E. G., 152 n., 154 n.
Ford, Simon, 135 n.
Fourth Advice to a Painter, The, 152, 155–7

Foxcroft, H. C., 228 n.
Foxley, William, 213
Frank, Joseph, 92 n.
Franke, Richard, 151
Free Conference Touching the Present State of England, A, 171
Frye, Northrop, 160
Fuller, Thomas, 68, 81, 117 n., 246 n.
Furley, O. W., 218 n.

Gardiner, S. R., 30, 43, 49 n., 81 n., 91, 111 n., 112 n., 119 n.
Garland, Augustine, 112
Gauden, John, 127 n.
Gee, Edward, 58–9
Goodwin, John, 120
Goodwin, Thomas, 120 n.
Gorboduc, 89 n.
Greene, Thomas, 245, 251 n.
Grey, Anchitell, *Debates*, 210 n.
Griffith, Matthew, 14
Grimstone, Sir Harbottle, 216
Grosart, A. B., 101 n., 134 n., 184 n.
Grotius, Hugo, 20, 32–5, 37, 38 n., 64, 84, 129 n.
Guazzo, Stefano, 89 n.
Guicciardini, Francesco, 35, 83
Gustavus Adolphus, 94

Hale, Sir Matthew, 5, 224 n.
Hales, John, 193, 207
Haley, K. H. D., 208 n.
Halifax, George Savile, first Marquis of, 163, 188, 230
Hall, Arthur, 25
Hall, Henry, 62
Hall, John, 5, 19
Hall, John, of Richmond, 113, 117–18, 134 n.
Hall, Joseph, 131
Hall, Thomas, 124
Haller, William, 17, 28
Hammond, Henry, 28
Harbord, Sir Charles, 173
Harley, Sir Edward, 196
Harris, John, 246 n.

Harrison, Thomas, 119
Harvey, Christopher, 237
Hawke, Michael, 113 n.
Haywood, William, 39
Hearnshaw, F. J. C., 19 n.
Heath, James, 126
Henry IV, 65
Herbert, George, 237
Herennium, Ad, 100, 101 n.
Herle, Charles, 9, 18, 21, 58 n., 133
Hexter, J. H., 11 n., 139
Heylyn, Peter, 246
Hickman, William, 90
Hicks, R. D., 254 n.
Hill, Christopher, 20 n., 80 n.
Hinks, D. A. G., 101 n.
History and Proceedings of the House of Lords, The, 221 n.
Hobbes, Thomas, 4–5, 16, 22, 35, 37, 54, 57, 62–4, 76, 82, 99, 190, 206, 235, 239
Holdsworth, W. S., 189 n., 224 n.
Holland, Sir John, 176–7
Holland, John, 134 n.
Hooker, Richard, 20
Hooker, Thomas, 127 n.
Horace, 73, 157–61, 163
Howell, James, 99, 252
Hudson, Michael, 16, 27
Hughes, Merritt Y., 14, 22 n., 242 n.
Hunting of the Foxes, The, 91
Hunton, Philip, 15, 24–5, 205, 230
Hunton, Samuel, 113, 117
Hyde, Anne, Duchess of York, 155
Hyman, Lawrence, 75, 122 n., 145 n.

Ingelo, Nathaniel, 107
Isidorus of Seville, 84 n.

James I, 13 n., 25
James II, formerly Duke of York, 152, 176 n., 207, 217–18
Japikse, N., 172
Jenkin, William, 51
Johnson, Samuel, 4, 6
Jones, Eldred, 247 n.

Jones, Inigo, 237 n.
Jones, J. R., 150 n.
Jonson, Ben, 104, 158–9
Jordan, Thomas, 140
Judson, Margaret, 11 n., 15 n.
Juvenal, 161

Karcher, Carolyn, 138 n.
Kempis, Thomas à, 88
Kermode, Frank, 242 n.
Kliger, Samuel, 89–90
Knevet, Ralph, 237

Lambert, John, 111
Lane, Edward, 125
Lapide, Cornelius, 129 n., 130 n.
Laslett, Peter, 22
Lauderdale, John Maitland, first Duke of, 208, 210
Legouis, Pierre, 99 n., 142 n., 145, 189 n., 196, 214
Leishman, J. B., 243
Lerner, L. D., 79–80
Leslie, Henry, 78
L'Estrange, Roger, 134, 193, 205, 227–8
Levine, J. A., 160 n.
Lightfoot, John, 50
Lilburne, John, 11, 48, 91
Lipsius, Justus, 256
Lisola, Baron, 172
Lister, T. H., 164 n.
Livy, 84 n.
Locke, John, 5, 22
Lord, George deF., 146, 152 n., 154, 156 n.
Louis XIV, 165–8, 170, 172, 184–5, 210
Lovelace, Richard, 104
Lucan, 71–4, 93, 98, 102
Lyra, Nicholas, 129
Lyttleton, Sir Thomas, 191

Machiavelli, Niccolo, 89
Macrobius, 253
Mallet, Sir John, 216
Malvezzi, Virgilio, 77, 116

Man in the Moon, The, 61, 91
Margoliouth, H. M., 89, 134 n., 146–7 n., 156, 173
Marshall, Stephen, 50–1
Marvell, Andrew: his loyalism and Hyde's, 2–3; as whig historian, 3–4; as typical loyalist, 5; comparison with Milton, 6–7; his combination of virtues, 7; animus against army in 1648, 30; elegiac mood 1648–9, 37; turning to history, 64; probable sympathy with the Engagers, 66; acceptance of verdict of history, 67
An Horatian Ode, 69–105: cruel choice of loyalties, 69; duality of Cromwell's rôle, 70–2; Cromwell and Caesar, 72–4; Cromwell's virtues, 75–8; attitude toward Charles's execution, 78–84; the need for a state architect, 84–5; Irish praise for Cromwell, 85–8; the theme of the ode, 88–90; the dictatorship issue, 90–2; refutation of Cromwell's detractors, 92–4; the necessity of invading Scotland, 94–8; justice and power, 99; rhetorical structure of the ode, 100–2; providence re-interpreting history, 102–3; comparison of ode with earlier poems, 103–4; the unenvious arts of the poet, 104–5
The First Anniversary, 106–44: self-conscious modesty, 106; desire for more active life, 107; wish for Cromwell's kingship, 108; unity of the poem, 109; vitality of kingship issue, 110–14; Cromwell contrasted with kings, 115; Cromwell as founder of mixed state, 116–18; desire for a Fifth Monarchy, 118–20; the call for grace, 121–6; consequence if Cromwell were not crowned, 126–9; Cromwell's fitness to rule, 129–32; Cromwell as pater patriae, 132–6; deliberative structure of

poem, 136–8; contradictory aspects of poem and Commonwealth, 138–41; *On the Victory... by Blake*, 141–2; *A Poem upon the Death of O. C.*, 143; implications of following providence, 144

The last Instructions to a Painter, 145–83: question of sincerity, 145–6; authenticity of texts, 146–7; growing dissatisfaction with government, 147–51; letter to Mayor Franke, 151; comparison with earlier *Advices*, 152–7; relation to *Ars Poetica*, 157–60; relation to Chaucer, 161–3; criticism of foreign policy, 163; St Albans and a French treaty, 164–5; the bad faith of Louis XIV, 165–7; England's relation to Holland, 168–9; Charles II's unreadiness, 169–70; dismissal of Clarendon, 170–1; attitudes after Dutch war, 171–3; battle over excise, 173–4; Marvell's respect for the royal prerogative, 174–8; loyal poet and subject, 179–83

The Rehearsal Transpros'd, 184–207: deteriorating government, 184–6; the Conventicle Act, 186–7; the constitutional balance, 187–8; Declaration of Indulgence, 188–91; difference from other apologists, 191–3; similarities with nonconformists, 193; expedience and discretion, 194; the middle ground, 195–7; the providential constitution, 197–8; impossibility of absolutism, 199–200; natural political laws, 200–1; the cause too good, 201–3; Marvell's detachment, 203; balance, moderation and expedience, 204–6; hope for a Christian administration, 207

An Account of the Growth of Popery, 207–31: growing disillusion, 207–8; *Mr Smirke*, 208–9; the Popish Plot, 209; court chicanery 210; a speaking out, 211–14; attitude to indulgence, 214; *An Act for... Securing the Protestant Religion*, 215–16; speech about the succession, 216–17; defence of prerogative, 217–18; problem of sincerity, 218; the constitutional fiction, 219–24; omission of whig 'reason' and history, 224–6; an early trimmer, 226–8; summary, 228–31

Upon Appleton House, 232–57: mirror of the microcosm, 232–4; a platonic-Christian rationale, 234–6; poem as building, 237–9; compared with Davenant's palace, 239–40; the poem vs. *Gondibert*, 240–1; Virgilian allusion, 242–3; good and bad retirement, 244–5; the meadow and mowers/moors, 246–7; possibilities of allegory, 248; the poet's debility, 248–9; a lesson from *Gondibert*, 249–50; the descent of Maria, 251; theme of the poem, 252; stoic and Christian background, 252–5; farewell to Fairfax, 255; conclusion, 255–7

Mary I, 13
Mather, Cotton, 127 n.
Mathieson, William L., 180 n.
Maxwell, John, 9, 14, 19, 24
May, Thomas, 73, 103–4
Maynwaring, Roger, 13 n.
Mazzeo, J. A., 75, 108, 127
McRae, K. D., 19 n.
Mendo, Andres, 117 n.
Mercurius Melancholicus, 28
Mercurius Politicus, 33 n., 92
Milton, John, 6–7, 31, 58, 66, 69, 88–9, 107, 142, 205
Milward, John, 173, 176 n., 177 n.
Miner, Earl, 152 n.
Mirrour for Magistrates, 89 n.
Moderate, The, 28

Moderate Intelligencer, The, 43
Moray, Sir Robert, 180
More, Henry, 50, 76
Morton, Thomas, 20–1
Mullett, Charles F., 132 n.

Nashe, Thomas, 256–7
Nedham, Marchamont, 6, 33 n. 63, 98, 113 n., 228
Nethersole, Sir Francis, 29–30
Nethway, J., 116
Nimrod, 24, 98, 102, 133
Norwood, Anthony, 93
Nuttall, Geoffrey, 125 n.

O'Brien, Gordon Worth, 236 n.
Oldham, John, 159
Omond, G. W. T., 181 n.
Osborne, Francis, 63, 77
Osborne, Mary Tom, 152 n., 157 n.
Oudart, Nicholas, 39 n.
Overall, John, 20, 133
Owen, John, 42, 192–3

Palme, Per, 237 n.
Palmer, A., 63–4
Paraeus, David, 98
Parker, Henry, 12, 17–19, 21, 76, 95, 97 n., 218
Parker, Samuel, 70, 187, 189–92, 194–8, 200, 205–7, 246
Paterculus, Velleius, 97–8
Patrick, Simon, 127 n., 195
Patrides, C. A., 120 n.
Paulucci, Lorenzo, 111
Penn, William, 192
Perfect Diurnall, A, 86–7, 96 n.
Perfect Occurrences, 85–6
Persius, 158
Pertinent and Profitable Meditation, A, 95 n.
Peters, Hugh, 41
Pickthorn, Sir Kenneth, 21 n.
Plato, 88, 234
Pliny, 247
Plutarch, 253
Pocock, J. G. A., 22, 25

Pollard, A. F., 20 n.
Poole, Matthew, 129 n.
Pope, Alexander, 116
Popple, William, 184, 186, 208
Potter, George R., 236 n.
Povey, Thomas, 28 n.
Proudfoot, L., 96 n.
Prynne, William, 50, 53, 96 n.
Pufendorf, Samuel, 88
Puttenham, George, 237–8
Pym, John, 139, 218

Quarles, Francis, 16, 20
Quarles, John, 135 n.
Quintilian, 100, 101 n.

Raleigh, Walter, 98
Ramsay, Andrew, 89 n.
Ramsden, John, 148
Ranke, Leopold von, 167, 171 n., 172 n.
Resolves of Parliament Touching...an Engagement, 48
Reynolds, Edward, 61
Richard II, 65
Richard III, 92
Richards, Thomas, 119 n.
Richardson, Samuel, 134 n.
Robbins, Caroline, 6, 145 n., 149, 173, 176, 224, 229
Roberts, Clayton, 177 n.
Robertson, Alexander, 181 n.
Rocket, John, 82
Røstvig, Maren-Sofie, 243
Rogers, Edward, 119 n.
Rollins, Hyder E., 135 n.
Ronalds, Francis S., 218 n.
Rous, Francis, 6, 45–6, 51–6, 58, 64, 98 n.
Royall Health to the Rising Sun, The 135 n.
Ruvigny, Henri de Massue, Marquis de, 172
Ruyter, Michael de, 169

Sadler, John, 79, 135 n.
St Albans, Henry Jermyn, Earl of, 161, 163–8, 170

Saint-Amant, Marc Antoine Gérard, sieur de, 243, 257
Sanderson, Robert, 39–40, 50 n., 61, 76 n., 97 n.
Sandys, George, 246 n.
Sansovino, Francisco, 96 n.
Saunders, Richard, 62, 98 n.
Schmitter, Dean Morgan, 196
Schramm, Percy Ernst, 123 n.
Scoular, K. W., 243
Seaman, Lazarus, 50–1
Seasonable Question and a Usefull Answer, A, 222
Second Advice to a Painter, The, 152–4, 157–8
Sedgwick, Obadiah, 127 n.
Segrais, Jean Regnauld de, 243 n.
Selden, John, 133 n.
Seneca, Lucius Annaeus, 88, 253–4
Sense of the Covenant, The, 44
Servius, 84 n.
Severall Proceedings in Parliament, 86–7
Shaftesbury, Anthony Ashley Cooper, first Earl of, 5, 112, 212–13, 220–1, 224
Shakespeare, William, 65, 246 n.
Shaw, John B., 113 n.
Sherlock, William, 65
Shirley vs. Fagg, 208, 213, 221
Short Reply unto a Declaration, A, 95 n.
Sidney, Algernon, 227
Simpson, Evelyn M., 236
Simpson, John, 134 n.
Sirluck, Ernest, 9, 27 n., 140 n.
Skinner, Quentin, 22 n., 37 n., 66–7
Smith, John, 127 n.
Snow, Vernon F., 183 n.
Solon, 88, 256
Solorzano, Juan de, 117 n.
Some Considerations in relation to the Act of 2 January, 60
Speed, John, 25, 96
Speght, Thomas, 162
Spelman, Sir John, 18, 24, 133
Spingarn, J. E., 235 n.
Spittlehouse, John, 119
Sprat, Thomas, 68

Spurstowe, William, 124
Starkey, Thomas, 89 n.
Stillingfleet, Edward, 150
Straka, Gerald, 65 n.
Summers, Joseph, 157 n.
Swadlin, Thomas, 15–16
Syfret, R. H., 70–1, 93
Sylvester, Matthew, 127 n.

Tasso, Torquato, 235
Taverner, Richard, 88
Taylor, Jeremy, 68
Temple, Sir William, 163, 168–9, 171–2
Third Advice to a Painter, The, 152–4, 157–8
Thomas, M. G. Lloyd, 114-15
Thurloe, John, 111 n., 126 n.
Tickell, John, 134 n.
Toliver, Harold E., 200
Tooke, Andrew, 116
Tooley, M. J., 19 n., 82 n.
Trapp, Joseph, 160
Trott, Sir John, 182
Turner, Sir Edward, 161
Turner, Thomas, 39
Tuve, Rosemond, 137
Tuveson, Ernest Lee, 118 n.

Underdown, David, 11 n.
Ussher, James, 133 n.

Vane, Sir Henry, the younger, 11
Vatablus, Franciscus, 129 n.
Villiers, Lord Francis, 30
Vines, Richard, 50
Virgil, 235, 241–3, 249, 251, 254
Vogel, Jane, 238 n.

Walker, Clement, 62, 92, 97, 100
Waller, Edmund, 5, 152, 157, 232, 243
Wallerstein, Ruth, 243
Walton, Izaak, 76 n.
Ward, Nathaniel, 48 n., 77
Wase, Christopher, 153–5
Wasserman, E. R., 232–3

INDEX

Weinberg, Bernard, 136
Weldon, Robert, 14 n.
Wenley, R. M., 10
Weston, Corinne Comstock, 13
Wharton, Philip, fourth Baron, 150
Whitelock, Bulstrode, 111
Wilkins, John, 64 n., 68
Wilkins, W. Walter, 91 n., 126 n.
Willett, Andrew, 134 n.
William III, 6, 208, 211
Williams, Griffith, 19, 23, 133, 134
Williamson, George, 75, 212
Wilson, Charles, 149 n.

Wilson, Richard, 149
Witcombe, D. T., 149 n.
Wither, George, 97, 112 n., 126, 135 n.
Wood, Anthony à, 30
Wormald, B. H. G., 1–3, 7, 11 n., 68 n., 70, 139
Wormuth, Francis D., 13 n., 76 n.
Wortley, Sir Francis, 117

Yule, George, 11 n., 79 n., 100 n.

Zagorin, Perez, 37